JOURNEYS IN
Math 4

RALPH D. CONNELLY
FRANK MARSH
JANICE SARKISSIAN
TREVOR CALKINS
JACK A. HOPE
THOMAS O'SHEA
J. NORMAN C. SHARP
HENRY TASCHUK
STELLA TOSSELL

GINN
AND
COM-
PANY

FOUNDED IN 1867

Ginn and Company
Educational Publishers

ISBN 0-7702-1413-4
C98084

EDITORS
Helen Nolan
Colin Baker
Shirley Miller
Janet Scully
Rosemary Tile
Dianne Brassolotto

DESIGNER
Hugh Michaelson

ILLUSTRATORS
Muriel Wood
Frances Clancy
Vesna Krstanovich
Marilyn Mets

TECHNICAL ILLUSTRATORS
Pat Code
Pam Kinney
Lorraine LeCamp
Dianna Little
Bruce Farquhar
John Piazza

COMPUTER MATERIAL
Gemini Education Group, Inc.

PHOTOGRAPHS
pages 16, 17 The Stock Market
pages 18, 20, 42, 52, 57(b), 66, 92,
        102 Miller Services
pages 170, 315(a), (b) courtesy of NASA
page 315(c) courtesy of Lucasfilm Ltd.
page 26 Royal Ontario Museum
All others, Harold Whyte Photography

Printed and bound in Canada
  BCDEFG 8987

Authors and Consultants

RALPH D. CONNELLY
Professor
College of Education
Brock University
St. Catharines, Ontario

FRANK MARSH
Program Coordinator
Mathematics and Science
Burin Peninsula Integrated
School Board
Burin, Newfoundland

JANICE SARKISSIAN
Supervisor of Programs
and Staff Development
Greater Victoria School
District 61
Victoria, British Columbia

TREVOR CALKINS
Principal
South Park Elementary School
Victoria, British Columbia

JACK A. HOPE
Associate Professor
Department of Curriculum Studies
University of Saskatchewan
Saskatoon, Saskatchewan

THOMAS O'SHEA
Associate Professor
Faculty of Education
Simon Fraser University
Burnaby, British Columbia

J. NORMAN C. SHARP
Former Mathematics Coordinator
Etobicoke Board of Education
Etobicoke, Ontario

HENRY A. TASCHUK
Elementary Mathematics Consultant
Edmonton, Public Schools
Edmonton, Alberta

STELLA TOSSELL
Mathematics Service Coordinator
Ginn and Company
Former Mathematics Consultant
North York Board of Education
North York, Ontario

Contents

Get Ready ... Get Set

Time

Give the numbers to complete the story.
"Get up, sleepy head, it's ☐**1**☐. The sun
has been up since ☐**2**☐. You have to leave
for school by ☐**3**☐. I'll have your lunch ready
for you at ☐**4**☐. Don't forget to meet
grandfather after school at ☐**5**☐."

8:20
12:15
7:35
4:30
9:45
6:05
2:10

What time does the clock show?

6.   **7.**    **8.**    **9.**

10.    **11.**    **12.**    **13.**

Draw a clock face to show the time you do this.

14.    **15.**    **16.**

Make your own digital clock.

1. Draw a shape like this and cut it out. Cut slits where the dotted lines are.

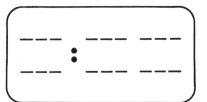

2. Take 3 strips of heavy paper that will fit through the slits. Write these numbers on them.

1	0	0
2	1	1
3	2	2
4	3	3
5	4	4
6	5	5
7		6
8		7
9		8
10		9
11		
12		

3. Put the number strips through the slits.

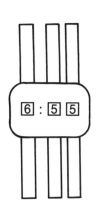

4. Tape the ends of each strip together. Use the clock to show times.

When it is 8:00 in the morning in Victoria, it is 11:00 in the morning in Toronto. The clock shows Victoria time. What time is it in Toronto?

5. (7:00)   **6.** (8:15)   **7.** (2:45)   **8.** (10:30)

3

Hidden Patterns

A chart with the numbers from 0 to 99 arranged like this has many patterns.

0	1	2	3	4	5	6	7	8	9
10	11	12	13	14	15	16	17	18	19
20	21	22	23	24	25	26	27	28	29
30	31	32	33	34	35	36	37	38	39
40	41	42	43	44	45	46	47	48	49
50	51	52	53	54	55	56	57	58	59
60	61	62	63	64	65	66	67	68	69
70	71	72	73	74	75	76	77	78	79
80	81	82	83	84	85	86	87	88	89
90	91	92	93	94	95	96	97	98	99

What is the pattern?

1. of each row

2. of each column

3. of a ↙ diagonal

4. of a ↘ diagonal

There are hidden patterns.

Add the digits of each number. What is the pattern in the sums?

30   31   32
3 + 0 = 3   3 + 1 = 4   3 + 2 = 5

5. of a row

6. of a column

7. of a ↙ diagonal

8. of a ↘ diagonal

Add the digits of each number in an L-shape.

24
34
44 45 46

9. What is the pattern in the sums?

Subtract the digits of each number in a ↘ diagonal.

10. What is the pattern in the differences?

11. Look for other patterns. Tell what they are.

More Patterns

What is the pattern? Copy and complete the square.

1.

88	98	
89		

2.

311	312	
321	322	

3.

	229	329
130	230	

4.

386		586
	496	596

5.

650		670
850		870

6.

442		
	543	
		644

Use the pattern, 1 green circle, 2 yellow circles.

7. What is the color of the 18th circle?

8. What is the color of the 29th circle?

Use the pattern, 2 green circles, 1 yellow circle, 1 white circle.

9. What is the color of the 17th circle?

10. What is the color of the 34th circle?

Look at this pattern.

11. What is the color of the 20th circle?

12. What is the color of the 30th circle?

Estimate

About how many are there?
Don't count. Guess which number is closest.

1.

5   7   9

2.

10   20   30

3.

12   20   40

4.

4   7   12

5.

10   15   20

6.

15   25   50

7.

12   20   30

8.

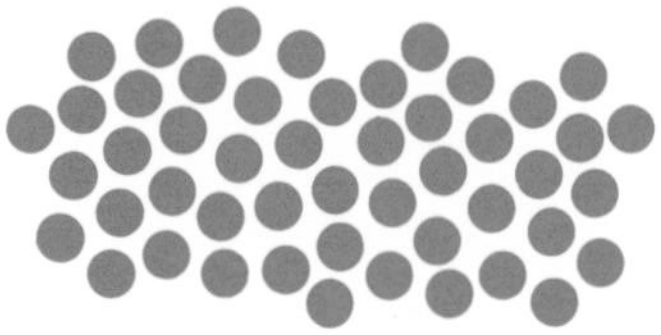

25   50   75

9.

70   100   200

Fact Families

Copy the chart.
Ring sets of 3 numbers
that make fact families.

6, 11, and 5 make this fact family.

6 + 5 = 11	11 − 6 = 5
5 + 6 = 11	11 − 5 = 6

The 3 numbers must
be next to each other
in a straight line
(row, column, or diagonal).

1. How many fact family sets
can you find? Write them.

6	11	5	2	4
4	7	9	4	4
16	5	13	8	5
4	9	2	12	7
8	15	7	3	2

**Copy the array. Find the fact family numbers in a triangle shape.
Draw each triangle in a different color.**

2.

5	11	2
•	•	•
14	9	17
•	•	•
1	10	8
•	•	•

3.

11	15	12
•	•	•
7	0	6
•	•	•
9	5	8
•	•	•

Look for a pattern in the row. Give the sums.

4. 2 + 7   **5.** 12 + 7   **6.** 22 + 7   **7.** 32 + 7

8. 5 + 8   **9.** 15 + 8   **10.** 25 + 8   **11.** 35 + 8

12. 7 + 5   **13.** 37 + 5   **14.** 57 + 5   **15.** 77 + 5

Addition Patterns

Use grid paper to make an addition table.
Fill in the sums for the colored squares.

1.

+	0	1	2	3	4	5	6	7	8	9
0	■									
1		■								
2			■							
3				■						
4					■					
5						■				
6							■			
7								■		
8									■	
9										■

2.

+	0	1	2	3	4	5	6	7	8	9
0	■	■	■	■	■	■	■	■	■	■
1	■									■
2	■									■
3	■									■
4	■									■
5	■									■
6	■									■
7	■									■
8	■									■
9	■	■	■	■	■	■	■	■	■	■

3.

+	0	1	2	3	4	5	6	7	8	9

4.

+	0	1	2	3	4	5	6	7	8	9

Show ways you can combine the stems to have this many flowers.

5. 6   **6.** 8   **7.** 9   **8.** 10   **9.** 12

10. If you also had a stem with 6 flowers, how many ways could you show 12?

Number Neighbors

Play "Neighbors Only."

You have 5 numbers in a row.
Make sums by adding numbers
that are neighbors.

For example,
suppose the 5 numbers are ① ② ③ ④ ⑤
and you want to show an addition for the sum 6.
You can use 1 + 2 + 3,
but you cannot use 1 + 5. Why not?

Copy and complete the game cards.

1. ① ② ③ ④ ⑤

Can you make this number?	If you can, show how.
6	1 + 2 + 3
7	
8	
9	
10	
11	
12	
13	
14	
15	

2. ① ⑤ ④ ② ③

Can you make this number?	If you can, show how.
6	4 + 2
7	
8	
9	
10	
11	
12	
13	
14	
15	

3. Some of the sums can be shown in more than one way.
Which ones? Show how.

Sum Fun

Copy and complete the wheel. Add the number in the centre to each number in the next circle.

1.

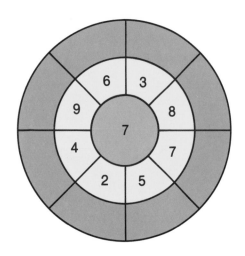

2.

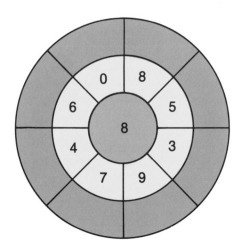

Give the sums in each row. Then give the sums in each column.

	9.	10.	11.	12.	13.	14.
3.	5 + 2	4 + 3	3 + 5	2 + 7	1 + 4	2 + 2
4.	3 + 9	3 + 4	8 + 7	0 + 9	3 + 8	7 + 7
5.	7 + 1	9 + 1	4 + 1	8 + 1	6 + 1	1 + 1
6.	6 + 8	1 + 9	7 + 5	3 + 6	9 + 7	6 + 6
7.	5 + 9	5 + 6	5 + 7	5 + 4	5 + 8	5 + 5
8.	7 + 8	6 + 5	9 + 4	7 + 2	6 + 9	8 + 8

15. Which row did you do the fastest? Why?

16. Which column did you do the fastest? Why?

Subtraction Action

Copy and complete the chart.

1.

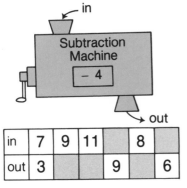

in	7	9	11		8	
out	3			9		6

2.

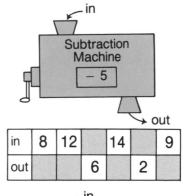

in	8	12		14		9
out			6		2	

3.

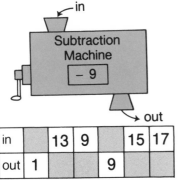

in		13	9		15	17
out	1			9		

4.

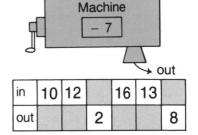

in	10	12		16	13	
out			2			8

Look for a pattern in the row. Subtract.

5. 9 − 4   **6.** 19 − 4   **7.** 29 − 4   **8.** 39 − 4

9. 12 − 6   **10.** 22 − 6   **11.** 32 − 6   **12.** 42 − 6

13. 17 − 8   **14.** 27 − 8   **15.** 37 − 8   **16.** 47 − 8

17. 18 − 9   **18.** 28 − 9   **19.** 38 − 9   **20.** 48 − 9

21. 15 − 7   **22.** 35 − 7   **23.** 55 − 7   **24.** 75 − 7

11

Calendar Calculator

Use a calendar as a "seven" calculator.

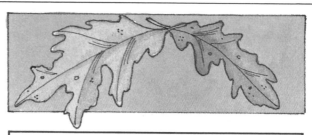

To add 7, go to the next week.
$\boxed{2} + 7 = \boxed{9}$

SEPTEMBER						
S	M	T	W	T	F	S
1	2	3	4	5	6	7
8	9	10	11	12	13	14
15	16	17	18	19	20	21
22	23	24	25	26	27	28
29	30					

To subtract 7, go back a week.
$\boxed{18} - 7 = \boxed{11}$

How can you add 14?

How can you subtract 21?

Use the calendar to find the sum or difference.

1. 8 + 7   **2.** 11 + 7   **3.** 7 + 13   **4.** 16 + 7

5. 3 + 14   **6.** 14 + 6   **7.** 15 + 14   **8.** 4 + 21

9. 13 – 7   **10.** 25 – 7   **11.** 22 – 7   **12.** 10 – 7

13. 30 – 14   **14.** 27 – 14   **15.** 29 – 21   **16.** 24 – 21

17. 21 + 7   **18.** 14 + 9   **19.** 17 – 14   **20.** 26 – 7

21. Make up a month with more days so you can add and subtract with larger numbers.

22. Make up a calendar with 6-day weeks. What numbers will you be able to add and subtract quickly?

Riddle

Why did the baker
stop making doughnuts?

To find out, follow these steps.

1. Copy this code.

| 8 | 6 | | 14 | 12 | 10 | | 10 | 1 | 3 | 6 | 0 |

| 12 | 9 | | 10 | 8 | 6 | | 8 | 12 | 16 | 6 |

| 11 | 2 | 17 | 1 | 7 | 6 | 17 | 17 |

2. Do these exercises to find the letters for the code.

7 + 4 = B	9 + D = 9	15 − 9 = E	8 + F = 17
6 + 8 = G	15 − H = 7	I + 2 = 3	7 + 9 = L
16 − N = 9	3 + 9 = O	11 − R = 8	8 + 9 = S
3 + 7 = T	9 − U = 7		

3. What is the answer to the riddle?

Copy the drawing.

4. How many squares can you find?

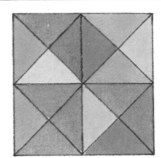

13

Degrees Celsius (°C)

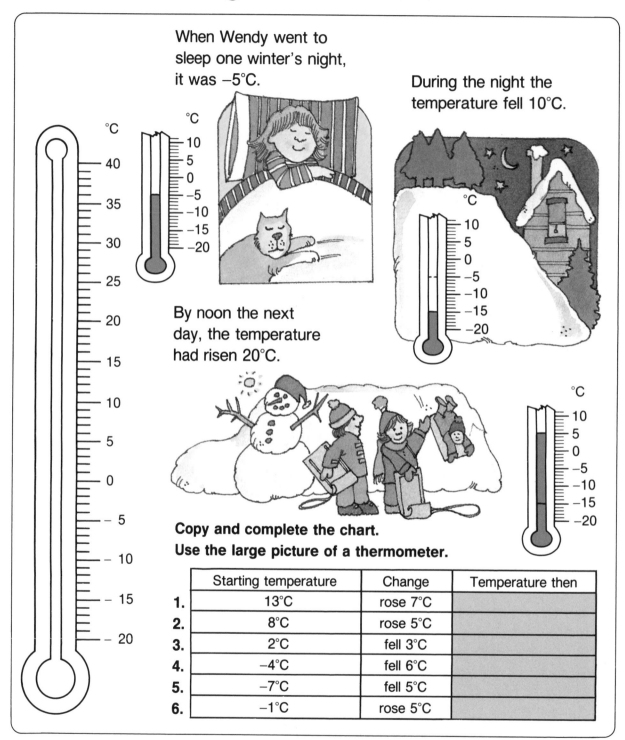

When Wendy went to sleep one winter's night, it was −5°C.

During the night the temperature fell 10°C.

By noon the next day, the temperature had risen 20°C.

Copy and complete the chart.
Use the large picture of a thermometer.

	Starting temperature	Change	Temperature then
1.	13°C	rose 7°C	
2.	8°C	rose 5°C	
3.	2°C	fell 3°C	
4.	−4°C	fell 6°C	
5.	−7°C	fell 5°C	
6.	−1°C	rose 5°C	

1/Numeration

In this chapter you will learn to read and write six-digit numbers.

Numbers to 999

There are 235 hot-air balloons in the festival.

10 tens equal 1 hundred.

hundreds	tens	ones
2	3	5

standard form   235

expanded form   200 + 30 + 5

words   two hundred thirty-five

WORKING TOGETHER

Show the number. Use ☐ for hundreds, ☐ for tens, ☐ for ones.

1. 173   **2.** 380   **3.** 546   **4.** 259   **5.** 482

Write the standard form. Then write the expanded form.

6. 4 hundreds 6 tens 7 ones   **7.** 2 hundreds 3 ones

8. 6 hundreds 2 tens 2 ones   **9.** 9 hundreds 6 tens

10. eighty-four   **11.** five hundred seventy

12. three hundred two   **13.** two hundred eleven

16

Write the standard form.

1. 7 hundreds 1 ten 3 ones

2. 6 hundreds 5 tens 1 one

3. 5 hundreds 3 tens

4. 3 hundreds 6 ones

5. 800 + 10 + 4

6. 200 + 90

7. 400 + 8

8. 100 + 5

9. one hundred forty-four

10. nine hundred sixteen

11. eight hundred seventy

12. six hundred four

Write the expanded form.

13. 215   14. 463   15. 807   16. 592   17. 320

Write the standard form for the number.
Then write the expanded form.

18. The first flights in hot-air balloons took place about two hundred ten years ago.

19. The first balloon trip across the Atlantic Ocean took one hundred thirty-seven hours.

20. Balloons are filled with air whose temperature reaches from eighty-five to one hundred degrees Celsius.

Try This

If 684 changes to 674, then 153 changes to 143.

Complete the change.

1. If 123 → 321, then 142 → ⬚.

2. If 907 → 917, then 659 → ⬚.

3. If 568 → 658, then 873 → ⬚.

4. If 425 → 525, then 401 → ⬚.

5. If 216 → 327, then 586 → ⬚.

6. If 873 → 651, then 942 → ⬚.

Numbers to 9999

There are 1345 containers aboard the cargo ship.

10 hundreds equal 1 thousand.

thousands	hundreds	tens	ones
1	3	4	5

standard form   1345

expanded form   1000 + 300 + 40 + 5

words   one thousand three hundred forty-five

WORKING TOGETHER

Show the number. Use ⬜ for thousands, ⬜ for hundreds, ⬜ for tens, □ for ones.

1. 1578   **2.** 3103   **3.** 2008   **4.** 4350

Write the standard form. Then write the expanded form.

5. 3 thousands 6 hundreds 8 tens 4 ones

6. 1 thousand 5 hundreds 2 ones   **7.** 7 thousands 9 tens 6 ones

8. 9 thousands   8 hundreds   1 ten   **9.** two thousand seven hundred thirty

10. four thousand fifty-eight   **11.** six thousand six

12. five thousand nine hundred twenty-five

EXERCISES

Write the standard form.

1. 6 thousands 6 hundreds 8 ones

2. 3 thousands 7 tens 6 ones

3. 1000 + 400 + 50 + 2

4. 5000 + 900 + 30 + 4

5. 7000 + 500 + 6

6. 1000 + 10 + 9

7. three thousand four hundred six

8. eight thousand one hundred

9. nine thousand eleven

10. two thousand four

11.
1 ten
2 thousands
3 hundreds
6 ones

12.
4 hundreds
8 ones
6 tens
5 thousands

13.
5 hundreds
7 ones
9 thousands
0 tens

Write the expanded form.

14. 1124   15. 4360   16. 7422   17. 8743   18. 4980

Write the standard form for the number.
Then write the expanded form.

19. The St. Lawrence Seaway opened in the year one thousand nine hundred fifty-nine.

20. The length of the St. Lawrence River is three thousand fifty-eight kilometres.

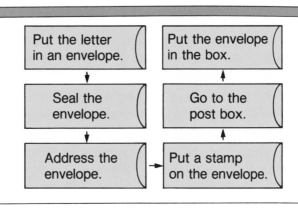

Computers cannot think for themselves. People must tell them what to do and when to do it.

1. Follow the steps in the **flow chart**. Then give the flow chart a title.

Put the letter in an envelope.

Seal the envelope.

Address the envelope.

Put the envelope in the box.

Go to the post box.

Put a stamp on the envelope.

Comparing and Ordering Numbers

During which month did the Maid of the Mist carry more passengers?

Month	Passengers
July	3485
August	3275

Look at the digits from left to right.

3485 The thousands are the same.
3275

3485 The hundreds are different.
3275

4 > 2, so 3485 > 3275

The steamer carried more passengers in July.

WORKING TOGETHER

In which place are the digits first different?

1. 1208
   1091

2. 5076
   5078

3. 3989
   4120

4. 2652
   2649

Use >, <, or = to make a true statement.

5. 966 ○ 976

6. 3574 ○ 3564

7. 4286 ○ 4000 + 200 + 80 + 6

List the numbers from least to greatest.

8. 4567, 4527, 4167, 4563

9. 4785, 6780, 780, 4980

EXERCISES

Use >, <, or = to make a true statement.

1. 2536 ⃝ 2653   **2.** 652 ⃝ 625   **3.** 1090 ⃝ 1000 + 9

4. 8118 ⃝ 8181   **5.** 2050 ⃝ 2005   **6.** 6572 ⃝ 7652

7. 4952 ⃝ 4935   **8.** 703 ⃝ 700 + 3   **9.** 3951 ⃝ 3941

Order from least to greatest.

10.
| 481 |
| 976 |
| 897 |
| 148 |

11.
| 5310 |
| 6922 |
| 4000 |
| 3939 |

12.
| 2493 |
| 397 |
| 2923 |
| 2402 |

13.
| 4443 |
| 4344 |
| 444 |
| 4444 |

14.
| 3275 |
| 3288 |
| 3263 |
| 236 |

15. Order the number of passengers from least to greatest.

Month	Passengers
May	1084
June	2139
September	2135
October	1048

16. Which falls are higher? Which falls are wider?

Falls	Height	Width
Canadian	57 m	640 m
American	59 m	338 m

Try This

Find the rain hats that show a true statement.
Use their letters to make a word that describes Niagara Falls.

A
229 < 292

D
9760 < 9607

M
6868 > 6686

U
3003 < 3030

S
5483 > 5438

O
767 > 757

L
2102 > 2120

F
872 < 882

Write the standard form.

1. 8 thousands 3 hundreds 8 tens 2 ones

2. 5 thousands 4 hundreds 1 ten 8 ones

3. 7 hundreds 9 ones   4. 3 thousands 2 tens

5. 600 + 20 + 5   6. 4000 + 100 + 20 + 4

7. 7000 + 600 + 4   8. 8000 + 7

9. seven thousand nine hundred fifty-two

10. five thousand six hundred eighteen

11. nine thousand one hundred   12. four hundred thirty

13. five thousand sixty-seven   14. one thousand twelve

Write the expanded form.

15. 356   16. 720   17. 7830   18. 1037   19. 2495

20. 3740   21. 6500   22. 6841   23. 2002   24. 804

Use >, <, or = to make a true statement.

25. 349 ◯ 314   26. 6509 ◯ 6905   27. 728 ◯ 700 + 20 + 8

28. 9726 ◯ 9784   29. 2643 ◯ 2943   30. 5181 ◯ 5118

Order from least to greatest.

31.	32.	33.	34.	35.
8798	5795	3124	6090	9229
8788	5579	344	6900	992
8797	575	3144	6099	2099
897	5759	142	6009	9022

How a Computer Works

How does a computer work? To help you understand, think about making a cake.

You need a recipe to tell you what to do. You need ingredients and tools to work with.

What happens?

1. if you do not have all the items

2. if you do not understand the recipe

> A computer needs **input** before it starts working.
> It needs a list of instructions, called a **program**.
> It works with words and numbers, called **data**.

Next, you make the cake. You follow the steps in the recipe.

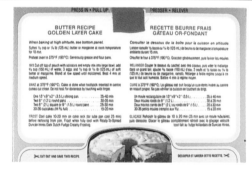

What happens?

3. if the steps are in the wrong order

4. if you forget to do a step

> A computer follows the instructions in a program one step at a time. This stage is called **processing**.

When you finish everything, you have a cake.

> A computer gives results called **output**.

Think about building a model airplane. Describe.

5. the program   6. the data   7. processing   8. the output

Rounding

In a car race, a car has travelled 1825 km.

Round to the nearest thousand.

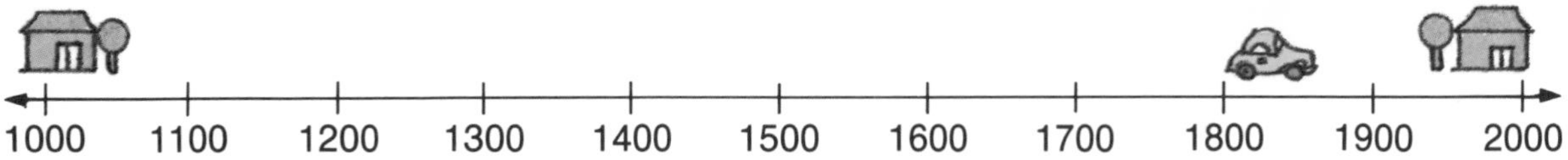

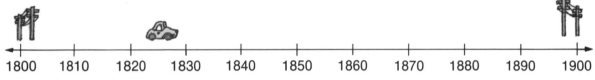

1825 is closer to 2000 than 1000.   1825 rounds to 2000.

Round to the nearest hundred.

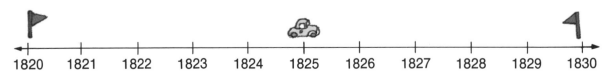

1825 is closer to 1800 than 1900.   1825 rounds to 1800.

Round to the nearest ten.

1820	1821	1822	1823	1824	1825	1826	1827	1828	1829	1830

1825 is **halfway** between 1820 and 1830.   1825 rounds to 1830.

WORKING TOGETHER

Copy and complete.

1. 22 is between 20 and ☐0.

2. 452 is between 400 and ☐00.

3. 3384 is between 3000 and ☐000.

4. 8707 is between ☐000 and 9000.

5. 645 is between 6☐0 and 650.

6. 1350 is between 1☐00 and 1400.

EXERCISES

Round to the nearest ten.

1. 64   **2.** 75   **3.** 36   **4.** 98   **5.** 117

6. 255   **7.** 439   **8.** 2439   **9.** 9360   **10.** 4733

Round to the nearest hundred.

11. 813   **12.** 1684   **13.** 901   **14.** 250   **15.** 353

16. 1011   **17.** 3449   **18.** 2550   **19.** 965   **20.** 5064

Round to the nearest thousand.

21. 9400   **22.** 4300   **23.** 1629   **24.** 7236   **25.** 2910

26. 7539   **27.** 8499   **28.** 6555   **29.** 1502   **30.** 2478

Copy and complete.

		Round to the nearest		
		ten	hundred	thousand
31.	2915			
32.	7350			
33.	1479			
34.	4495			

Shuffle cards from 1 to 18. Put them in a pile, face down.
Start with a 5 in a calculator display.
Take turns.

| 5 |

(5.)

Turn over a card. Add or subtract
once on the calculator to make the
display show the number on the card.

| + || 7 || = |

(12.)

25

Numbers to 999 999

When the moon is closest
to the earth, the distance
between them is 356 411 km.

10 one thousands equal 1 ten thousand.
10 ten thousands equal 1 hundred thousand.

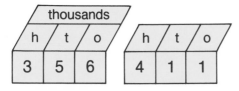

thousands					
h	t	o	h	t	o
3	5	6	4	1	1

standard form　　356 411

expanded form　　300 000 + 50 000 + 6000 + 400 + 10 + 1

words　　three hundred fifty-six thousand four hundred eleven

WORKING TOGETHER

Read the number.

1. 6437　　　　2. 63 948　　　　3. 50 601　　　　4. 597 425

5. 604 975　　　6. 918 302　　　7. 805 026　　　8. 700 760

Write the standard form. Then write the expanded form.

9. 4 hundred thousands 7 ten thousands 5 thousands
   6 hundreds 1 ten 3 ones

10. 3 ten thousands 1 thousand 5 tens 9 ones

11. two hundred thirty-three thousand one hundred eighty-four

12. twenty-five thousand sixty-two

Write the standard form.

1. 9 ten thousands 2 thousands 6 hundreds 5 tens 2 ones

2. 4 hundred thousands 6 ten thousands 1 thousand 2 hundreds

3. 100 000 + 20 000 + 3000 + 400 + 50 + 6

4. 50 000 + 300 + 20 + 7   5. 300 000 + 9000 + 800 + 4

6. seven hundred thirty-two thousand five hundred ninety-three

7. one hundred twelve thousand   8. two hundred six thousand five

Write the expanded form.

9. 652 378   10. 902 517   11. 86 001   12. 300 303

Write the standard form for the number.
Then write the expanded form.

13. The distance around the moon is ten thousand
nine hundred nineteen kilometres.

14. The distance to the moon is three hundred eighty-four thousand
four hundred three kilometres.

15. The distance to the moon when it is farthest from the earth is
four hundred six thousand six hundred ninety-seven kilometres.

KEEPING SHARP

Arrange these events in order.

1981 first re-usable spacecraft   1984 first Canadian in space
1966 first soft landing on moon   1969 first human on moon
1957 first satellite launched   1963 first woman in space
1959 first spacecraft on moon   1961 first human in space

Roman Numerals

What chapter is Sara reading?

1	2	3	4	5	6	7	8	9
I	II	III	IV	V	VI	VII	VIII	IX

When I comes before V or X, subtract 1.

10	20	30	40	50	60	70	80	90	100
X	XX	XXX	XL	L	LX	LXX	LXXX	XC	C

When X comes before L or C, subtract 10.

Chapter **X X I V**
20 4

Sara is reading Chapter 24.

WORKING TOGETHER

Write the standard form.

1. XLIV   2. LXXXIX   3. XCVIII   4. LXX   5. LXVII

Write the Roman numeral.

6. 56   7. 99   8. 39   9. 45   10. 18

EXERCISES

Write the Roman numeral.

1. 7   **2.** 90   **3.** 44   **4.** 29   **5.** 34

6. 51   **7.** 100   **8.** 85   **9.** 96   **10.** 63

Copy and continue the pattern.

11. V, X, XV, ☐, ☐, ☐   **12.** X, XX, XXX, ☐, ☐, ☐

13. VI, XVI, XXVI, ☐, ☐, ☐   **14.** IV, XIV, XXIV, ☐, ☐, ☐

15. IV, IX, XIV, ☐, ☐, ☐   **16.** II, IV, VI, ☐, ☐, ☐

17. XI, XXII, XXXIII, ☐, ☐, ☐   **18.** LV, LXVI, LXXVII, ☐, ☐, ☐

Which page comes before? Which page comes after?

19.    **20.**    **21.**

22.    **23.**    **24.**

Try This

Use toothpicks to make the number sentence.
Then make the sentence true by moving one toothpick.

1.  IX – VI = V   **2.**  IX + V = III

3.  IV = IV – I   **4.**  VIII = VI – II

29

Write the standard form.

1. 8 ten thousands 7 thousands 2 hundreds 4 tens 5 ones

2. 1 hundred thousand 3 ten thousands
   4 thousands 9 hundreds 6 tens 8 ones

3. 5 ten thousands 4 hundreds   4. 2 hundred thousands 9 tens

5. 200 000 + 50 000 + 8000 + 400 + 30 + 3

6. 400 000 + 8000 + 60 + 7   7. 20 000 + 3000 + 500 + 70 + 5

8. 10 000 + 300 + 6   9. 700 000 + 80 000 + 4

10. eighteen thousand two hundred ninety-five

11. four hundred forty-eight thousand three hundred eighty-seven

12. twenty thousand sixteen   13. eight hundred thousand six

Write the expanded form.

14. 78 564   15. 52 068   16. 40 902   17. 93 010

18. 528 326   19. 323 012   20. 106 409   21. 620 071

Copy and complete.

		Round to the nearest		
		ten	hundred	thousand
22.	4968			
23.	7029			
24.	3556			

Write the standard form.

25. LXIV   26. XCIII   27. LXXIX   28. XVIII

29. XXXII   30. LV   31. XXVIII   32. XLVI

Know Your Numbers

7643	**3769**	**2935**
793	**5013**	
2854	**6321**	**9875**
3160	**2785**	

Check. The digits in the answer add up to this.

Use a calculator.

1. Add the numbers that have 7 in the hundreds place. 21

2. Subtract the least number from the greatest. 19

3. Add the numbers between 2000 and 5000. 14

4. Add the numbers that have 3 in the ones place. 21

5. Subtract the number closest to 5000 from the number closest to 8000. 11

6. Add the numbers between 3000 and 9000. 22

7. Subtract the number closest to 800 from the number closest to 3000. 9

8. Add all the numbers greater than 5000. 25

9. Add the even numbers. 11

10. Add the number closest to 6000 to the least number. 13

11. Subtract the number closest to 3000 from the greatest number. 19

How to Solve a Problem

Here is a problem to solve.

Jason lives near his school.
How can he get to school on time?

First **think** about
the different ways.

Next choose one way. Then **plan and do**.

 or

or

Then **look back** to see
if the way you chose works.

Jason decides
to ride his bicycle.

Next time he should check his bicycle earlier.
Or, next time he should choose a different way.

Use this guide to help you solve problems.

Think.	What is the problem about?
	What am I asked to find?
Plan and do.	What can I do? Try it.
	Plan and solve the problem.
Look back.	Does my solution make sense? Check it.
	Are there other solutions?
	Are there other questions to ask?

How can Carol walk to and from school?

1. **Think.** Does Carol walk on the sidewalks or across people's yards?

2. **Plan and do.** Find one route on the map that Carol might use. How many blocks would she walk?

3. **Look back.** Find another route. Is it better than the other? Why?

4. Carol has to pick up some milk for dinner. What route could she take to and from school?

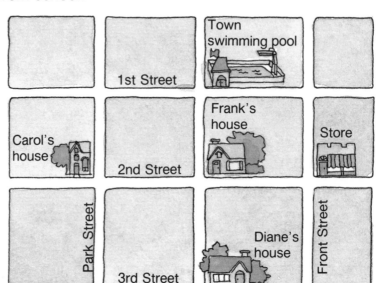

5. Describe three different ways that Frank can solve the problem.

I need more milk to make this. How can I have pudding for dinner?

PROBLEMS

1. Describe three different ways that Diane can solve the problem.

The baseball game starts in an hour. I need to wear my running shoes to play.

2. Name each picture as **Think**, **Plan and do**, or **Look back**.

a.    b.    c.

Describe two ways that you could solve the problem.
Use **Think**, **Plan and do**, and then **Look back**.

3. Which kite flies better?

4. How can the lawn be cut?

5. Which textbook has more pictures?

6. Is there enough room on the bus for the whole class?

7. Is there enough wrapping paper to wrap the gift?

8. How big can you print HAPPY BIRTHDAY on the envelope?

9. How many families in your town are named Jones?

10. What route should you take to visit a friend?

Chapter Checkup

Write the standard form.

1. 4 thousands 8 tens 5 ones

2. 9 hundreds 8 ones

3. 3 hundred thousands 5 ten thousands 8 thousands 4 tens

4. 9 hundred thousands 6 ten thousands 4 hundreds 2 ones

5. 300 + 80 + 7

6. 1000 + 600 + 2

7. 5000 + 400 + 4

8. 10 000 + 800 + 50

9. five thousand forty

10. three hundred eight

11. nine thousand fifty-six

12. twelve thousand ten

13. seven hundred four thousand ninety-six

Write the expanded form.

14. 4375

15. 8009

16. 21 407

17. 11 054

18. 90 610

19. 983 620

20. 100 836

21. 479 022

Use >, <, or = to make a true statement.

22. 673 ◯ 648

23. 4032 ◯ 4302

24. 2390 ◯ 2903

25. 507 ◯ 500 + 70

26. 7696 ◯ 7696

27. 200 + 20 ◯ 220

Copy and complete.

		Round to the nearest		
		ten	hundred	thousand
28.	6315			
29.	2021			
30.	9360			

Write the standard form.

31. XLII

32. LXIV

33. XXXVI

34. XCI

36

2/Addition

In this chapter you will learn to do
additions like 527 + 64 + 35 + 19.

Addition, No Regrouping

Add. 327 + 312
Use models and a chart.

You can write it this way.

Add ones.	Add tens.	Add hundreds.
3 2 **7** + 3 1 **2** **9**	3 **2** 7 + 3 **1** 2 **3** 9	**3** 2 7 + **3** 1 2 **6** 3 9

WORKING TOGETHER

Write the addition.

1.

tens	ones
▦▦▦▦▦▦▦	▤
▮	▤

2.

hundreds	tens	ones
▦ ▦	▮▮▮	▤
▦ ▦ ▦	▮▮▮	▤

Add.

3.   43
        + 36

4. $3.64
        + 5.24
        $.

5. $2.57 + $1.32

6. 406 + 91

Find the sum.

1. 41
+ 18

2. 257
+ 240

3. 3414
+ 5074

4. 79
+ 520

5. 8375
+ 613

6. 713
+ 25

7. 7213
+ 1456

8. $8.43
+ 1.03
$.

9. $3.10
+ 0.66
$.

10. $0.26
+ 1.33
$.

Line up the places. Then add.

11. 12 + 80

12. 602 + 311

13. 531 + 66

14. 9783 + 105

15. 516 + 201

16. 243 + 52

17. $5.32 + $3.64

18. $4.27 + $0.41

Solve.

19. Josh worked for 2 days. He earned $25 for yard work and $33 for painting. How much did he earn in all?

20. On Monday, 153 workers were hired. On Tuesday, 46 workers were hired. How many workers were hired both days?

21. The parts for repairs cost $432. The labor costs $126. What is the total cost?

22. Rosa needs 13 shelves. Only 5 shelves have been delivered. How many more does she need?

KEEPING SHARP

Use >, <, or = to make a true statement.

1. 9470 ○ 9740

2. 663 ○ 636

3. 7042 ○ 700 + 40 + 2

4. 4464 ○ 4644

5. 2004 ○ 2040

6. 400 + 60 + 1 ○ 461

7. 3113 ○ 3131

8. 1161 ○ 1116

Addition, Regrouping Ones

Lee filled 26 baskets with potatoes. Ray filled 18 baskets. How many baskets did they fill altogether?

Add. 26 + 18

Add ones.	Regroup 10 ones.	Add tens.
$\begin{array}{r} 2\,6 \\ +\ 1\,8 \\ \hline 4 \end{array}$	$\begin{array}{r} {}^{1} \\ 2\,6 \\ +\ 1\,8 \\ \hline 4 \end{array}$	$\begin{array}{r} {}^{1} \\ 2\,6 \\ +\ 1\,8 \\ \hline 4\,4 \end{array}$

Lee and Ray filled 44 baskets with potatoes.

WORKING TOGETHER

Do you need to regroup?

1. $\begin{array}{r} 38 \\ +55 \\ \hline \end{array}$
2. $\begin{array}{r} 16 \\ +23 \\ \hline \end{array}$
3. $\begin{array}{r} \$4.26 \\ +1.37 \\ \hline \end{array}$
4. $\begin{array}{r} 938 \\ +42 \\ \hline \end{array}$
5. $\begin{array}{r} 44 \\ +702 \\ \hline \end{array}$

Find the sum.

6. $\begin{array}{r} 47 \\ +28 \\ \hline \end{array}$
7. $\begin{array}{r} 674 \\ +217 \\ \hline \end{array}$
8. 48 + 315
9. $2.73 + $10.19

EXERCISES

Find the sum.

1. 39
  + 27

2. 38
  + 46

3. 61
  + 23

4. $8.15
  + 1.39

5. 259
  + 18

6. 45
  + 48

7. 342
  + 19

8. 28
  + 628

9. $5.18
  + 3.61

10. 227
  + 535

Line up the places. Then add.

11. 57 + 37

12. 24 + 75

13. 226 + 147

14. $5.43 + $0.19

15. 58 + 727

16. 32 + 18

17. 164 + 26

18. $9.23 + $0.58

Solve.

19. One row has 36 potato hills. The next row has 35 hills. How many hills are there altogether?

20. One field has 38 rows of potatoes. Another field has 24 rows. How many rows are there in all?

21. Lee's basket has 108 potatoes. Ray's basket has 86 potatoes. How many potatoes are there in both baskets?

22. The boys sold a large sack for $1.05 and a small sack for $0.75. How much did they get for both sacks?

Try This

Arrange the numbers 1 to 9 in place of the potatoes.
The sum along each side must be 17.

Addition, Regrouping Tens or Hundreds

The ranchers sold 282 cattle from one roundup and 341 cattle from another. How many cattle were sold in all?

Add. 282 + 341

Add ones.	Add tens. Regroup 10 tens.	Add hundreds.

2 8 2
+ 3 4 1
‾‾‾‾‾‾‾
    3
	1
	2 8 2
	+ 3 4 1
	‾‾‾‾‾‾‾
	  2 3
		1
		2 8 2
		+ 3 4 1
		‾‾‾‾‾‾‾
		6 2 3

There were 623 cattle sold.

WORKING TOGETHER

In which place do you need to regroup?

1. 653
   + 91

2. 2543
   + 1815

3. 7618
   + 731

4. 4020
   + 1680

5. 542
   + 653

Find the sum.

6. 744
   + 273

7. $16.08
   + 17.20

8. 94 + 422

9. 6081 + 358

EXERCISES

Add. Use the sums to solve the riddle.

1.

| A 346
+ 291 | C 267
+ 82 | D 4458
+ 2270 | E 3604
+ 485 | G 548
+ 4931 |

| H 3494
+ 473 | M 1883
+ 2416 | N 164
+ 228 | O 2506
+ 307 | P 78
+ 551 |

| R 2630
+ 1189 | T 945
+ 642 | U 234
+ 1595 | Y 2837
+ 4231 | Z 5123
+ 935 |

Riddle: How are cattle and the numbers 25 and 35 alike?

They are ___3819___ ___2813___ ___1829___ ___392___ ___6728___ ___4089___ ___6728___ ___1829___ ___629___.

Solve.

2. Helen sold her two cows for $1177 and $782. How much did she get in all?

3. On Friday 1503 rodeo tickets were sold. On Saturday 3498 were sold. How many were sold both days?

Try This

1. Replace the letters with the digits 1, 2, 3, 4, 5, 6, 7, 8, 9 to make a true addition statement.

```
  P I G
+ M U D
  J O Y
```

2. Try it using the digits 0, 1, 2, 3, 4, 5, 6, 7, 8.

43

Addition, Two Regroupings

What is the mass of the tiger and the camel together?

267 kg   396 kg   573 kg   568 kg

Add.   267 + 568

Add ones. Regroup.	Add tens. Regroup.	Add hundreds.
$\begin{array}{r} 1 \\ 2\,6\,7 \\ +\,5\,6\,8 \\ \hline 5 \end{array}$	$\begin{array}{r} 1\,1 \\ 2\,6\,7 \\ +\,5\,6\,8 \\ \hline 3\,5 \end{array}$	$\begin{array}{r} 1\,1 \\ 2\,6\,7 \\ +\,5\,6\,8 \\ \hline 8\,3\,5 \end{array}$

The mass of the tiger and the camel together is 835 kg (kilograms).

WORKING TOGETHER

In which places do you need to regroup?

1. 687
   + 273

2. 934
   + 69

3. 6554
   + 137

4. 1736
   + 2098

5. $2.28
   + 4.91

Find the sum.

6. 724
   + 198

7. $4.67
   + 0.46

8. 8379 + 275

9. 143 + 99

44

Find the sum.

1.   537
   + 296

2. $3.79
   + 0.38

3.   3195
   + 5626

4. $4.47
   + 3.84

5.   54
   + 688

Copy. Then add across and down.

6.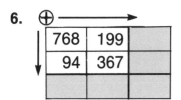

768	199	
94	367	

7.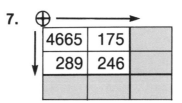

4665	175	
289	246	

8.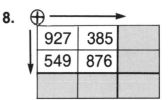

927	385	
549	876	

Solve. Use the masses given on the opposite page.

9. Find the combined mass of the two lightest animals.

10. What is the total mass of the camel and the bear?

11. What is the mass of the bison and the tiger together?

12. Find the combined mass of the two heaviest animals.

A person gives **input** to a computer. The instructions that tell it what to do are the **program**. The information that the computer works with is the **data**.

Pretend that you are a computer. Follow each step in the program, using the data. Give the results or **output**.

Program	Data
1. Read a number. 2. Round the number to the nearest ten. 3. Print the rounded number. 4. Go to step 1. 5. Stop.	24, 77, 8, 45, 113

Find the sum.

1. 67
   + 32

2. 18
   + 81

3. 40
   + 56

4. 37
   + 24

5. 39
   + 48

6. $1.39
   + 2.43

7. $3.05
   + 6.85

8. 63
   + 48

9. 147
   + 282

10. 326
   + 590

11. 367
   + 651

12. 265
   + 349

13. 112
   + 299

14. 457
   + 184

15. $6.62
   + 2.49

16. 14 + 55

17. 39 + 25

18. 48 + 27

19. 62 + 29

20. 432 + 480

21. 399 + 800

22. $1.81 + $1.39

23. 348 + 732

Solve.

24. The pigs eat 2487 kg of feed in three months. The turkeys eat 1910 kg of feed. How much feed do the pigs and the turkeys eat?

25. The apple crop sold for $4625. The pear crop sold for $3563. How much did the two crops sell for?

26. The farmer spends $5.79 for rope and $1.20 for nails. How much does he spend altogether?

27. To repair the fence costs $78.75. The paint costs $20.50. How much do the repairs and the paint cost?

Parts of a Computer

Pretend that you want a computer to find the sum of five numbers. First you make a list of instructions to tell the computer what to do. Then you decide which five numbers to add.

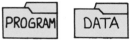

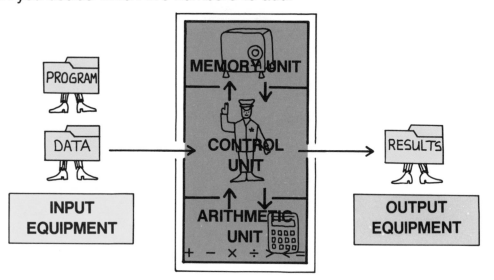

Follow these steps on the diagram to see what happens.

1. You use the **input equipment** to give the program and the data to the computer.

2. The **control unit** receives them. Then it sends them to the **memory unit** for storage.

3. The control unit gets the first instruction from memory and reads it. Then it gets the first number from memory.

4. The control unit gets the next instruction from memory. It sends the number to the **arithmetic unit** for adding.

5. The control unit takes the total and sends it to memory.

6. Steps 3, 4, and 5 are repeated with each of the other numbers.

7. The control unit gets the last total from memory and sends it out.

8. The sum is printed on the **output equipment**.

Estimating Sums

There are 487 peanuts in one jar and 345 raisins in another jar. About how many peanuts and raisins are there in all?

Round to the nearest hundred. Add to estimate the sum.

$$\begin{array}{r} 487 \\ + 345 \end{array} \longrightarrow \begin{array}{r} 500 \\ + 300 \\ \hline 800 \end{array}$$

There are about 800 raisins and peanuts.
Do you think the exact sum is more or less than 800?

WORKING TOGETHER

Round to the nearest ten.

1. 24   2. 89   3. 55   4. 32   5. 99

Round to the nearest hundred.

6. 645   7. 947   8. 551   9. 773   10. 139

Estimate.

11. 69 + 19   12. 602 + 325   13. 373 + 28

EXERCISES

Estimate the sum.

1. 68 + 42

2. 439 + 88

3. 76 + 21

4. 157 + 263

5. 224 + 713

6. 397 + 114

7. 345
      + 83

8. $2.57
      + 0.76

9. 487
      + 397

10. 569
      + 93

11. $3.48
      + 2.65

12. 584
      + 266

13. 855
      + 479

14. $0.78
      + 3.84

15. 696
      + 175

16. 555
      + 349

Estimate how many in all.

17.

345
raisins

554
pumpkin seeds

18.

554
pumpkin seeds

396
banana chips

19.

396
banana chips

668
popcorn kernels

20.

668
popcorn kernels

538
sunflower seeds

KEEPING SHARP

Write the standard form.

1. 3000 + 700 + 40 + 8

2. 8000 + 80 + 8

3. 7000 + 600 + 5

4. 5000 + 70

5. 2000 + 400 + 80 + 3

6. 400 + 90

7. 600 + 50 + 9

8. 1000 + 6

9. 900 + 9

10. 800 + 20 + 4

49

Addition, More Than Two Numbers

Michelle sold 86 beets, 93 squash, 75 cabbages and 34 cucumbers. How many vegetables did she sell in all?

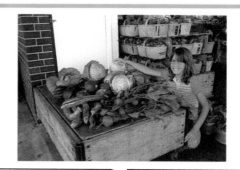

Add. 86 + 93 + 75 + 34

Round. Add to estimate.		
86	→	90
93	→	90
75	→	80
+ 34	→	+ 30
		290

Add ones. Regroup.

$$\begin{array}{r} {}^{1} \\ 86 \\ 93 \\ 75 \\ +\ 34 \\ \hline 8 \end{array}$$

Add tens. Regroup.

$$\begin{array}{r} {}^{1} \\ 86 \\ 93 \\ 75 \\ +\ 34 \\ \hline 288 \end{array}$$

288 is close to 290. The sum is reasonable.
Michelle sold 288 vegetables.

WORKING TOGETHER

Estimate.

1. 46 + 274 + 89

2. 38 + 406 + 97

3. 54 + 369 + 6 + 14

4. 483 + 79 + 26 + 14

Line up the places. Then find the sum.

5. 527 + 54 + 46

6. 96 + 57 + 38 + 72

7. 794 + 545 + 283

8. 83 + 21 + 543 + 37

Find the sum.

1.	2.	3.	4.	5.
74	16	493	80	668
28	49	68	735	843
65	257	54	24	+ 555
+ 17	+ 32	+ 105	+ 8	

Find the sum of the numbers.

6. inside the square

7. inside the rectangle

8. inside the triangle

9. inside the circle

10. inside both the circle and the square

11. inside both the circle and the rectangle

12. only in the triangle

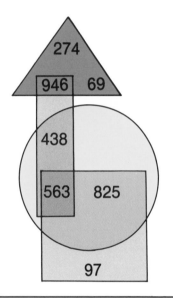

Do one addition to make the calculator display change to the next number.

1. (5261,) → (5265,) → (5275,) → (5775,)

2. (3487,) → (3490,) → (3590,) → (4090,)

3. (1045,) → (7045,) → (7050,) → (7100,)

4. (2813,) → (2820,) → (3020,) → (3200,)

5. (6209,) → (6299,) → (6999,) → (7000,)

Addition, Three Regroupings

On Saturday, 4679 people went to the fair.
On Sunday, 3485 people went. How many
people went to the fair on the weekend?

Add.   4679 + 3485

Round. Add to estimate.

$$
\begin{array}{r}
4679 \\
+\,3485 \\
\end{array}
\quad\longrightarrow\quad
\begin{array}{r}
5000 \\
+\,3000 \\
\hline
8000 \\
\end{array}
$$

Add ones. Regroup.	Add tens. Regroup.	Add hundreds. Regroup.	Add thousands.
1 4 6 7 9 + 3 4 8 5 —————— 4	1 1 4 6 7 9 + 3 4 8 5 —————— 6 4	1 1 1 4 6 7 9 + 3 4 8 5 —————— 8 1 6 4	1 1 1 4 6 7 9 + 3 4 8 5 —————— 8 1 6 4

8164 is close to 8000. The sum is reasonable.
There were 8164 people at the fair.

WORKING TOGETHER

Estimate.

1. 3156 + 2609   **2.** 5555 + 1820   **3.** 4948 + 4498

In which places do you need to regroup?

4. 3649 + 2487	**5.** 2975 + 519	**6.** 7286 + 1965	**7.** $83.74 + 15.29	**8.** 994 + 2057

Add. Match each sum with a letter.
Then decode the message.

D matches
1234 + 999

1.

+	2879	777	3876	999
1234	A	B	C	D
5678	E	F	I	K
1357	L	M	O	R
2468	S	T	U	V

2011		8557

5110	4113	2356	8557	6455	6344	4236

4113	3467	5233	9554	2233

2134	9554	5347	3245	4113	6677	8557	5347

Solve.

2. The Shaw family spent $26.78 at the fair. The Wong family spent $34.53. How much did both families spend?

3. 3245 hamburgers sold.
   2786 hot dogs sold.
   How many hamburgers and hot dogs sold in all?

> **Try This**

Write five different additions using the numbers from the gameboard.

A D D S			
A	7468	1539	5377
D	8835	9025	3648
D			
S	5187	6726	8265

```
  5187
+ 3648
------
  8835
```

PRACTICE

Estimate how many in all.

1. 78
figs
 130
apricots

2. 53
dates
 84
prunes

3.  96
walnuts
 112
almonds

4. 255
raisins
 246
peanuts

Estimate.

5. 5378
+ 2843

6. 6666
+ 444

7. $30.89
+ 19.32

8. $92.46
+ 1.94

9. 24 + 85 + 97

10. 604 + 136 + 62

11. 262 + 487 + 141

Find the sum.

12. 2958
+ 4357

13. $57.27
+ 3.88

14. $16.79
+ 39.49

15. 969
+ 8053

16. 7346 + 975

17. 64 + 17 + 352

18. 83 + 55 + 91 + 72

Solve. Use the pictures above.

19. How many figs, dates, and prunes are there?

20. How many walnuts, almonds, and peanuts are there?

21. Which contain more fruit, the bags of apricots, dates, and raisins
or the bags of figs, prunes, and raisins?

54

Estimate First

When you use a calculator to add, follow these steps.

Estimate mentally.   421 → 400
                     + 397 → + 400
                             800

Calculate.   4 2 1 + 3 9 7 = (818.)

Compare.   818 is close to 800.

Which total is probably correct?

1. 84 + 21 + 53   (1508.)   (158.)   (1058.)

2. 622 + 283   (805.)   (905.)   (8105.)

3. 791 + 534   (1225.)   (12125.)   (1325.)

Copy the gameboard. Use a calculator and two different kinds of markers. Play with a partner. Take turns.

Choose two numbers from the pool. Calculate the sum. If the sum is on the gameboard, put one of your markers on it.

The first player to get 4 in a row wins.

Pool

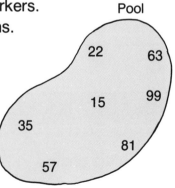

22   63
15   99
35
81
57

Gameboard

85	120	144	57
37	162	180	98
103	79	156	134
50	114	72	138

Find the Information

Read the letter. **Think** about the facts in it.

October 1

Dear Pen pal,

I am 9 years old. My brother David is 11, and my sister Dorothy is 14. We live on a big farm and help with the chores every day. In the barn there are 14 hens, 1 rooster, 25 milk cows, 3 cats named Fritz, Leo, and Fluff, and our pony Star.

There are always lots of eggs to collect. I gathered 8 eggs on Thursday, 5 eggs on Friday, and 9 eggs on Saturday. Dorothy collects the eggs during the rest of the week.

David helps my father milk the cows every morning and night. They use 2 shiny milking machines to get the milk.

I help my sister feed the cats and Star. In the summer Fritz had 6 kittens. I guess Fritz isn't a male! Fluff had 4 kittens a month ago. We had to give all the kittens away last week.

I hope you like the picture. Write soon.

Your friend,
Shirley

WORKING TOGETHER

1. Name each person and animal in the photo.

2. Which person in the photo wrote the letter?

Find the facts in the letter to solve the problem.

1. What animals live in the barn?

2. How many animals live in the barn?

3. How much older is David than Shirley?

4. How many kittens were given away?

5. Who collects the eggs?

6. How many eggs did Shirley gather?

7. How many days in a week does Dorothy collect the eggs?

8. Which cat did not have kittens?

9. How many more kittens were born in the summer than were born last month?

10. If all the cows, hens, roosters, and pony are in the barn now, how many legs are there?

Think. What facts do you need to solve each problem below?
Then **plan and do**.
Look back to see if your answer makes sense.

11. How many cats and kittens were there at the end of September?

12. How many cows is each milking machine used for?

Problem Solving Review

Describe two ways that you could solve the problem.
Use **Think**, **Plan and do**, and then **Look back**.

1. Are there enough pencils in the box for the class?

2. How can you cut a heart shape out of cardboard?

3. Where do you fold a piece of paper to get 4 equal parts?

4. Which of your friend's jigsaw puzzles is easier to put together?

Tell whether the picture for the problem shows
Think, **Plan and do**, or **Look back**.

5. Is there enough wallpaper to cover the wall?

6. How can we share the cookies equally?

Find the facts in the sign to solve the problem.

7. Where is the carnival?

8. How many hours is the carnival open?

9. How much does it cost for 2 adults and 3 students to attend?

FALL CARNIVAL

Place: Darwin School

Open: 4:00 p.m. to 6:00 p.m. Friday
11:00 a.m. to 3:00 p.m. Saturday

Admission: Students 20¢   Adults 50¢

Chapter Checkup

Find the sum.

1. 823
  + 134

2. 32
  + 965

3. 426
  + 567

4. 524
  + 39

5. $7.08
  + 0.96

6. 754
  + 175

7. 2245
  + 813

8. 878
  + 43

9. 596
  + 287

10. $6.35
  + 0.79

11. $79.98
  + 14.62

12. 546
  + 5869

13. 6563
  + 1477

14. $30.95
  + 9.68

15. 637 + 8594

16. 297 + 4361

17. 8932 + 406

18. 259 + 368 + 107

19. 64 + 798 + 27

20. 56 + 89 + 74 + 45

Estimate the sum.

21. $4.15
  + 3.82

22. 608
  + 139

23. 546
  + 75

24. 3649
  + 2498

25. 755 + 266 + 433

26. 316 + 548 + 299

27. 172 + 85 + 63

Solve.

28. The mass of a tractor is 3188 kg. The mass of a loaded wagon is 2876 kg. How heavy are they together?

29. Andy buys feed three times a year. Last year he bought 470 kg, 195 kg, and then 248 kg. How much feed did he buy?

30. Andy's equipment used 438 L of gas in July and 247 L in August. How much (litres) of gas in July and 247 L

31. The pens held 47 sheep, 136 cows, and 39 pigs. How many animals were in the pens?

Cumulative Checkup

Write the standard form.

1. 9 hundred thousands 4 tens
2. 8 thousands 6 tens 8 ones
3. 8 hundreds 5 tens 8 ones
4. 3 thousands 9 hundreds 2 tens
5. 10 000 + 6000 + 50 + 8
6. 600 000 + 300 + 20 + 9
7. 30 000 + 600 + 20
8. four thousand sixty-five
9. three hundred twenty thousand four hundred eighty-one
10. eight hundred seventy-five thousand fifty

Write the expanded form.

11. 4672
12. 5093
13. 23 716
14. 63 045
15. 40 706
16. 379 218
17. 750 624
18. 160 084

Order from least to greatest.

19. 678, 867, 786, 768
20. 1045, 1450, 986, 1050
21. $9.32, $9.73, $9.27, $9.81
22. 30 627, 41 268, 300 620, 45 318

Write the Roman numeral.

23. 73
24. 55
25. 19
26. 97
27. 8
28. 37
29. 26
30. 81
31. 62
32. 44

Round to the nearest ten.

33. 172
34. 384
35. 36
36. 6043
37. 5287

Round to the nearest hundred.

38. 653
39. 542
40. 4324
41. 1216
42. 251

Round to the nearest thousand.

43. 8240
44. 6825
45. 9562
46. 7499
47. 17 114

3/Subtraction

In this chapter you will learn to do
subtractions like 4003 − 1875.

Subtraction, No Regrouping

Subtract. 568 − 325
You can use models
and a chart.

You can write it this way.

Subtract ones.
5 6 **8**
− 3 2 **5**
3

Subtract tens.
5 **6** 8
− 3 **2** 5
4 3

Subtract hundreds.
5 6 8
− **3** 2 5
2 4 3

WORKING TOGETHER

Write the subtraction.

1.

tens	ones
||||||‖ XXX	XXXXX XX □

2.

hundreds	tens	ones
⊠ ▦ ▦ ▦	‖‖	XXXX □□

Subtract.

3. 59
  − 37

4. $7.67
  − 3.25

5. $5.48 − $2.12

6. 974 − 23

62

1. Subtract. Use the matching letters to decode the joke.

743	586	497	947	898
− 622	− 453	− 264	− 32	− 781
A	B	C	D	E

68	869	753	93	479
− 22	− 542	− 321	− 62	− 135
G	H	I	L	N

635	927	86	578	696
− 24	− 523	− 32	− 56	− 274
O	R	S	T	W

Knock! Knock!   422 327 611' 54   522 327 117 404 117?

522 432 31 915 121.   522 432 31 915 121   422 327 611?

522 432 31 915 121   133 117 31 31   404 432 344 46 54.

Solve.

2. Anna delivers 528 newspapers. Tony delivers 414 newspapers. How many more newspapers does Anna deliver than Tony?

3. 176 homes receive the late edition. 64 homes receive the early edition. How many fewer homes receive the early edition?

KEEPING SHARP

Add.

1. 7 + 7	**2.** 8 + 4	**3.** 6 + 7	**4.** 5 + 6	**5.** 3 + 9
6. 9 + 7	**7.** 4 + 7	**8.** 9 + 8	**9.** 8 + 5	**10.** 9 + 2
11. 8 + 3	**12.** 9 + 9	**13.** 6 + 9	**14.** 8 + 8	**15.** 5 + 7
16. 4 + 9	**17.** 7 + 8	**18.** 8 + 6	**19.** 5 + 9	**20.** 6 + 6

Subtraction, Regrouping Tens

The hobby shop has 74 model cars. Of these, 48 are antique cars. How many are not antique?

Subtract. 74 – 48

Round. Estimate.	Need more ones. Regroup 1 ten.	Subtract ones.	Subtract tens.
$\begin{array}{r} 7\,2 \to 7\,0 \\ -4\,8 \to -5\,0 \\ \hline 2\,0 \end{array}$	$\begin{array}{r} ^{6}^{12} \\ \not7\,\not2 \\ -4\,8 \\ \hline \end{array}$	$\begin{array}{r} ^{6}^{12} \\ \not7\,\not2 \\ -4\,8 \\ \hline 4 \end{array}$	$\begin{array}{r} ^{6}^{12} \\ \not7\,\not2 \\ -4\,8 \\ \hline 2\,4 \end{array}$

24 is close to 20. The difference is reasonable.
24 cars are not antique.

WORKING TOGETHER

Regroup 1 ten as 10 ones.

   ☐16   6 ☐

1. 4̸8̸   2. 7̸2̸   3. 84   4. 130   5. 169

Find the difference.

6. $\begin{array}{r} 45 \\ -26 \\ \hline \end{array}$ 7. $\begin{array}{r} 897 \\ -469 \\ \hline \end{array}$ 8. 48 – 16   9. $7.64 – $0.56

EXERCISES

Estimate.

1. 80 − 28	**2.** 878 − 35	**3.** 43 − 9	**4.** 560 − 319	**5.** 57 − 29

Find the difference.

6. 152 − 27	**7.** 74 − 68	**8.** 968 − 726	**9.** 377 − 65	**10.** 56 − 18

11. 794 − 545	**12.** 60 − 33	**13.** $6.84 − 4.63	**14.** 43 − 27	**15.** $2.64 − 0.39

16. 62 − 35   **17.** 178 − 19   **18.** 854 − 46   **19.** $7.91 − $2.83

20. 30 − 18   **21.** 460 − 329   **22.** 85 − 40   **23.** $2.47 − $0.28

Solve.

24. 43 model planes are on display. 92 model planes are in stock. How many more are in stock?

25. 174 model cars sold. 56 model planes sold. How many models sold in all?

26. 96 model spaceships sold. 38 model boats sold. How many fewer boats were sold?

27. 65 models are on sale. 47 models have been sold. How many models are left?

Try This

Randy named his model spaceships and arranged them like this.

Ace   Star   Lunar   Apollo   Eclipse   ___?___

Which of these names should be given to the last spaceship?

Orion, Enterprise, Sputnik, Voyageur, Saturn

Subtraction, Regrouping Hundreds or Thousands

The veterinarian gave rabies shots to 758 dogs this year. Last year the vet gave shots to 575 dogs. How many more shots were given this year?

Subtract. 758 − 575

Round. Estimate.	Subtract ones. Need more tens.	Regroup 1 hundred.	Subtract tens. Subtract hundreds.

758 → 800
−575 → −600
 200
	758
	−575
	   3
		6 15
		7̸ 5̸ 8
		−5 7 5
		     3
			6 15
			7̸ 5̸ 8
			−5 7 5
			 1 8 3

183 is close to 200. The difference is reasonable.
This year, 183 more shots were given.

WORKING TOGETHER

Regroup 1 hundred as 10 tens.

    ☐12   4 ☐
1. 3 2 7   **2.** 5 0 9   **3.** 4425   **4.** 2138   **5.** 7306

Regroup 1 thousand as 10 hundreds.

    ☐13   2 ☐
6. 8 3 8 7   **7.** 3 4 5 2   **8.** 2830   **9.** 5024   **10.** 1685

Subtract.

11.   549
  − 292   **12.**   6502
  − 3192   **13.** $74.68
  − 32.25   **14.** 2716 − 423

EXERCISES

Estimate.

1. 589	2. 1405	3. 7265	4. 2843	5. 768
− 294	− 122	− 4555	− 1212	− 495

Find the difference.

6. 6086	7. $5.29	8. 5586	9. $52.07	10. $62.43
− 536	− 4.87	− 1722	34.05	31.81

11. 9478	12. 549	13. $32.48	14. $72.77	15. $85.34
− 517	− 406	− 6.37	− 6.63	− 32.81

16. 678 − 384   **17.** 454 − 72   **18.** $93.69 − $75.41

19. 7805 − 4361   **20.** 3465 − 282   **21.** $60.90 − $8.50

Solve.

22. 2524 stray dogs were found this year. 2397 stray dogs were found last year. How many more were found this year?

23. The shelter spent $8265 for food this year. Last year it spent $7825. How much less did it spend last year?

Play with a partner. Enter 100 on a calculator.
Take turns subtracting any number from 1 to 9 from the display.
The player who reaches any of these numbers gets points.

75.	- 1 point
50.	- 2 points
30.	- 3 points
0.	- 4 points

The player who has more points when 0 is reached wins.

Subtraction, Two Regroupings

The music shop sold 2724 records and 1056 tapes. How many more records than tapes were sold?

Subtract. 2724 − 1056

Round. Estimate.	Regroup 1 ten. Subtract ones.	Regroup 1 hundred. Subtract tens.	Subtract hundreds. Subtract thousands.
2724→ 3000 −1056→−1000 2000	1 14 27 2̸ 4̸ −1 0 5 6 8	11 6 7̸ 14 27 2̸ 4̸ −1 0 5 6 6 8	11 6 7̸ 14 27 2̸ 4̸ −1 0 5 6 1 6 6 8

1668 is close to 2000. The difference is reasonable.
There were 1668 more records sold than tapes.

WORKING TOGETHER

Regroup 1 ten. Then regroup 1 hundred.

1. 496　　**2.** 224　　**3.** 5738　　**4.** 2647　　**5.** 4555

Regroup 1 hundred. Then regroup 1 thousand.

6. 3389　　**7.** 9162　　**8.** 7819　　**9.** 6114　　**10.** 1926

Estimate. Then subtract.

11.　8513
　　− 4274

12.　5238
　　− 2396

13. 1457 − 563

14. $4.05 − $1.22

EXERCISES

1. Subtract. Use the matching letters to decode the joke.

365	730	642	832	4516
− 178	− 86	− 468	− 579	− 1238
A	D	E	I	K

2473	7936	5563	4629	8115
− 284	− 4259	− 1670	− 3874	− 3742
L	M	N	O	R

3448	6524	6157	2840	9805
− 768	− 5135	− 373	− 158	− 4921
S	T	U	Y	♪♪

What did the music teacher say to the class?

253 1389' 2680   1389 253 3677 174   2682 755 5784

2189 174 187 4373 3893 174 644   1389 755

3677 187 3278 174   3893 755 1389 174 2680 4884

Solve.

2. 336 record albums sold.
178 single records sold.
How many records sold in all?

3. A record set costs $14.55. A tape set costs $16.90. How much more does the tape set cost?

 One tape player costs exactly $12.34 more than another. What are the prices of the two players?

$53.06 $59.38 $79.22

$71.72 $32.89 $38.72

$55.23 $65.98

Try This

69

Estimate.

1. 5351
   − 470

2. 9254
   − 3808

3. 9104
   − 5553

4. 567
   − 419

5. $62.79
   − 6.52

Subtract.

6. 836
   − 359

7. 673
   − 43

8. $9.23
   − 4.66

9. $73.92
   − 8.77

10. 923
    − 116

11. 8588
    − 7673

12. 2513
    − 267

13. 747
    − 316

14. 5350
    − 1948

15. $79.66
    − 48.83

16. 6218 − 572

17. 6638 − 3748

18. $7.82 − $1.26

19. 4748 − 345

20. $22.55 − $6.28

21. 650 − 97

Subtract. Use the differences to form a Magic Square.

22.

7551 − 5632	1017 − 407	9394 − 7849
3299 − 2315	2767 − 1409	5212 − 3480
6843 − 5672	8552 − 6446	999 − 202

Add across, down, or diagonally to get 4074 in the Magic Square.

Solve.

23. There are 375 pieces to the puzzle. 196 have been put together. How many pieces are left to be put together?

24. A jigsaw puzzle costs $7.21. Bill gives the clerk $9.01. How much money does Bill get back from the clerk?

The Subtraction Constant

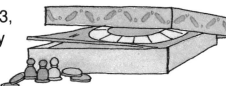

Four children each want to buy a game that costs $8. Paul has saved $17, Sue $23, Rita $11, and David $21. How much money will each child have left over?

$17 − $8 = $9 $23 − $8 = $15 $11 − $8 = $3 $21 − $8 = $13

Here is a short method. Do not press C between the parts.

[1][7][−][8][=]   [2][3][=]   [1][1][=]   [2][1][=]
    9.   15.   3.   13.

What number was subtracted from each of the others?
Where is it shown in the program?

Use the short method to complete the chart.

1.

	− 357
832	
1408	
501	
724	

2.

	− 492
501	
870	
2314	
940	

3.

	− 278
462	
689	
705	
1123	

Solve.

4. Three children each bought a $15 fish tank and some fish. How much did each child's fish cost?

Pierre

tank and angelfish, $19

Sarah

tank and goldfish, $21

Karen

tank and fancy guppies, $34

71

Subtraction, Three Regroupings

There are 4113 fiction books and 1875 sports books. How many more fiction than sports books are there?

Subtract. 4113 − 1875

Regroup 1 ten. Subtract ones.	Regroup 1 hundred. Subtract tens.	Regroup 1 thousand. Subtract hundreds.	Subtract thousands.
0 13 4 1 1̸ 3̸ −1 8 7 5 　　　8	10 0 0̸ 13 4 1̸ 1̸ 3̸ −1 8 7 5 　　3 8	10 10 3 0̸ 0̸ 13 4̸ 1̸ 1̸ 3̸ −1 8 7 5 　2 3 8	10 10 3 0̸ 0̸ 13 4̸ 1̸ 1̸ 3̸ −1 8 7 5 2 2 3 8

There are 2238 more fiction books than sports books.

WORKING TOGETHER

Regroup 1 ten. Regroup 1 hundred. Then regroup 1 thousand.

1. 8651　　2. 6922　　3. 4816　　4. 5624　　5. 7520

Round to estimate. Then subtract.

6.　8217
　　− 2258

7.　4141
　　− 2794

8.　$65.68
　　− 28.47

9. 3742 − 953

Find the difference.

1. 2523
    – 1678

2. 4292
    – 703

3. 3431
    – 1552

4. 9414
    – 3682

5. $68.47
    – 29.78

6. $36.76
    – 8.88

7. 2375
    – 1685

8. $71.46
    – 50.48

9. 3526
    – 1869

10. 4753
    – 958

11. $66.32 – $17.58

12. 2438 – 749

13. 1775 – 588

Solve.

14. How many more social studies books are there than biography books?

15. How many fewer science books are there than fiction books?

16. How many social studies and sports books are there? How many fewer of these are there than fiction books?

Library Inventory

Biography	649 books
Fiction	4113 books
Science	1179 books
Social Studies	2104 books
Sports	1873 books

Ink was spilled on the library's record book.
Complete a new page for the record book.

Try This

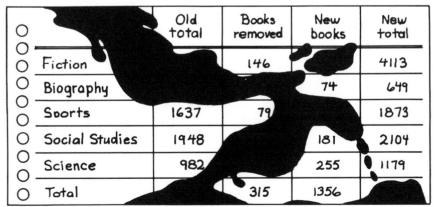

	Old total	Books removed	New books	New total
Fiction		146		4113
Biography			74	649
Sports	1637	79		1873
Social Studies	1948		181	2104
Science	982		255	1179
Total		315	1356	

Subtraction, Regrouping Zero

A sporting goods store sold 4000 baseball caps. Of these, 2974 were Toronto Blue Jay caps. How many were not Blue Jay caps?

Subtract. 4000 − 2974

Need more ones. 0 in tens place.	Regroup one of the 400 tens.	Subtract ones. Subtract tens.	Subtract hundreds. Subtract thousands.
$\begin{array}{r} 4\,0\,0\,0 \\ -2\,9\,7\,4 \\ \hline \end{array}$	$\begin{array}{r} 3\,9\,9\,10 \\ \cancel{4\,0\,0\,0} \\ -2\,9\,7\,4 \\ \hline \end{array}$	$\begin{array}{r} 3\,9\,9\,10 \\ \cancel{4\,0\,0\,0} \\ -2\,9\,7\,4 \\ \hline 2\,6 \end{array}$	$\begin{array}{r} 3\,9\,9\,10 \\ \cancel{4\,0\,0\,0} \\ -2\,9\,7\,4 \\ \hline 1\,0\,2\,6 \end{array}$

1026 of the caps were not Blue Jay caps.

WORKING TOGETHER

Copy and complete the regroupings.

1. $\begin{array}{r} 4\,9\,9\,\square \\ \cancel{5\,0\,0\,0} \end{array}$
2. $\begin{array}{r} \square\,13 \\ 3\,\cancel{0}\,\cancel{8}\,8 \end{array}$
3. $\begin{array}{r} \square\,15 \\ 2\,\cancel{4}\,\cancel{0}\,\cancel{5} \end{array}$
4. $\begin{array}{r} \square\,12 \\ \cancel{1}\,\cancel{0}\,\cancel{0}\,\cancel{2} \end{array}$
5. $\begin{array}{r} \square\,10 \\ 7\,\cancel{5}\,\cancel{0}\,\cancel{0} \end{array}$

Copy and complete.

6. $\begin{array}{r} \square\ \ \square \\ \$3\cancel{0}.\cancel{4}9 \\ -2.75 \\ \hline 4 \end{array}$

7. $\begin{array}{r} \square\,\square \\ \cancel{2\,0\,0\,0} \\ -1\,8\,2\,4 \\ \hline \end{array}$

8. $\begin{array}{r} 4\,6\,0\,2 \\ -1\,2\,3\,4 \\ \hline \end{array}$

9. 5005 − 1726

EXERCISES

Find the difference.

1.	6048 − 3265	**2.**	7004 − 3957	**3.**	3800 − 665	**4.**	7028 − 1154	**5.**	$15.02 − 5.79
6.	802 − 254	**7.**	3030 − 883	**8.**	8000 − 3078	**9.**	4701 − 2815	**10.**	$20.28 − 19.32
11.	6073 − 1478	**12.**	1002 − 266	**13.**	$32.01 − 22.57	**14.**	$50.00 − 4.64	**15.**	$26.03 − 8.84

16. 6005 − 2849   **17.** 7046 − 392   **18.** $91.01 − $9.66

Solve.

19. The city had $5000 for a baseball field. It spent $4027. How much money was left?

20. A team ordered 17 uniforms. Each cost $32.09. Sid brought $40.00 for his. How much change did he receive?

21. Babe Ruth's home run record was 714, Willie Mays's was 660, and Hank Aaron's was 755. What was the total of all three players?

22. 2400 fans were at the Junior League game. Of them 1869 were children. How many fans were adults?

KEEPING SHARP

Copy and complete.

		Round to the nearest		
		ten	hundred	thousand
1.	4945			
2.	3653			
3.	5815			
4.	1274			

Using Addition to Check Subtraction

The bicycle costs $79.95.
Melanie has saved $62.50.
How much more money does
she need to buy the bicycle?

Subtract. $79.95 − $62.50

Round. Estimate.	Subtract.	Add to check.
$79.95 → $80.00 −62.50 → −60.00 $20.00	$79.95 −62.50 $17.45	$17.45 +62.50 $79.95

$17.45 is close to $20.00
Melanie needs $17.45 more to buy the bicycle.

WORKING TOGETHER

Which numbers do you add to check the subtraction?

| 1. | 624
− 296
328 | 2. | 245
− 69
176 | 3. | 8283
− 3386
4897 | 4. | 4004
− 2985
1019 | 5. | 6123
− 347
5776 |

Subtract. Then add to check.

6. 836
   − 499

7. $72.80
   − 44.57

8. $55.01
   − 7.95

9. 5136 − 2847

EXERCISES

Subtract. Then add to check using a calculator.

1. 735 − 201	**2.** 942 − 473	**3.** 900 − 618	**4.** 5231 − 3997	**5.** 3312 − 1879
6. 2130 − 699	**7.** 9100 − 7457	**8.** 7823 − 5658	**9.** $86.40 − 29.98	**10.** $35.02 − 13.55
11. 9360 − 3748	**12.** 4120 − 899	**13.** $32.75 − 8.29	**14.** $53.11 − 16.48	**15.** 6521 − 1637

16. 6187 − 1844   **17.** 1125 − 632   **18.** $40.64 − $4.06

Solve. Then add to check.

19. Mike's bike repairs cost $7.82. He paid with a ten-dollar bill. How much change did he receive?

20. Tony had his slot car repaired for $0.79. How much change did he receive from one dollar?

21. The plumber charged $25.61. How much change did she give for 3 ten-dollar bills?

22. Sara's shoe repairs cost $5.65. New laces cost $1.25. She has eight dollars. Does she have enough money?

Computer equipment is called **hardware**.

1. Name the equipment in this computer system.

2. Name some other equipment that can be connected to a computer.

PRACTICE

Find the difference.

1. 2461 – 1683	**2.** 4036 – 868	**3.** 6284 – 2896	**4.** $81.94 – 63.95	**5.** 7248 – 579
6. 6000 – 898	**7.** 5600 – 1367	**8.** 3000 – 462	**9.** $40.00 – 28.15	**10.** 8008 – 2189

11. 5397 – 1698   **12.** $42.75 – $8.86   **13.** 6002 – 2165

14. 8432 – 953   **15.** 7000 – 546   **16.** $32.46 – $13.59

Add to check the subtraction. Correct any mistakes.

17. 3378 – 489 2888	**18.** 8352 – 5811 3541	**19.** 786 – 299 467	**20.** 6639 – 4572 2067	**21.** 8743 – 6259 1484

Solve.

22. The shoe store had 3432 pairs of shoes in April. 1775 pairs were sold. How many pairs were left at the end of April?

23. The store sold 1700 pairs of shoes in July. 588 pairs were sports shoes. How many pairs sold were not sports shoes?

24. The store held a special sale. $3000 worth of shoes were sold for $1768. How much less did the shoes cost on sale?

78

Input and Output Equipment

Tell whether the devices named below receive input or give output.

1.

A game is shown on a **monitor**. You can use a **joystick** to move your player. Sounds come from a **speaker** when you win the game.

2.

A floppy disk is inserted into a **disk drive**. You can use a **light pen** to point to pictures or words shown on a **touch screen**.

3.

You can use a **mouse** or **trackball** to move numbers, words, or pictures on the screen in any direction. A **printer** can show results on paper.

4.

A **turtle robot** can act out the Logo commands you type on a **keyboard**. It can draw designs with its pen down.

More Than One Step

How many books are in Ken's bookcase?
There are 36 books on the top shelf. The
middle shelf has 17 fewer books than the
top shelf. The bottom shelf has twice as
many books as the middle shelf.

36 books
17 less than 36
twice as many as middle

Think. Draw a picture. Ask questions about it.

Do I need to know what the books are about?

Does it matter how the books are arranged?

Plan and do. First find the number of books on each shelf.

	Top	Middle	Bottom
	3 6	2 16 $\cancel{3}\cancel{6}$ − 1 7 ——— 1 9	1 1 9 +1 9 ——— 3 8

Then find the total.

```
  2
  3 6
  1 9
+ 3 8
-----
  9 3
```

Look back. Ken found the total another way.

There are 93 books in all.

```
   1            1
   3 6          5 5
 + 1 9        + 3 8
 -----        -----
   5 5          9 3
```

WORKING TOGETHER

1. How many books are on the bottom shelf?

2. Solve the problem another way.

168 books in all
54 books
23 books
▢ books

80

PROBLEMS

Solve the problem. Show the steps.

1. How many cars are parked in the garage?

   ☐ cars parked in all

63 cars parked on the 3rd level
86 cars parked on the 2nd level
75 cars parked on the 1st level

2. How many records are on the third shelf?

   317 records in all

63 records on the top shelf
128 records on the 2nd shelf
☐ records on the 3rd shelf
92 records on the bottom shelf

3. Kevin had $5.00. He spent $2.89. He earned $2.50 more. Now how much money does Kevin have?

4. How much money does Lynne have left? She had $10.00. She spent $1.47 in one store and $3.75 in another store.

5. How much money do you have left from $4.00? You bought as many notebooks as you could.

   Notebooks
   $1.20 each

6. There are 62 eggs to pack in cartons. How many full cartons can you pack?

7. A mystery book has 212 pages. Beth read 98 pages of the book on Monday. She finished the book on Tuesday. How many more pages did she read on Tuesday than on Monday?

8. 495 children at Macdonald School and 347 children at Laurier School had to have booster shots. The nurses have given 516 shots already. How many children still need their shots?

Problem Solving Review

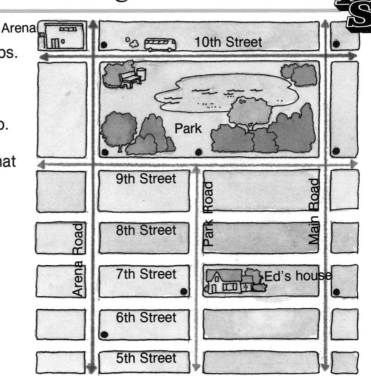

The colored lines show bus routes. The dots show bus stops.

1. How can Ed get to the Arena by bus? He walks from his house to a bus stop.

2. Describe two other routes that Ed can take.

3. Which route do you think is the best? Why?

Solve.

4. Pat receives 25¢ each day for walking her neighbor's dog. How much does she earn in 6 days?

5. Ben left for school at 8:15 a.m. He came home at 3:15 p.m. How long was he away?

6. Altogether, how many pencil crayons are missing from the two packs?

7. How many windows are along the front of the three office buildings?

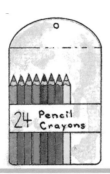

Chapter Checkup

Estimate.

1. $83.26
   − 47.58

2. 2049
   − 976

3. $58.42
   − 12.71

4. 1720
   − 716

Do the first three exercises in each set. Use the pattern to find the answer for the fourth exercise.

5. 9655
   − 8421

6. 2687
   − 1353

7. 2030
   − 596

8. 7883
   − 6349

9. 7823
   − 5658

10. 8464
    − 2852

11. 8502
    − 6337

12. 9681
    − 4069

13. 2000
    − 779

14. 2928
    − 486

15. 5311
    − 1648

16. 6501
    − 1617

Subtract. Then add to check.

17. 7000 − 4826

18. 7123 − 1154

19. 3807 − 665

20. 6073 − 1478

21. 5132 − 464

22. $15.02 − $5.79

Solve.

23. The drive-in theatre holds 562 cars. 374 cars came Friday night. How many more cars can the drive-in hold?

24. 374 cars were at the theatre. 259 were on time for the first movie. How many cars were late?

25. After the first movie, 314 people visited the snack bar. 178 visited it after the second movie. How many visited in all?

26. The first movie lasts 145 min (minutes). The second movie lasts 98 min. How much longer is the first movie?

Cumulative Checkup

Use >, <, or = to make a true statement.

1. XXVI ⊙ XIX   **2.** XL ⊙ LXX   **3.** LX ⊙ XXXV

4. 2750 ⊙ 2570   **5.** 9628 ⊙ 9682   **6.** 700 + 50 ⊙ 705

7. 10 000 + 400 + 50 + 3 ⊙ 10 435   **8.** 8567 ⊙ 8000 + 500 + 70 + 7

Order from least to greatest.

9. $6.73, $7.04, $6.39, $7.50   **10.** 396, 636, 963, 369

11. 4971, 7194, 7419, 4719   **12.** 5832, 5383, 5823, 5288

13. $12.63, $16.20, $12.30, $15.00   **14.** XXIV, XXII, XIX, X

Estimate.

15. 632 + 493   **16.** 805 + 655   **17.** 434 + 212

Add.

18.	**19.**	**20.**	**21.**	**22.**
638 + 261	436 + 259	167 + 284	460 + 239	28 + 49

23.	**24.**	**25.**	**26.**	**27.**
43 32 60 + 85	170 340 25 + 458	167 322 + 506	90 136 28 + 14	931 286 + 138

28.	**29.**	**30.**	**31.**
4327 + 1826	8075 + 784	1629 + 3582	741 + 3389

32.	**33.**	**34.**	**35.**
2674 + 2346	5264 + 777	3284 + 1988	1625 + 493

4/Geometry

In this chapter you will learn about geometric shapes. You will see these shapes in your environment.

Lines and Line Segments

This marking suggests a **line segment**.

The shoulder marking suggests a **line**.

A **line** is a straight path that continues without end.

A **line segment** is a straight path that connects two end points.

WORKING TOGETHER

Does the figure show a line?

1.
2.
3.
4.
5.

Does the figure show a line segment?

6.
7.
8.
9.
10.

Which part of the picture suggests a line or a line segment?

11.
12.
13.

EXERCISES

True or false?

1.  — — — — a line segment

2.  a line

3.  ← – – → a line

4.  a line segment

5.  •———• a line segment

6.  a line segment

7.  •———→ a line

8.  ←———→ a line

Which part of the picture suggests a line or a line segment?

9.

10.

11.

12.

13.

14.

15. How many lines are there?

16. How many line segments are there?

These words and numbers are **palindromes**. What is the same about them?

OTTO   3773
RADAR
141   MOM

Take a number. Reverse the digits and add the two numbers. Repeat until you get a palindrome.

1. 75   ⑦ ⑤ ⊞ ⑤ ⑦ ⊟ (132)   ⊞ ② ③ ① ⊟ (   )

2. 16   **3.** 47   **4.** 78   **5.** 138   **6.** 762

Which number needed the most repetitions?

Angles

The hands on a clock suggest an **angle**.

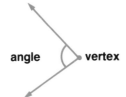

angle   vertex

The **vertex** names the angle.

S

This is **angle S**, or ∠**S**.

P

An angle that makes a square corner is a **right angle**.
Angle P, or ∠P, is a right angle.

WORKING TOGETHER

Name the angle.

1.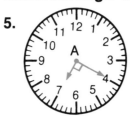

2.

3.

4.

Match the angle with its description.

5.

6.

7.

8.

| a right angle | an angle smaller than a right angle | an angle larger than a right angle |

EXERCISES

Use the classroom.

1. List ten objects that suggest angles.

Name the red angle.

2.

3.

4.

Match the angle with its description.

5.   **6.**   **7.**   **8.**

a right angle	an angle smaller than a right angle	an angle larger than a right angle

Draw a clock. Show the hands making the angle.

9. an angle smaller than a right angle

10. a right angle

11. an angle larger than a right angle

---

1. Draw an angle smaller than a right angle.

2. Make the arms of the angle 12 cm long.

3. Mark dots 1 cm apart on each arm, beginning at the vertex.

4. Join the outside dots of one arm to the inside dots of the other arm. Use different colors.

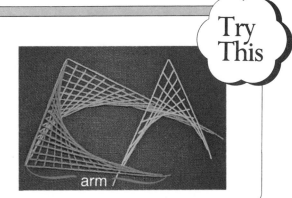

arm

Try This

Polygons

A closed figure whose sides are line segments is a **polygon**.

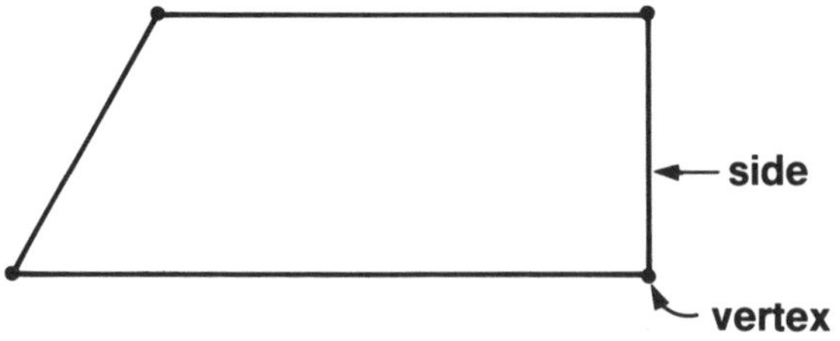

← side

vertex

A **triangle** is a polygon with 3 sides.

A **quadrilateral** is a polygon with 4 sides.

A **pentagon** is a polygon with 5 sides.

A **hexagon** is a polygon with 6 sides.

An **octagon** is a polygon with 8 sides.

Special jobs need special tools.

A **rectangle** is a quadrilateral with opposite sides equal and 4 right angles.

A **square** is a quadrilateral with 4 equal sides and 4 right angles.

WORKING TOGETHER

Is the figure a polygon?

1.

2.

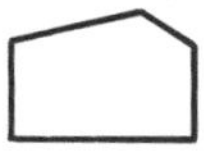

3.

4.

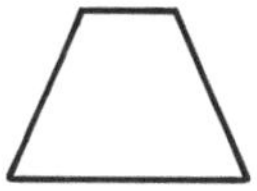

5.

Use the picture.

1. List examples of polygons.

Is the figure a polygon?

2.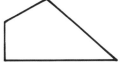

3.

4.

5.

Write the kind of polygon.

6.

7.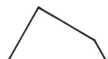

8.

9.

10. 3 vertices   **11.** 6 sides   **12.** 4 vertices   **13.** 5 sides

Draw a polygon with the following.

14. 6 vertices   **15.** 4 equal sides   **16.** 5 vertices   **17.** 3 sides

---

Try This

These are marms.

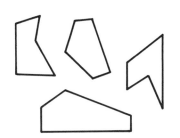

These are not marms.

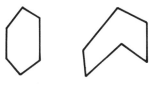

Which of these are marms?

1.   **2.**

3.   **5.**   **4.**

91

Solids

What solid shapes
do you see?

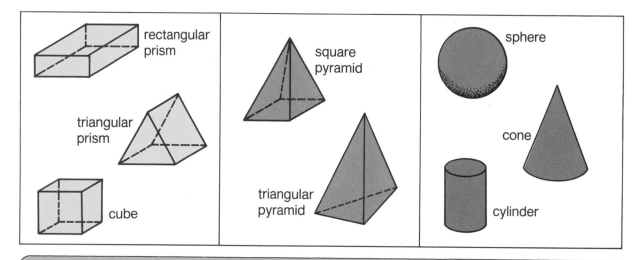

rectangular prism

triangular prism

cube

square pyramid

triangular pyramid

sphere

cone

cylinder

WORKING TOGETHER

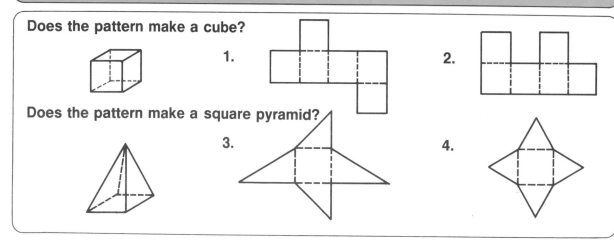

Does the pattern make a cube?

1.

2.

Does the pattern make a square pyramid?

3.

4.

Which solid shape is suggested?

1.

2.

3.

4.

Does the pattern make this solid shape?

8.
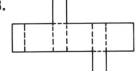

9.

10.

11.

12.
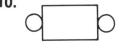

13.

Try This

Prisms cost 20¢ each. Pyramids cost 15¢ each.
Cones, cylinders, and spheres cost 10¢ each.
Make a building that will cost $1.00.

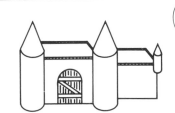

Face, Edge, and Vertex

A **face** of a solid is a flat surface.

Faces meet at an **edge**.
Edges meet at a **vertex**.

You can use straws and pipecleaners to make
the edges and vertices of solid shapes.

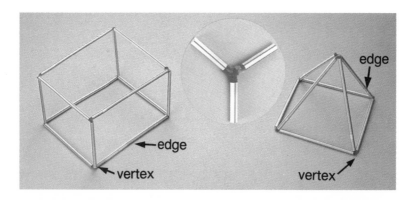

WORKING TOGETHER

How many?

1. edges

2. vertices

3. faces

What is the shape of the face?

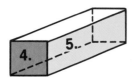 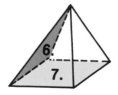

94

EXERCISES

How many straws are needed to make the edges?

1.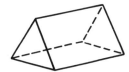

2.

3.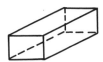

How many vertices need pipe cleaners?

4.

5.

6.

How many?

7. faces

8. edges

9. vertices

10. edges

11. vertices

12. faces

Write the shape of the face.

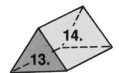
13. **14.**

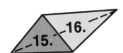
15. **16.**

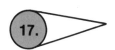
17.

KEEPING SHARP

Add.

1.	31 + 14	**2.**	223 + 35	**3.**	425 + 253	**4.**	570 + 108	**5.**	58 + 23
6.	237 + 45	**7.**	461 + 59	**8.**	536 + 387	**9.**	281 + 309	**10.**	526 + 688

PRACTICE

Name the angles.

1. larger than a right angle

2. a right angle

3. smaller than a right angle

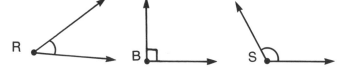

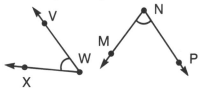

Write the kind of polygon.

4.

5.

6.

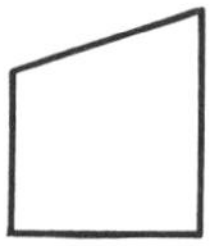

7.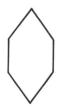

8.

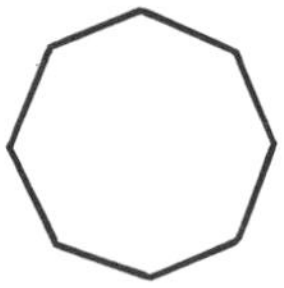

9.

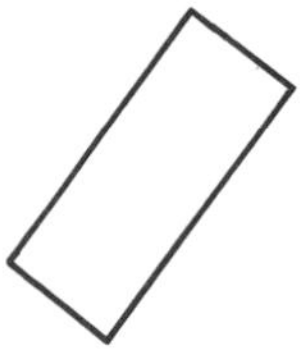

10.

11.

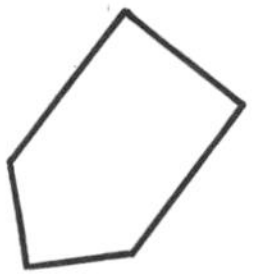

Name the solid.

12.

13.

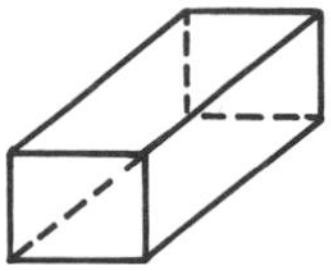

14.

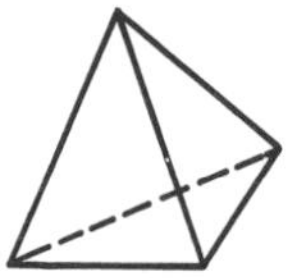

15.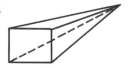

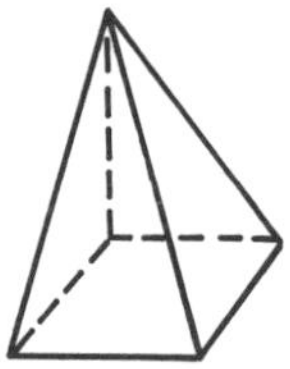

How many?

16. edges

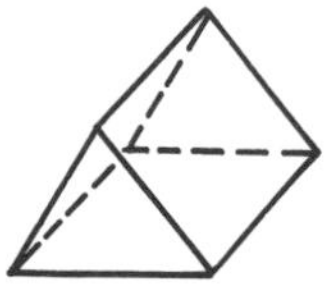

17. vertices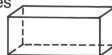

18. faces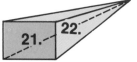

Write the shape of the face.

96

Codes

A	B	C	D	E	F	G	H	I
131	132	133	134	135	136	137	138	139

J	K	L	M	N	O	P	Q	R
140	141	142	143	144	145	146	147	148

S	T	U	V	W	X	Y	Z	space
149	150	151	152	153	154	155	156	157

Some codes use the numbers just as they are.

The code for CAT is   133   131   150.

Other codes make you calculate.

A code for CAT could be   67 + 66   198 − 67   82 + 68.

                              133   131   150

Use a calculator to decode the message.

1. 107 + 31   151 − 16   75 + 67   325 − 179

2. 207 − 74   73 + 72   418 − 275   106 + 29   391 − 234
     81 + 57   192 − 57   65 + 83   620 − 485

Write a code.

3. DOG   **4.** HOUSE   **5.** COME TO MY HOUSE

6. Make up a message for a friend. Code it.

7. You know where a treasure is hidden. Write a code for the location.

97

Line Symmetry

The flag can be folded so that
one part matches the other part.

The flag has
line symmetry.

The fold line is the
line of symmetry.

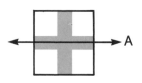 A

Line A is a
line of symmetry.

Line B is not a
line of symmetry.

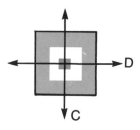 D

Both line C and line D
are lines of symmetry.

Which is a line of symmetry?

1.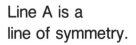
A ← → B

2.
C
D

3.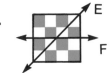
E
F

Trace the figure. Draw the line of symmetry.

4.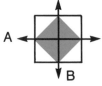

5.

6.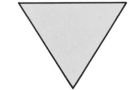

EXERCISES

Which is a line of symmetry?

1.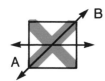

2.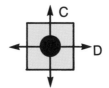

3.

Trace the picture. Draw the line of symmetry.

4.

5.

6.

Line M is the line of symmetry. Copy and complete the figure.

7.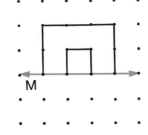

8.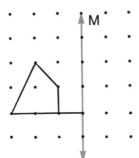

9.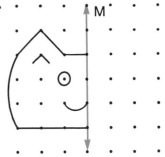

Draw the picture. Show a line of symmetry.

10. a rectangle

11. the letter A

12. the numeral eight

KEEPING SHARP

Subtract.

1. 78	**2.** 335	**3.** 596	**4.** 73	**5.** 214	**6.** 560
− 56	− 24	− 354	− 56	− 37	− 374

Flips

Flip one page about the
flip line.

The two pictures match.
They are **flip images**.

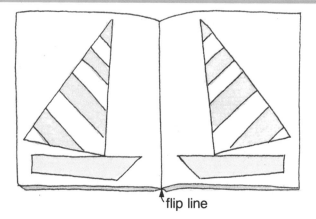

flip line

Finding the Flip Image

Trace the red shape and the two dots.

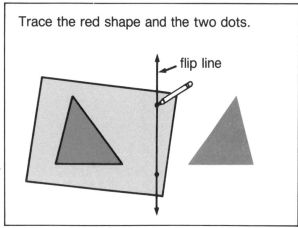

flip line

Flip the tracing over. Match the two pairs of dots.

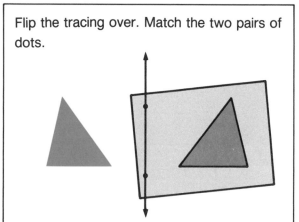

The tracing matches the blue shape.
The blue shape is the flip image of the red shape.

WORKING TOGETHER

Use tracing paper. Is the blue shape the flip image of the red shape?

1.

2.

100

Does the picture suggest a flip?

1.    **2.**    **3.**

Use tracing paper. Is the blue shape the flip image of the red shape?

4.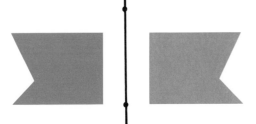

5.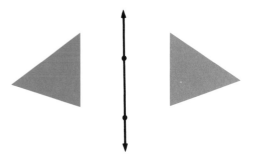

6.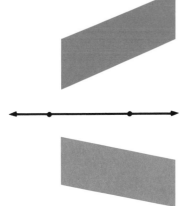

7.

A triangle is flipped to make the tiling pattern.

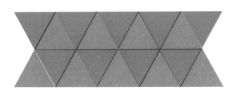

Make a tiling pattern by flipping a hexagon.

Try This

Slides

The **slide arrow** shows the direction
and the distance that the toboggan
slides.

Finding the Slide Image

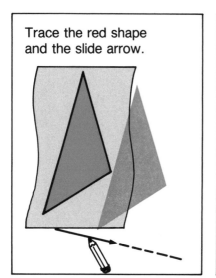

Trace the red shape
and the slide arrow.

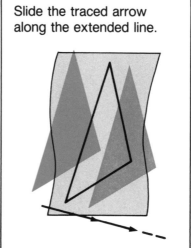

Slide the traced arrow
along the extended line.

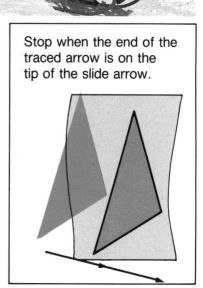

Stop when the end of the
traced arrow is on the
tip of the slide arrow.

The tracing matches the blue shape.
The blue shape is the **slide image** of the red shape.

WORKING TOGETHER

**Use tracing paper. Is the blue shape the slide image of the red shape
for the given slide arrow?**

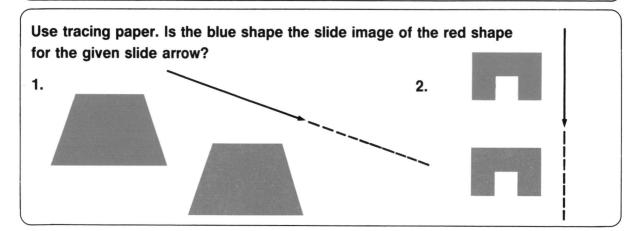

1.

2.

EXERCISES

Does the picture suggest a slide?

1.

2.

3.

Use tracing paper. Is the blue shape the slide image of the red shape for the given slide arrow?

4.

5.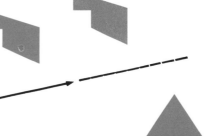

6.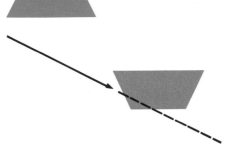

7.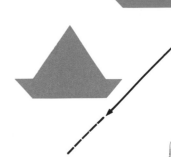

People invent machines to help them solve problems.

Match the problem with the invention that solves it.

1. How can I travel quickly to the top floor of a tall building?

2. How can I write something that is hard to erase?

3. How can the names, addresses, and numbers for a telephone book be sorted?

4. How can the Prime Minister be seen and heard by most Canadians?

COMPUTER

TELEPHONE

TELEVISION

SNOWMOBILE

BALLPOINT PEN

ZIPPER

ELEVATOR

Turns

Each swing turns about a point.
The point is the **turn centre**.

Finding the Turn Image

Trace the red shape. Mark a dot at the end of the **turn arrow**.	Press a pencil point on the turn centre. Turn the tracing to move the dot along the turn arrow.	Stop when the dot is on the tip of the arrow.

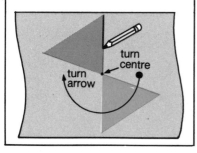

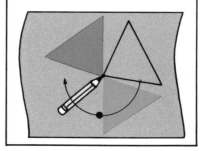

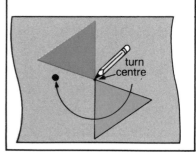

The traced shape matches the blue shape.
The blue shape is the **turn image** of the red shape.

WORKING TOGETHER

Use tracing paper. Is the blue shape the turn image of the red shape?

1.

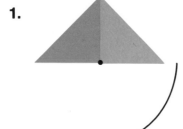

2.

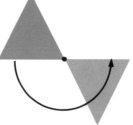

Does the picture suggest a turn?

1.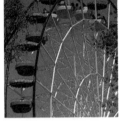

2.

3.

Use tracing paper. Is the blue shape the turn image of the red shape?

4.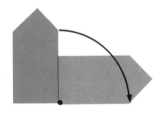

5.

6.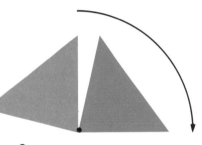

7.

8.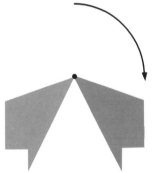

9.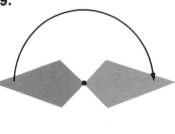

Try This

Where will the arrow be?

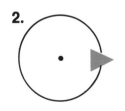
turn centre $\frac{1}{4}$ turn

$\frac{1}{2}$ turn

1.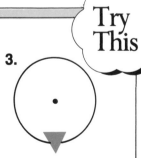
after $\frac{1}{4}$ turn

2.
after $\frac{1}{2}$ turn

3.
after $\frac{1}{4}$ turn

Congruent Shapes

Use tracing paper to find the button that matches the button on Kyle's sleeve.

Objects that have the same size and shape are **congruent**.

Finding Congruent Shapes

Trace the red triangle.	Move the tracing over the blue triangle.	The tracing matches the blue triangle.

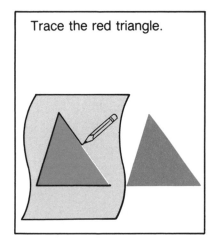 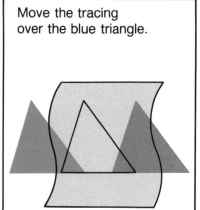 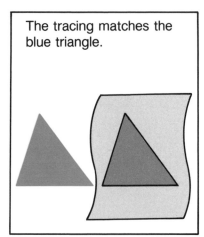

The blue triangle is **congruent** to the red triangle.

WORKING TOGETHER

Use tracing paper. Is the blue shape congruent to the red shape?

1.

2.

3.

Use tracing paper. Is the blue shape congruent to the red shape?

1.

2.

3.

4.

5.

6.

Use tracing paper. Find pairs of congruent figures.

7.

8.

9.

10.

11.

12.

13.

Try This

Use tangram pieces to construct the bear and the giraffe.

Construct a shape of your own.

Trace the figure. Draw the lines of symmetry.

1.

2.

3.

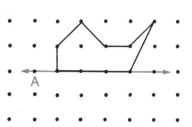

Line A is the line of symmetry. Copy and complete the figure.

4.

5.

6.

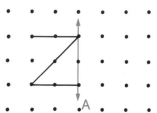

Does the picture suggest a slide, a flip, or a turn?

7.

8.

9.

10.

Use tracing paper. Is the blue shape a slide, flip, or turn image?

11.

12.

13.

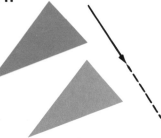
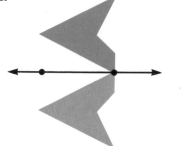
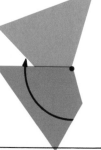

What Computers Can Do

There are many sizes and types of computers.
Some are large enough to fill a room.
Some are small enough to fit in your pocket.

People use computers to help them solve problems.

Some computers can do only
one special job:
help scientists steer a rocket
help postal workers sort mail
help athletes test their fitness

Other computers can do many
different jobs:
help doctors care for patients
help librarians keep track of books
help secretaries produce reports

Suppose you want to make a telephone book for your school.
Think of the tasks involved.

Step 1: Print the last name, first name, address, and phone number
of each student on a card.
Step 2: Sort all the cards alphabetically by last name.
Step 3: List the sorted information on blank pages to make a book.

1. Use the steps above to make a
phone book for your class.

2. What do you think a computer
could do to help you?

Draw a Picture

How many rungs does the ladder have?

A fireman stood on the middle rung of the ladder to spray water on a burning building. When the fire died down he climbed up 3 rungs. Then the fire flared up again so he climbed down 5 rungs. Later he climbed up 6 rungs and put the fire out. Finally he climbed up the last 4 rungs and stepped onto the roof.

Start

Think.   Act out the problem.

Plan and do.   Draw a picture.

Look back.   Which solution makes sense? Why?

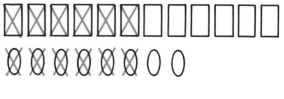

The ladder has 11 rungs.

No, the ladder has 17 rungs.

WORKING TOGETHER

Use the picture to solve the problem.

1. Jim bought 12 buns and 8 wieners. He made 6 hot dogs. How many more hot dogs can he make?

2. There are 12 houses on Key Street. Every fourth house has a garage. How many do not have a garage?

Copy and complete the picture. Then solve the problem.

1. Mr. and Mrs. Rogers have 4 daughters. Each daughter has 3 children. How many grandchildren do the Rogers have?

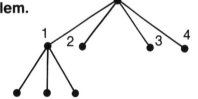

2. Len built a pyramid with 28 blocks. In which row from the bottom does the 15th block go?

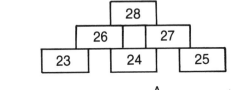

3. Anne, Bob, and Clare can form pairs in 3 ways. How many ways can Anne, Bob, Clare, Daniel, and Earl form pairs?

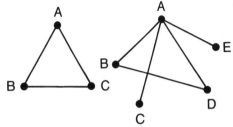

4. Who is the oldest and who is the youngest? Lena, Joy, Kurt, and Pierre were born the same year. Lena's birthday is in the 8th month. Joy's birthday is 6 months before Lena's. Kurt's birthday is 4 months after Joy's. Pierre's birthday is exactly halfway between Joy's and Kurt's.

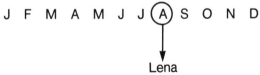

Draw a picture to help you solve the problem.

5. Ray has 1 black marble and 2 white marbles. How many different color patterns can he make with 3 marbles in a row?

6. There are 4 elephants in a parade. Each elephant is 3 m (metres) long. The spaces between them are 2 m long. How long is the line?

7. Marcy puts a thumbtack in each corner of a picture. What is the least number of tacks she needs to put up 4 pictures?

Problem Solving Review

Solve.

1. Susan scored 143 points in a game. Peter scored 151 points, John scored 156 points. Karen scored 160 points. Who scored more points, the boys, or the girls? How many more?

2. How many pieces will you have if you cut straight across a pie three times?

3. What is the cost for 2 adults and 4 children to go on the water slide?

4. Six children and their leader from Shady Summer Camp went on the water slide. The camp leader paid with a $20 bill. How much change did she receive?

WATER SLIDE RIDES
Adults $3
Children $2

5. Becky is shorter than Ted. Ted is shorter than Fran. Who is the shortest? Who is the tallest?

6. What time did Roland wake up? He went to bed three hours before midnight. Then he slept for ten hours.

7. You get on an elevator at the ground floor. You go up 7 floors, down 4 floors, up 8 floors, down 3 floors, down 6 floors, and up 2 floors. Then you get off the elevator. What floor are you on?

8. A litre of milk provides 5 glasses of milk. How many litres of milk are needed for a party for your class?

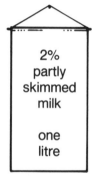

2% partly skimmed milk

one litre

Chapter Checkup

Match the shape with the word.

1.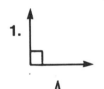
2.
3.
4.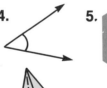
5.

6.
7.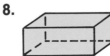
8.
9.
10. ·———————·

| octagon | hexagon | pyramid | line segment | cone | cylinder |
| square | prism | angle | right angle | line | cube |

How many?

11. vertices 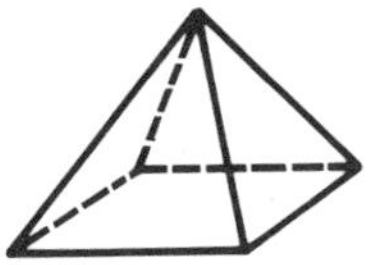
12. edges
13. faces

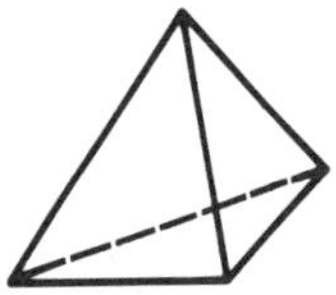

Trace the figure. Is the red line a line of symmetry?

14.
15.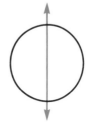
16.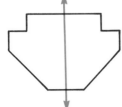

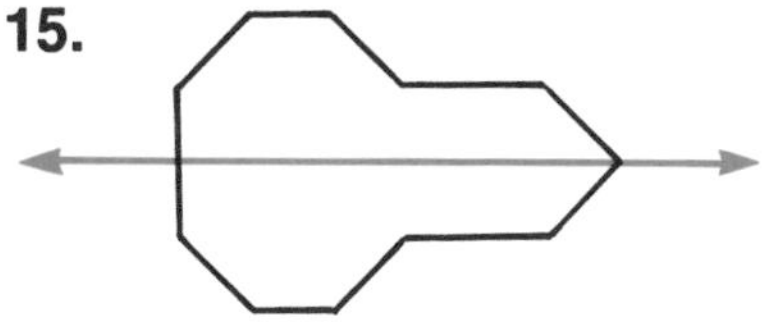

Use tracing paper. Is the blue shape congruent to the red shape?

17.
18.

Cumulative Checkup

Write the numbers that come before and after.

1. ☐, 4229, ☐

2. ☐, 10 330, ☐

3. ☐, 999, ☐

4. ☐, 42 681, ☐

5. ☐, XXIX, ☐

6. ☐, XC, ☐

Add or subtract.

7. 458
+ 297

8. 306
+ 588

9. 934
+ 76

10. 825
+ 174

11. 907
+ 27

12. 6254
+ 1896

13. 3078
+ 933

14. 7004
+ 1997

15. 2659
+ 2659

16. 8000
− 2432

17. 6409
− 2819

18. 5067
− 2878

19. 3600
− 921

20. $7062
− 3473

21. $20.60
− 19.75

22. $40.85
− 18.90

23. $3000
− 2892

Solve.

24. The corner store sold 3625 packs of gum. 1270 of the packs were bubble gum. How many were not?

25. The store sells 320 morning papers and 583 evening papers each day. How many papers are sold each day?

26. The store sold 2640 popsicles last year and 1960 this year. How many more popsicles were sold last year?

27. In one week the store took in 5300 pennies and 4670 nickels. How many more pennies than nickels were taken in?

28. The store sold 429 magazines last week and 387 this week. How many magazines were sold in the two weeks?

29. The store sold 2725 bags of 2% milk and 1286 bags of skim milk last month. How many bags of milk were sold in all?

5/Multiplication

In this chapter you will learn more
about factors, products, and multiples.
You will see them in different settings,
from nature to supermarkets,
hockey leagues, and picnics.

Multiplication to 9 × 5

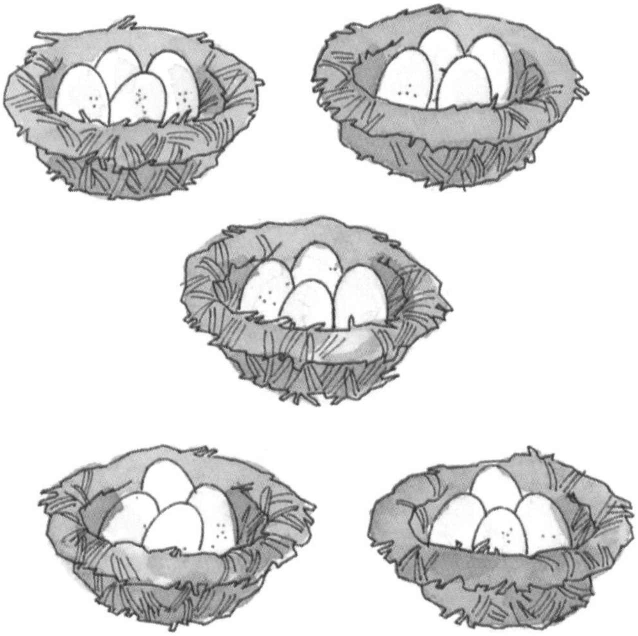

Tom sees 5 birds' nests.
Each nest has 4 eggs.
How many eggs are there in all?

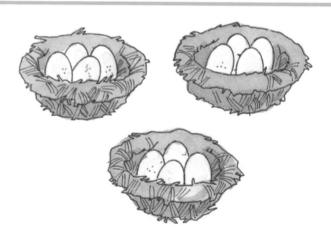

Tom adds.

4 + 4 + 4 + 4 + 4 = 20

He can also multiply.

$$\begin{array}{r} 4 \\ \times 5 \\ \hline 20 \end{array}$$

5 × 4 = 20   or

factor   factor   product

There are 20 eggs in all.

WORKING TOGETHER

Skip count.

1. by 5's to 45   **2.** by 3's to 27   **3.** by 2's to 18

Copy and complete the number sentences.

4. 2 + 2 + 2 + 2 + 2 = ☐
5 × 2 = ☐

5. 3 + 3 + 3 + 3 = ☐
4 × 3 = ☐

Multiply.

6. 4 × 1   **7.** $\begin{array}{r} 3 \\ \times 3 \\ \hline \end{array}$ **8.** $\begin{array}{r} 2 \\ \times 9 \\ \hline \end{array}$ **9.** $\begin{array}{r} \times 5 \\ \hline 6 \end{array}$

Write a multiplication fact for the picture.

1.   2.

Multiply. Draw a picture if you need to.

3. 3×4 4. 7×1 5. 4×5 6. 3×3 7. 5×0

8. 9×2 9. 8×3 10. 4×4 11. 6×2 12. 6×5

13. $\begin{array}{r} 4 \\ \times\,2 \\ \hline \end{array}$ 14. $\begin{array}{r} 3 \\ \times\,7 \\ \hline \end{array}$ 15. $\begin{array}{r} 5 \\ \times\,5 \\ \hline \end{array}$ 16. $\begin{array}{r} 1 \\ \times\,6 \\ \hline \end{array}$ 17. $\begin{array}{r} 2 \\ \times\,8 \\ \hline \end{array}$

18. $\begin{array}{c|c} \times & 0 \\ \hline 4 & \\ \end{array}$ 19. $\begin{array}{c|c} \times & 4 \\ \hline 8 & \\ \end{array}$ 20. $\begin{array}{c|c} \times & 3 \\ \hline 9 & \\ \end{array}$ 21. $\begin{array}{c|c} \times & 5 \\ \hline 8 & \\ \end{array}$ 22. $\begin{array}{c|c} \times & 4 \\ \hline 7 & \\ \end{array}$

Solve.

23. Tom filled 8 bird feeders. He put 2 scoops of seed into each feeder. How many scoops did he use?

24. There are 2 birds at each feeder. How many birds are at 7 feeders?

25. There are 6 chickadees and 3 finches at a feeder. How many birds in all are at the feeder?

Try This

Every apartment in this building has 2 windows. How many apartments have windows that face this way? Jack says 21. Clare says 28.

Who is correct?

117

6 and 7 as Factors

Mia and Tim arranged stamps in arrays.
How many stamps does each array have?

Mia

Tim

$6 \times 3 = 18$

$7 \times 2 = 14$

$3 \times 6 = 18$

$2 \times 7 = 14$

Mia's array has 18 stamps.

Tim's array has 14 stamps.

WORKING TOGETHER

**Copy and complete. Does changing the order
of the factors change the product?**

1. $6 + 6 + 6 + 6 + 6 + 6 + 6 = \square$
$7 \times 6 = \square$

2. $7 + 7 + 7 + 7 + 7 + 7 = \square$
$6 \times 7 = \square$

3. $5 + 5 + 5 + 5 + 5 + 5 = \square$
$6 \times 5 = \square$

4. $6 + 6 + 6 + 6 + 6 = \square$
$5 \times 6 = \square$

5. $\begin{matrix} \cdot\cdot\cdot\cdot\cdot\cdot\cdot \\ \cdot\cdot\cdot\cdot\cdot\cdot\cdot \\ \cdot\cdot\cdot\cdot\cdot\cdot\cdot \end{matrix}$ $\quad 3 \times 7 = \square$
$7 \times 3 = \square$

6. $\begin{matrix} \cdot\cdot\cdot\cdot\cdot\cdot \\ \cdot\cdot\cdot\cdot\cdot\cdot \\ \cdot\cdot\cdot\cdot\cdot\cdot \\ \cdot\cdot\cdot\cdot\cdot\cdot \end{matrix}$ $\quad 6 \times 4 = \square$
$4 \times 6 = \square$

EXERCISES

Copy and complete.

1.

×	0	1	2	3	4	5	6	7	8	9
6	0	6	12							

2.

×	0	1	2	3	4	5	6	7	8	9
7	0	7	14							

Multiply.

3. $\begin{array}{r} 2 \\ \times 6 \\ \hline \end{array}$
4. $\begin{array}{r} 6 \\ \times 2 \\ \hline \end{array}$
5. $\begin{array}{r} 7 \\ \times 5 \\ \hline \end{array}$
6. $\begin{array}{r} 5 \\ \times 7 \\ \hline \end{array}$
7. $\begin{array}{r} 6 \\ \times 6 \\ \hline \end{array}$

8. $\times \dfrac{7}{0}$
9. $\times \dfrac{6}{9}$
10. $\times \dfrac{7}{7}$
11. $\times \dfrac{8}{7}$
12. $\times \dfrac{7}{8}$

Solve.

13. Lou put 6 stamps on each page of an album. He filled 7 pages. How many stamps does he have?

14. A letter carrier walks 7 km each day. What distance is walked in 5 days?

15. There are 4 piles of mailbags. Each pile has 6 bags. How many mailbags are there?

16. Jim bought eight 6¢ stamps. Joe bought seven 7¢ stamps. Who paid more? How much more?

Work with a partner to calculate each pair of products.
Compare your results.

1. 489×8 8×489

2. 67×58 58×67

3. 1265×3 3×1265

4. $13 \times 52 \times 27$ $27 \times 13 \times 52$

Does changing the order of the factors change the product?

119

8 and 9 as Factors

How many boxes of corn flakes?   How many boxes of bran flakes?

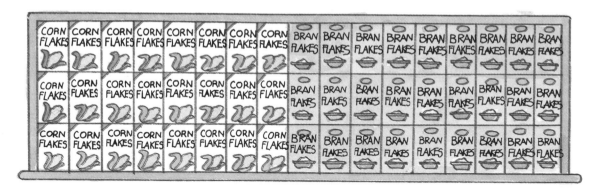

Multiply.

$3 \times 8 = 24$ $3 \times 9 = 27$
   or   or
$8 \times 3 = 24$ $9 \times 3 = 27$

There are 24 boxes   There are 27 boxes
of corn flakes.   of bran flakes.

WORKING TOGETHER

Copy and complete.

1. $5 + 5 + 5 + 5 + 5 + 5 + 5 + 5 = \square$ **2.** $8 + 8 + 8 + 8 + 8 = \square$
       $8 \times 5 = \square$ $5 \times 8 = \square$

3. $4 + 4 + 4 + 4 + 4 + 4 + 4 + 4 + 4 = \square$ **4.** $9 + 9 + 9 + 9 = \square$
        $9 \times 4 = \square$ $4 \times 9 = \square$

5. $4 \times 8 = \square$ **6.** $5 \times 9 = \square$
      $8 \times 4 = \square$ $9 \times 5 = \square$

EXERCISES

Copy and complete.

1.

×	0	1	2	3	4	5	6	7	8	9
8	0	8	16							

2.

×	0	1	2	3	4	5	6	7	8	9
9	0	9	18							

Multiply.

3. 8
     × 4

4. 8
     × 1

5. 9
     × 3

6. 9
     × 6

7. 8
     × 8

8. × | 5
    8 |

9. × | 7
    9 |

10. × | 7
    8 |

11. × | 6
    8 |

12. × | 9
    9 |

13. 1 × 9   **14.** 5 × 8   **15.** 9 × 2   **16.** 5 × 9   **17.** 9 × 6

18. 6 × 8   **19.** 7 × 8   **20.** 8 × 0   **21.** 9 × 8   **22.** 7 × 9

Solve.

23. There are 8 muffins in a package. How many are in 5 packages?

24. Peggy buys 8 cans of soup and 7 cans of vegetables. How many cans does she buy?

25. Tim can fill 8 shelves in 1 hour. How many shelves can he fill in 6 hours?

26. Cans of cat food are in stacks of 9. How many cans are in 4 stacks?

KEEPING SHARP

Draw an abacus to show the number.
Then write the standard form.

THOUSANDS

1. 3 thousands 0 hundreds 4 tens 5 ones
2. 8 ten thousands 2 hundreds 9 ones
3. seven hundred thirty-two thousand
4. ninety-seven thousand ninety-seven
5. 40 000 + 3000 + 700 + 5
6. 3 tens 6 hundred thousands 6 ones 8 thousands

A Multiplication Table

When the multiplication facts are in a table they are easy to find.

For the product of 3 and 8:

Look across from 3.
Stop under the 8.

or

Look across from 8.
Stop under the 3.

×	0	1	2	3	4	5	6	7	8	9
0	0	0	0	0	0	0	0	0	0	0
1	0	1	2	3	4	5	6	7	8	9
2	0	2	4	6	8	10	12	14	16	18
3	0	3	6	9	12	15	18	21	24	27
4	0	4	8	12	16	20	24	28	32	36
5	0	5	10	15	20	25	30	35	40	45
6	0	6	12	18	24	30	36	42	48	54
7	0	7	14	21	28	35	42	49	56	63
8	0	8	16	24	32	40	48	56	64	72
9	0	9	18	27	36	45	54	63	72	81

The product of 3 and 8, 24, can be found either way.

The **multiples** of 3 in this table are
0, 3, 6, 9, 12, 15, 18, 21, 24, 27.
Find them in the table.

WORKING TOGETHER

Use the table. Give the multiples of the number.

1. 8   **2.** 5   **3.** 0   **4.** 9   **5.** 4

Use the table. Give the product.

6. across from 4, down from 7   **7.** across from 8, down from 5

8. across from 9, down from 6   **9.** across from 6, down from 8

Write the product. Use the table to check your answer.

10. 3×7 **11.** 7×3 **12.** 9×4 **13.** 6×7 **14.** 5×5

Multiply.

1. 8×4 2. 3×6 3. 2×9 4. 9×8 5. 8×6

6. 9×3 7. 6×4 8. 0×8 9. 5×6 10. 7×1

11. $\begin{array}{r} 0 \\ \times 6 \\ \hline \end{array}$ 12. $\begin{array}{r} 8 \\ \times 8 \\ \hline \end{array}$ 13. $\begin{array}{r} 7 \\ \times 4 \\ \hline \end{array}$ 14. $\begin{array}{r} 5 \\ \times 1 \\ \hline \end{array}$ 15. $\begin{array}{r} 9 \\ \times 8 \\ \hline \end{array}$

16. $\begin{array}{c|c} \times & 3 \\ \hline 8 & \\ \end{array}$ 17. $\begin{array}{c|c} \times & 6 \\ \hline 9 & \\ \end{array}$ 18. $\begin{array}{c|c} \times & 7 \\ \hline 7 & \\ \end{array}$ 19. $\begin{array}{c|c} \times & 1 \\ \hline 9 & \\ \end{array}$ 20. $\begin{array}{c|c} \times & 8 \\ \hline 6 & \\ \end{array}$

Copy and complete.

21. $4 \times 5 = 5 \times \square$ 22. $9 \times 7 = \square \times 9$ 23. $8 \times 6 = 6 \times \square$

24. $7 \times 8 = \square \times \square$ 25. $6 \times 7 = \square \times \square$ 26. $5 \times 9 = \square \times \square$

Solve.

27. There are 4 screwdrivers in a pack. How many screwdrivers are in 6 packs?

28. Hammers cost $9 each. On Saturday, 5 people each bought a hammer. How much did the hammers cost altogether?

29. One box had 8 wrenches. Frank sold 6 of the wrenches. How many are left?

30. Some screws are sold with 7 in a package. How many screws are in 8 packages?

Try This

Linda invented this tool.

Use the table to find out what she called the tool.

×	4	8	5
6	E	I	L
9	M	P	R
7	S	T	U

36   35   30   56   48   72   30   48   24   45   28

Find the product.

1. 6
   ×3

2. 4
   ×8

3. 0
   ×5

4. 9
   ×6

5. 8
   ×9

6. 9
   ×4

7. 1
   ×8

8. 1
   ×1

9. 8
   ×7

10. 7
    ×6

11. 4
    ×0

12. 3
    ×5

13. 7 × 3

14. 0 × 7

15. 9 × 9

16. 6 × 8

17. 1 × 5

18. × | 6
    8 |

19. × | 6
    5 |

20. × | 5
    9 |

21. × | 7
    7 |

22. × | 6
    6 |

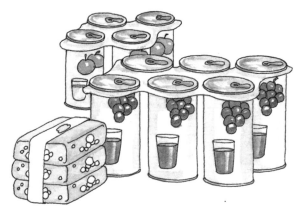

Solve.

23. Tim baked 3 packages of cinnamon rolls. How many rolls did he bake?

24. Ravi bought 2 packages of brownies. How many brownies did he buy?

25. How many cans of apple juice are there in 5 packs?

26. How many bars of soap are there in 6 packages?

27. Mr. Venza put 6 boxes of fish sticks into his freezer. How many fish sticks did he put there?

28. Jenny bought 3 packs of grape juice. Mark bought 4 packs of apple juice. Who bought more cans of juice?

Multiples

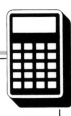

You can use repeated addition to find the multiples of a number.

$7 + 7 + 7 + 7 + 7 +$

7,   14,   21,   28,   35,

You can also skip count to find the multiples.

$0 + 7 = = = = =$

7, 14, 21, 28, 35,

Calculate.

1. Find the multiples of 9 to 90.

2. Find the multiples of 12 to 144.

3. Find the multiples of 13 less than 150.

4. Find the multiples of 27 less than 280.

5. Find the multiples of 6 between 45 and 100.

6. Find the multiples of 8 between 60 and 125.

7. List the first six multiples of 14.

8. List the first six multiples of 17.

Skip count to find the answer.

9. 578 people will take the bus. Each bus carries 42 people. How many buses are needed?

10. Peter has 178 pennies in his piggy bank. How many piles of 25 pennies can he make?

125

10 and 100 as Factors

How many apples are in 4 bags?

$10 + 10 + 10 + 10 = 40$

$$\begin{array}{c} 1 \\ \times 4 \\ \hline 4 \end{array} \quad \blacktriangleright \quad \begin{array}{c} 1 \text{ ten} \\ \times 4 \\ \hline 4 \text{ tens} \end{array} \quad \blacktriangleright \quad \begin{array}{c} 10 \\ \times 4 \\ \hline 40 \end{array}$$

There are 40 apples in 4 bags.

How much toothpaste is in 3 tubes?

$100 + 100 + 100 = 300$

$$\begin{array}{c} 1 \\ \times 3 \\ \hline 3 \end{array} \quad \blacktriangleright \quad \begin{array}{c} 1 \text{ hundred} \\ \times 3 \\ \hline 3 \text{ hundreds} \end{array} \quad \blacktriangleright \quad \begin{array}{c} 100 \\ \times 3 \\ \hline 300 \end{array}$$

There are 300 mL of toothpaste in 3 tubes.

WORKING TOGETHER

Copy and complete.

1.
$$\begin{array}{c} 1 \\ \times 5 \\ \hline \square \end{array} \quad \begin{array}{c} 1 \text{ ten} \\ \times 5 \\ \hline \square \text{ tens} \end{array} \quad \begin{array}{c} 10 \\ \times 5 \\ \hline \square \end{array}$$

2.
$$\begin{array}{c} 1 \\ \times 6 \\ \hline \square \end{array} \quad \begin{array}{c} 1 \text{ hundred} \\ \times 6 \\ \hline \square \text{ hundreds} \end{array} \quad \begin{array}{c} 100 \\ \times 6 \\ \hline \square \end{array}$$

3. $2 \times 10 = \square$ **4.** $6 \times 10 = \square$ **5.** $9 \times 10 = \square$

6. $4 \times 100 = \square$ **7.** $5 \times 100 = \square$ **8.** $7 \times 100 = \square$

Write a multiplication sentence for the picture.

9.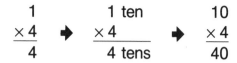

10.

Multiply.

1. 10
   × 2

2. 10
   × 5

3. 100
   × 4

4. 100
   × 3

5. 10
   × 8

6. 100
   × 9

7. 100
   × 6

8. 10
   × 6

9. 10
   × 9

10. 100
    × 7

Find the product of the factors.

11. 3 and 10

12. 2 and 100

13. 6 and 10

14. 10 and 4

15. 5 and 100

16. 7 and 10

17. 8 and 100

18. 100 and 3

Solve.

19. A chess set costs $10. What is the cost of 5 chess sets?

20. There are 100 cm in 1 m. How many centimetres are there in 7 m?

21. On a long trip, a car travels 100 km each hour. How far does it travel in 4 hours?

22. Pencils cost 10¢ each. Anders buys 3 of them. How much change does he get from $1.00?

Try This

Who Am I?

1. I am an odd number.
   My tens digit is odd.
   My ones digit is less than 6.
   The difference of my digits is 8.

2. I am greater than 30.
   I am less than 50.
   One of my factors is 5.
   The product of my digits is 15.

3. I am an odd number.
   I am less than 30.
   My tens digit is one greater than my ones digit.

4. I am less than 70.
   I am a multiple of 4.
   I am a multiple of 6.
   The sum of my digits is 9.

Multiplying Tens and Hundreds

There are 60 minutes in 1 hour. How many minutes are there in 3 hours?

Multiply.   3 × 60

$$
\begin{array}{r} 6 \\ \times 3 \\ \hline 18 \end{array}
\quad\blacktriangleright\quad
\begin{array}{r} 6 \text{ tens} \\ \times 3 \\ \hline 18 \text{ tens} \end{array}
\quad\blacktriangleright\quad
\begin{array}{r} 60 \\ \times 3 \\ \hline 180 \end{array}
$$

There are 180 minutes in 3 hours.

There are 400 sheets of paper in 1 package. How many sheets are in 6 packages?

Multiply.   6 × 400

$$
\begin{array}{r} 4 \\ \times 6 \\ \hline 24 \end{array}
\quad\blacktriangleright\quad
\begin{array}{r} 4 \text{ hundreds} \\ \times 6 \\ \hline 24 \text{ hundreds} \end{array}
\quad\blacktriangleright\quad
\begin{array}{r} 400 \\ \times 6 \\ \hline 2400 \end{array}
$$

There are 2400 sheets in 6 packages.

WORKING TOGETHER

Copy and complete.

1.
$$
\begin{array}{r} 3 \\ \times 5 \\ \hline \square \end{array}
\qquad
\begin{array}{r} 3 \text{ tens} \\ \times 5 \\ \hline \square \text{ tens} \end{array}
\qquad
\begin{array}{r} 30 \\ \times 5 \\ \hline \square 0 \end{array}
$$

2.
$$
\begin{array}{r} 4 \\ \times 3 \\ \hline \square \end{array}
\qquad
\begin{array}{r} 4 \text{ hundreds} \\ \times 3 \\ \hline \square \text{ hundreds} \end{array}
\qquad
\begin{array}{r} 400 \\ \times 3 \\ \hline \square 00 \end{array}
$$

3. 2 × 20 = ▢

4. 8 × 50 = ▭

5. 6 × 80 = ▭

6. 5 × 900 = ▭

7. 4 × 700 = ▭

8. 2 × 600 = ▭

Write a multiplication sentence for the picture.

9.

10.

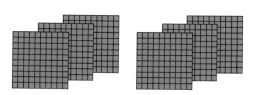

Copy and complete the table.

1.

×	3	4	5	6
3				

2.

×	30	40	50	60
3				

3.

×	5	6	7	8
5				

4.

×	500	600	700	800
5				

Find the product.

5. $\begin{array}{r} 40 \\ \times 7 \\ \hline \end{array}$
6. $\begin{array}{r} 60 \\ \times 6 \\ \hline \end{array}$
7. $\begin{array}{r} 300 \\ \times 3 \\ \hline \end{array}$
8. $\begin{array}{r} 500 \\ \times 2 \\ \hline \end{array}$
9. $\begin{array}{r} 80 \\ \times 4 \\ \hline \end{array}$

10. 5×600
11. 7×300
12. 8×90
13. 9×600
14. 4×30

Solve.

15. Jason bought 3 boxes of drinking straws. Each box contains 50 straws. How many straws did Jason buy?

16. The mass of a carton of cottage cheese is 500 g. What is the mass of 3 cartons?

17. Tom drives 400 km each week. How many kilometres does he drive in 8 weeks?

18. A box of aluminum foil contains 80 cm of foil. Tess uses 9 cm. How much foil remains?

KEEPING SHARP

Multiply, then add. Write only the answer.

1. $4 \times 3 + 2$
2. $5 \times 4 + 1$
3. $9 \times 2 + 3$
4. $3 \times 7 + 2$

5. $4 \times 6 + 1$
6. $7 \times 5 + 4$
7. $8 \times 8 + 1$
8. $6 \times 1 + 3$

9. $2 \times 8 + 1$
10. $6 \times 9 + 3$
11. $4 \times 0 + 2$
12. $3 \times 5 + 2$

13. $7 \times 6 + 4$
14. $8 \times 5 + 2$
15. $9 \times 4 + 3$
16. $7 \times 9 + 6$

Multiplying a Two-Digit Number

There are 19 players on each
Minor Atom hockey team.
How many players are needed
to make up a 4-team league?

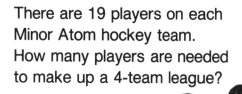

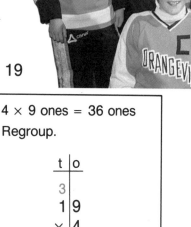

```
  3
  1 9
  1 9
  1 9
+ 1 9
  7 6
```

Multiply. 4 × 19

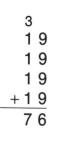

| 4 × 9 ones = 36 ones |
| Regroup. |

```
  t | o
  3 |
  1 | 9
× | 4
    | 6
```

| 4 × 1 ten = 4 tens |
| Add the 3 extra tens. |

```
  t | o
  3 |
  1 | 9
× | 4
  7 | 6
```

To make up 4 teams, 76 players are needed.

WORKING TOGETHER

Copy and complete.

```
       1
1.   8 5
   × 3
   ☐ 5
```

```
     ☐
2.   6 9
   × 6
   ☐ 4
```

```
3.   3 2
   × 4
   ☐ 8
```

```
     ☐
4.   9 8
   × 5
   ☐ ☐
```

```
5.   4 1
   × 8
   ☐ ☐
```

EXERCISES

Find the product.

1. 12
   × 9

2. 32
   × 3

3. 27
   × 4

4. 46
   × 5

5. 52
   × 4

6. 37
   × 6

7. 60
   × 8

8. 74
   × 5

9. 21
   × 7

10. 56
    × 9

11. 3 × 43

12. 16 × 9

13. 8 × 35

14. 44 × 6

15. 62 × 7

16. 5 × 92

17. 4 × 38

18. 30 × 7

Solve.

19. The Minor Atom hockey league has 27 players who have scored 6 goals each. How many goals have these players scored in all?

20. Each team plays 44 games in a season. Each game has 3 periods. How many periods does a team play in a season?

21. 24 of the Grade 4 students play hockey. Of these, 8 are girls. How many are boys?

22. The teams buy pucks in boxes of 48. How many pucks are in 5 boxes?

Try This

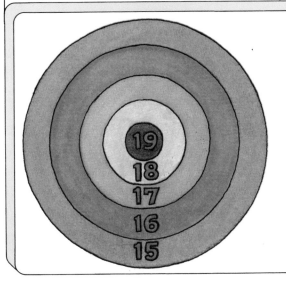

Sophia scored 99 in this dart game.

1. How many darts did she throw?

2. Where did they hit the target?

131

Multiplying a Three-Digit Number

Centennial Park has 3 picnic
areas. Each area has tables
for 286 people. How many people
can eat there at one time?

Multiply. 3 × 286

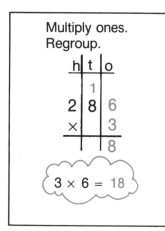

Multiply ones.
Regroup.

```
   1
 h t o
 2 8 6
 ×   3
     8
```

3 × 6 = 18

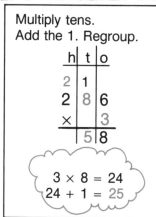

Multiply tens.
Add the 1. Regroup.

```
 2 1
 h t o
 2 8 6
 ×   3
   5 8
```

3 × 8 = 24
24 + 1 = 25

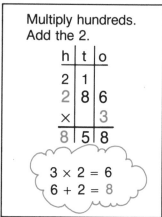

Multiply hundreds.
Add the 2.

```
 2 1
 h t o
 2 8 6
 ×   3
 8 5 8
```

3 × 2 = 6
6 + 2 = 8

858 people can eat there at one time.

WORKING TOGETHER

Copy and complete.

1.
```
  □1
 2 4 3
 ×   4
 9 □ 2
```

2.
```
  □4
 5 4 7
 ×   6
 3 □□2
```

3.
```
 5 2
 2 8 4
 ×   7
 �_____
```

4.
```
  □
 3 9 1
 ×   5
 ___5
```

5.
```
  2
 6 0 8
 ×   3
 _____
```

6.
```
  1
 7 8 3
 ×   2
 _____
```

7.
```
 □□
 1 2 3
 ×   8
 _____
```

8.
```
 2 0 3
 ×   2
 _____
```

Find the product.

1. 384 ×5	2. 241 ×6	3. 307 ×3	4. 342 ×2	5. 441 ×5
6. 281 ×4	7. 115 ×6	8. 897 ×6	9. 227 ×5	10. 743 ×9

Multiply.

11. 2×610 12. 345×3 13. 4×452 14. 698×7 15. 807×4

16. 8×254 17. 3×215 18. 9×921 19. 7×615 20. 709×8

Solve.

21. Colored ribbon comes in rolls of 175 cm. The students bought 8 rolls to make awards. How much ribbon did they buy?

22. Students work in teams of 2 for a scavenger hunt. There are 136 teams. How many students take part?

23. The students need 858 wieners. A package contains 8 wieners. Will 108 packages be enough?

24. 436 students are enrolled in the school. 7 were absent on the day of the picnic. How many students attended the picnic?

Calculators and electronic toys are not real computers. But they contain some computer parts.

Is the statement true or false?	COMPUTER	CALCULATOR	ELECTRONIC TOY
1. A person gives input.	T or F	T or F	T or F
2. The machine can be taught to do almost anything.	T or F	T or F	T or F
3. The machine can save results in its memory.	T or F	T or F	T or F

More Than Two Factors

Jeanne and Marc each have
3 boxes of 8 crayons.
How many crayons are there in all?
Multiply 2, 3, and 8.

Try multiplying 2 × 3 first.

$$
\begin{array}{rl}
3 & \text{boxes each} \\
\times 2 & \text{children} \\
\hline
6 & \text{boxes in all}
\end{array}
\qquad
\begin{array}{rl}
8 & \text{crayons in a box} \\
\times 6 & \text{boxes in all} \\
\hline
48 & \text{crayons in all}
\end{array}
$$

Then try multiplying 3 × 8 first.

$$
\begin{array}{rl}
8 & \text{crayons in a box} \\
\times 3 & \text{boxes each} \\
\hline
24 & \text{crayons each}
\end{array}
\qquad
\begin{array}{rl}
24 & \text{crayons each} \\
\times 2 & \text{children} \\
\hline
48 & \text{crayons in all}
\end{array}
$$

The products are the same.

There are 48 crayons in all.

WORKING TOGETHER

Copy and complete.

1. 2 × 5 × 6

$$
\begin{array}{rl}
5 \\
\times 2 \\
\hline
\square
\end{array}
\nearrow
\begin{array}{rl}
\square \\
\times 6 \\
\hline
\square
\end{array}
$$

2. 3 × 7 × 5

$$
\begin{array}{rl}
5 \\
\times 7 \\
\hline
\square
\end{array}
\nearrow
\begin{array}{rl}
\square \\
\times 3 \\
\hline
\square
\end{array}
$$

3. 4 × 8 × 3

$$
\begin{array}{rl}
3 \\
\times 4 \\
\hline
\square
\end{array}
\nearrow
\begin{array}{rl}
\square \\
\times 8 \\
\hline
\square
\end{array}
$$

Multiply.

4. 2 × 3 × 7

5. 4 × 6 × 9

6. 20 × 3 × 3

Multiply the numbers on each crayon.
Use the letters to decode the colorful telephone story.

1.

A 2,2,3	B 3,2,4	C 4,5,1	E 6,2,5
G 7,3,4	I 8,5,4	K 4,4,4	L 2,9,7
N 7,2,8	O 5,5,8	P 7,3,2	R 3,8,4
W 8,2,0,3	Y 9,2,3,2		

$\underline{84}$ $\underline{96}$ $\underline{60}$ $\underline{60}$ $\underline{112}$, $\underline{84}$ $\underline{96}$ $\underline{60}$ $\underline{60}$ $\underline{112}$

$\underline{108}$ $\underline{60}$ $\underline{126}$ $\underline{126}$ $\underline{200}$ $\underline{0}$

$\underline{24}$ $\underline{126}$ $\underline{12}$ $\underline{20}$ $\underline{64}$, $\underline{24}$ $\underline{126}$ $\underline{12}$ $\underline{20}$ $\underline{64}$, $\underline{24}$ $\underline{126}$ $\underline{12}$ $\underline{20}$ $\underline{64}$,

$\underline{42}$ $\underline{160}$ $\underline{112}$ $\underline{64}$!

Solve.

2. A paint box holds 9 pots of paint. There are 6 paint boxes on each of 3 shelves. How many pots are there?

3. Barb and her friends can each make 3 stencil prints in 1 minute. How many prints can 4 children make in 5 minutes?

Try This

As I was going to Halifax,
I met a man with 7 sacks.
Every sack had 7 cats.
Every cat had 7 kits.
Man, kits, cats, and sacks,
How many were going to Halifax?

Find the product.

1. 10
   × 2

2. 37
   × 5

3. 100
   × 8

4. 384
   × 2

5. 50
   × 3

6. 42
   × 8

7. 800
   × 7

8. 783
   × 3

9. 60
   × 3

10. 29
    × 7

11. 500
    × 9

12. 207
    × 9

13. 10
    × 7

14. 83
    × 5

15. 200
    × 6

16. 415
    × 5

17. 30
    × 9

18. 74
    × 6

19. 100
    × 5

20. 928
    × 4

21. 40
    × 3

22. 87
    × 8

23. 700
    × 2

24. 586
    × 6

25. 608
    × 5

Multiply.

26. 70×9

27. 4×46

28. 600×7

29. 9×814

30. $6 \times 2 \times 9$

31. 6×93

32. $14 \times 1 \times 4$

33. 702×2

34. 316×6

35. $7 \times 4 \times 3$

36. 300×7

37. $5 \times 4 \times 9$

38. 5×933

39. 4×100

40. $3 \times 2 \times 7 \times 3$

Solve.

41. One bottle of shampoo contains 250 mL. How many millilitres are in 3 bottles?

42. A package of sliced meat has a mass of 175 g. What is the mass of 4 packages?

43. Liam is packing 18 cookies in each box. There are 128 cookies in all. Can he pack 7 boxes?

44. There are 15 bags of herbal tea in a box. There are 3 kinds of tea. Mrs. Cartier bought 2 boxes of each kind. How many tea bags did she get?

Coding on Punch Cards

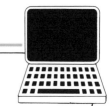

The telephone company uses a computer system.
It keeps track of each customer's monthly bill.
In Ontario, information such as the phone number and
the amount to be paid is given on **computer punch cards.**

1. Examine a computer punch
card from the telephone
company. Describe it.

2. The first and last groups of holes
show the phone number and
amount. Find them.

The computer needs special input equipment to
read the cards. A **card reader** decodes the
arrangement of the holes. Then this information
is processed by the computer.

You can code words on another type of punch card.
Each letter is coded by punching two special holes in a column.

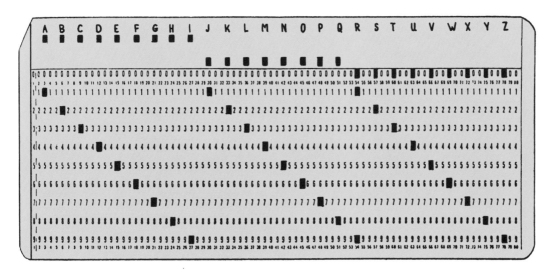

3. How many letters can be coded
on one card?

4. Code your name on a computer
punch card.

Look for a Pattern

Lee cuts a pie so that all cuts
go through the centre.

How many pieces are there after 7 cuts?

Think. How many pieces are there
after 1 cut?
after 2 cuts?
after 3 cuts?

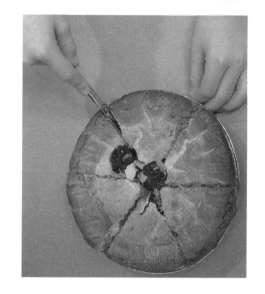

Plan and do. Make a table. Look for a pattern.

Number of cuts	1	2	3	4	5
Number of pieces	2	4	6	8	10

Lee sees a pattern
and states this rule.

The number of pieces
is twice the number
of cuts.

Look back. Use Lee's rule to find the number of pieces
after 7 cuts. Give the answer in a sentence.

WORKING TOGETHER

Use Lee's rule to solve the problem.

1. How many pieces are there
after 9 cuts?

2. How many cuts would you have to
make to get 22 pieces?

Copy and continue the pattern.

3. 1, 3, 5, 7, ☐, ☐, ☐

4. 2, 6, 10, 14, ☐, ☐, ☐

PROBLEMS

Copy and continue the pattern.

1. 4, 8, 12, 16, ☐, ☐, ☐   **2.** 85, 78, 71, 64, ☐, ☐, ☐

3. ⊞, ⊞, ⊞, ⊞, ?, ?, ?   **4.** •, •᛫•, •᛫᛫•, •᛫᛫᛫•, ?, ?, ?

Copy and complete the table. Solve the problems.

Fence posts go around a square garden.

5. How many posts are there? There are 10 posts on each side.

6. There are 48 posts altogether. How many posts are on each side?

Number of posts on each side	2	3	4	5	6	7
Number of posts in all	4					

Marty earns $2.50 a week for doing chores around the yard.

Week	1	2	3	4	5	6	7	8	9
Money	$2.50								

7. How much does he earn in 7 weeks?

8. How many weeks must he work to earn $10.00?

Solve.

Beth is making a row of triangles.

9. How many toothpicks does she need to make 6 triangles?

10. How many triangles can she make with 21 toothpicks?

139

Problem Solving Review

Solve.

1. How many times do you cut a drinking straw to get 10 pieces?

2. How many triangles can you make with 6 toothpicks?

3. Steve started washing dishes at 3:45. He worked for 20 minutes. What time did he finish?

4. A bookcase has 25 books. 5 books are on each shelf. 2 books on each shelf are new. How many new books are in the bookcase?

5. I bought 1 record last week and 2 records this week. How much did the 3 records cost?

6. How much can you save if you buy 3 records at one time?

RECORD PRICES	
1 record	$6
2 records	$11
3 records	$16
5 records	$25

7. Copy and continue the table for square windows.

Number of panes on a side	1	2	3			
Number of panes in all	1	4				

Copy and continue the pattern.

8. 1, 12, 123, ☐, ☐, ☐

9. °, ⠿, ⣿, ?, ?, ?

10. 0 + 1 + 2 = 3,   1 + 2 + 3 = 6,   2 + 3 + 4 = 9, ☐, ☐, ☐

Chapter Checkup

Find the product.

1. 6×2
2. 8×1
3. 5×3
4. 2×9
5. 8×3
6. 4×7

7. 6×9
8. 7×0
9. 6×8
10. 3×9
11. 0×1
12. 7×8

Multiply.

13. 1×1
14. 5×4
15. 0×0
16. 7×9
17. 9×5

18. 10×4
19. 7×43
20. 8×100
21. 10×6
22. 2×47

23. 7×100
24. 813×3
25. 7×35
26. 5×98
27. 3×486

Find the product.

28. 18×9
29. 327×4
30. 500×6
31. 80×2
32. 94×9

33. 70×7
34. 600×9
35. 521×8
36. 27×5
37. 684×6

Multiply.

38. 7×28
39. 40×8
40. $5 \times 6 \times 2$
41. $1 \times 8 \times 6 \times 2$

42. 5×320
43. $9 \times 7 \times 3$
44. 419×6
45. 7×600

Solve.

46. A kit contains 45 m of cord. How much cord is in 7 kits?

47. A model train set costs $78. What is the cost of 3 sets?

48. One jigsaw puzzle contains 525 pieces. How many pieces are in 6 puzzles?

49. Leo and Jane each bought 4 spools of thread. Each spool holds 46 m of thread. How many metres of thread did they buy in all?

Cumulative Checkup

Write in expanded form.

1. 6152
2. 9010
3. 17 008
4. 61 400
5. 102 307

Order from greatest to least.

6. 7142, 7412, 7124, 7241
7. 386 544, 389 244, 398 244

Add or subtract.

8.
```
   42
 + 37
```

9.
```
   48
 − 25
```

10.
```
   84
 −  7
```

11.
```
    7
 + 31
```

12.
```
  319
 − 107
```

13.
```
   15
 + 43
```

14.
```
  738
 + 250
```

15.
```
  886
 − 543
```

16.
```
  563
 + 224
```

17.
```
  907
 − 281
```

18.
```
  614
 − 189
```

19.
```
   57
 + 26
```

20.
```
  829
 + 48
```

21.
```
  718
 − 192
```

22.
```
  923
 − 564
```

23.
```
   73
 + 587
```

24.
```
  4304
 − 1981
```

25.
```
  465
 + 296
```

26.
```
  708
 + 137
```

27.
```
  6215
 − 1782
```

Match the angle with its description.

28.
29.
30.
31.

a right angle	an angle smaller than a right angle	an angle larger than a right angle

Name the polygon.

32.
33.
34.
35.

6/Division

You can use division to find the number of equal groups
or to find the size of equal groups.

Basic Division Facts, Divisors to 5

Michelle has a 20-letter message to encode.
She does it by writing the letters in groups of 5.
How many groups are there?

divisor   quotient

Divide. $20 \div 5 = 4$

$$4 \longleftarrow \text{quotient}$$
$$\text{divisor} \longrightarrow 5\,\overline{)\,20}$$

There are 4 groups of 5 in 20.

WORKING TOGETHER

Copy the array. Ring the groups. Tell how many groups.

1. • • • • •
   • • • • •
   • • • • •
   How many 3's?
   How many 5's?

2. • • • •
   • • • •
   • • • •
   How many 3's?
   How many 4's?

3. • • • • •
   • • • • •
   How many 2's?
   How many 5's?

Copy and complete. Draw an array to help.

4. $15 \div 3 = \square$

5. $4\,\overline{)\,12}^{\,\square}$

6. $5\,\overline{)\,10}^{\,\square}$

7. $12 \div 2 = \square$

8. $2\,\overline{)\,8}^{\,\square}$

9. $18 \div 3 = \square$

10. $24 \div 4 = \square$

11. $5\,\overline{)\,30}^{\,\square}$

Divide. Draw an array for exercises 1, 2, and 3.

1. $4\overline{)20}$ 2. $3\overline{)21}$ 3. $4\overline{)28}$ 4. $5\overline{)40}$ 5. $2\overline{)16}$

6. $3\overline{)18}$ 7. $5\overline{)25}$ 8. $4\overline{)12}$ 9. $2\overline{)14}$ 10. $5\overline{)45}$

11. $27 \div 3$ 12. $35 \div 5$ 13. $24 \div 4$ 14. $18 \div 2$ 15. $9 \div 3$

16. $32 \div 4$ 17. $10 \div 2$ 18. $12 \div 3$ 19. $20 \div 5$ 20. $16 \div 4$

Solve.

21. Tim has 12 photos. He places 4 on each page. How many pages does he use?

22. 8 girls are Guides. They have earned 4 badges each. How many badges have they earned in all?

23. Michelle gets a coded message that contains 45 letters. How many 5-letter groups are there?

24. 15 cookies are shared. Each child gets 3 cookies. How many children share the cookies?

Try This

Be a detective! Find the missing numerals.

1.
```
   4 9 □
 + □ 0 4
 ─────────
 □ 3 □ 1
```

2.
```
   3 6 □
 - 1 □ 3
 ─────────
 □ 8 2
```

3.
```
   2 8 1
   3 4 7
 + □ □ □
 ─────────
   8 5 4
```

4.
```
 □ □ □ □
 - 2 8 5 2
 ─────────
   2 1 8 4
```

5.
```
   6 7 □
   5 □ 6
 +   9 8
 ─────────
 □ □ 1 4
```

6.
```
   □ 4 8
 - 1 □ 6
 ─────────
   5 7 □
```

7.
```
     □ 6 2
 + □ 4 □ □
 ─────────
   2 8 2 0
```

8.
```
   5 □ 6 1
 + □ 6 □ 7
 ─────────
   7 0 1 □
```

9.
```
   8 □ 4
 - 3 8 □
 ─────────
   □ 4 6
```

10.
```
   □ 0 8 5
 - □ □ 9
 ─────────
   3 6 5 □
```

Missing Factor

Derek shared 12 pancakes among 4 people. How many pancakes did each person have?

4 people
■ pancakes each
12 pancakes in all

$4 \times \square = 12$

Use the multiplication table to find the missing factor.

Find the 4 row.
Look across to 12.
Look up the column from 12.
The other factor is at the top.

	column									
×	0	1	2	3	4	5	6	7	8	9
0	0	0	0	0	0	0	0	0	0	0
1	0	1	2	3	4	5	6	7	8	9
2	0	2	4	6	8	10	12	14	16	18
3	0	3	6	9	12	15	18	21	24	27
4	0	4	8	12	16	20	24	28	32	36
5	0	5	10	15	20	25	30	35	40	45
6	0	6	12	18	24	30	36	42	48	54
7	0	7	14	21	28	35	42	49	56	63
8	0	8	16	24	32	40	48	56	64	72
9	0	9	18	27	36	45	54	63	72	81

row (label for row 4)

Each person had 3 pancakes.

WORKING TOGETHER

Which row of the table do you use?

1. $4 \times \square = 28$ **2.** $7 \times \square = 56$ **3.** $\square \times 6 = 48$ **4.** $\square \times 9 = 54$

Which column of the table do you look up?

5. $8 \times \square = 56$ **6.** $\square \times 9 = 36$ **7.** $\square \times 5 = 0$ **8.** $8 \times \square = 32$

Copy and complete. Use the table.

9. $\square \times 5 = 30$ **10.** $3 \times \square = 27$ **11.** $7 \times \square = 42$ **12.** $4 \times \square = 24$

EXERCISES

Copy and complete.

1. $2 \times \square = 14$ **2.** $6 \times \square = 24$ **3.** $\square \times 9 = 45$ **4.** $\square \times 1 = 4$

5. $3 \times \square = 12$ **6.** $8 \times \square = 48$ **7.** $\square \times 70 = 210$ **8.** $\square \times 5 = 150$

9.
$$\begin{array}{r} 5 \\ \times\, \square \\ \hline 20 \end{array}$$
10.
$$\begin{array}{r} \square \\ \times\, 7 \\ \hline 49 \end{array}$$
11.
$$\begin{array}{r} 8 \\ \times\, \square \\ \hline 40 \end{array}$$
12.
$$\begin{array}{r} \square \\ \times\, 2 \\ \hline 12 \end{array}$$
13.
$$\begin{array}{r} 7 \\ \times\, \square \\ \hline 0 \end{array}$$
14.
$$\begin{array}{r} \square \\ \times\, 5 \\ \hline 15 \end{array}$$

15.
$$\begin{array}{r} 9 \\ \times\, \square \\ \hline 72 \end{array}$$
16.
$$\begin{array}{r} \square \\ \times\, 5 \\ \hline 35 \end{array}$$
17.
$$\begin{array}{r} 4 \\ \times\, \square \\ \hline 32 \end{array}$$
18.
$$\begin{array}{r} \square \\ \times\, 6 \\ \hline 36 \end{array}$$
19.
$$\begin{array}{r} \square \\ \times\, 2 \\ \hline 100 \end{array}$$
20.
$$\begin{array}{r} \square \\ \times\, 3 \\ \hline 270 \end{array}$$

Solve.

21. Mr. Baker made 27 muffins. He put 9 on each plate. How many plates did he use?

22. The total mass of 8 pancakes is 320 g. What is the mass of 1 pancake?

23. There were 24 slices of bread. Derek and Ingrid each ate 3 slices. How many slices are left?

24. Ms. Miller had 400 mL of juice. She divided it equally into 4 glasses. How many millilitres of juice went into each glass?

Companies mail out thousands of form letters each year. They hope these will convince people to buy their products.

1. Examine form letters that are printed by computers.

2. Why might people think that a form letter was written just for them?

3. Does the computer really know the person it prints a letter for?

4. Why do you think a computer is used to print out these letters?

Using a Multiplication Table to Divide

For 5 $\overline{)\,35}$ or 35 ÷ 5,
start at the 5 row.
Look across to 35.
Look up the column from 35.
The quotient is at the top.

×	0	1	2	3	4	5	6	7	8	9
0	0	0	0	0	0	0	0	0	0	0
1	0	1	2	3	4	5	6	7	8	9
2	0	2	4	6	8	10	12	14	16	18
3	0	3	6	9	12	15	18	21	24	27
4	0	4	8	12	16	20	24	28	32	36
5	0	5	10	15	20	25	30	35	40	45
6	0	6	12	18	24	30	36	42	48	54
7	0	7	14	21	28	35	42	49	56	63
8	0	8	16	24	32	40	48	56	64	72
9	0	9	18	27	36	45	54	63	72	81

start ⟶ 5

$\overset{7}{5\,\overline{)\,35}}$ quotient

WORKING TOGETHER

Where do you start on the table?

1. 3 $\overline{)\,18}$ 2. 4 $\overline{)\,28}$ 3. 3 $\overline{)\,27}$ 4. 45 ÷ 5   5. 32 ÷ 4

How far across do you look?

6. 18 ÷ 2   7. 4 $\overline{)\,20}$ 8. 3 $\overline{)\,12}$ 9. 9 ÷ 3   10. 25 ÷ 5

Find the quotient. Use the table.

11. 16 ÷ 2   12. 4 $\overline{)\,16}$ 13. 9 ÷ 1   14. 3 $\overline{)\,21}$ 15. 40 ÷ 5

EXERCISES

Divide.

1. $4\overline{)28}$ 2. $3\overline{)15}$ 3. $4\overline{)8}$ 4. $2\overline{)12}$ 5. $2\overline{)10}$

6. $4\overline{)24}$ 7. $5\overline{)30}$ 8. $1\overline{)8}$ 9. $4\overline{)4}$ 10. $3\overline{)24}$

11. $5\overline{)20}$ 12. $3\overline{)12}$ 13. $5\overline{)40}$ 14. $2\overline{)6}$ 15. $3\overline{)21}$

16. $3 \div 3$ 17. $20 \div 5$ 18. $27 \div 3$ 19. $8 \div 2$ 20. $5 \div 5$

21. $12 \div 4$ 22. $36 \div 4$ 23. $15 \div 5$ 24. $14 \div 2$ 25. $32 \div 4$

Solve.

26. Students put the same amount of soil in each of 4 planters. They used 12 pails of soil in all. How many pails of soil were in each planter?

27. There are 24 bean plants in 4 equal rows. How many plants are in each row?

28. There are 3 rows of radishes. There are twice as many rows of peas. How many rows of peas and radishes are there in all?

What numbers complete this comic strip?

Try This

Add ☐   Divide by ☐   Ta Da!

149

Related Multiplication and Division Facts

Gerry has 12 tarts.
She makes this array.

12 tarts in 3 rows

$12 \div 3 = 4$ or $3\overline{)12}$ with quotient 4

12 tarts in 4 columns

$12 \div 4 = 3$ or $4\overline{)12}$ with quotient 3

3, 4, and 12 give a family
of multiplication and division facts.

$3 \times 4 = 12$ $4 \times 3 = 12$ $12 \div 4 = 3$ $12 \div 3 = 4$

WORKING TOGETHER

Write two multiplication facts and two division facts for the array.

1.

2.

Copy and complete. Draw an array.

3. $4 \times 7 = \square$ $28 \div 7 = \square$
   $7 \times 4 = \square$ $28 \div 4 = \square$

4. $\dfrac{\times\ |3}{3\ |\square}$ $3\overline{)9}$ with quotient $\square$

EXERCISES

Write the family of facts for the array.

1.

2.

3.

4.

Copy and complete. Draw an array.

5. $3 \times 9 = \square$ $\square \times 9 = 27$

   $\overset{\square}{3 \overline{)\,27}}$ $\overset{\square}{9 \overline{)\,27}}$

6. $4 \times \square = 20$ $5 \times \square = 20$

   $\overset{\square}{4 \overline{)\,20}}$ $\overset{\square}{5 \overline{)\,20}}$

Copy the fact. Write the other facts of the family.

7. $2 \times 7 = 14$ **8.** $3 \times 8 = 24$ **9.** $24 \div 4 = 6$ **10.** $16 \div 2 = 8$

11. $5 \times 1 = 5$ **12.** $25 \div 5 = 5$ **13.** $7 \times 3 = 21$ **14.** $45 \div 5 = 9$

Write the family of facts for the set of numbers.

15. 2, 8, 4   **16.** 5, 10, 2   **17.** 6, 2, 3   **18.** 4, 4, 16

19. 5, 30, 6   **20.** 32, 8, 4   **21.** 4, 9, 36   **22.** 7, 6, 42

KEEPING SHARP

Use >, <, or = to make a true statement.

1. $593 \times 4 \bigcirc 447 \times 5$ **2.** $4846 + 706 \bigcirc 694 \times 8$

3. $555 + 897 \bigcirc 798 + 666$ **4.** $863 \times 7 \bigcirc 683 \times 9$

5. $4692 - 1839 \bigcirc 9 \times 317$ **6.** $1234 + 5678 \bigcirc 9876 - 3456$

7. $7803 - 1234 \bigcirc 8730 - 2341$ **8.** $5 \times 879 \bigcirc 4444 - 49$

Divide.

1. $3\overline{)15}$ 2. $5\overline{)10}$ 3. $4\overline{)16}$ 4. $5\overline{)15}$ 5. $4\overline{)32}$

6. $36 \div 4$ 7. $24 \div 3$ 8. $12 \div 2$ 9. $6 \div 3$ 10. $30 \div 5$

Copy and complete.

11. $\begin{array}{r} 6 \\ \times\ \square \\ \hline 54 \end{array}$
12. $\begin{array}{r} \square \\ \times\ 4 \\ \hline 24 \end{array}$
13. $\begin{array}{r} 9 \\ \times\ \square \\ \hline 45 \end{array}$
14. $\begin{array}{r} 3 \\ \times\ \square \\ \hline 21 \end{array}$
15. $\begin{array}{r} \square \\ \times\ 6 \\ \hline 48 \end{array}$

16. $\begin{array}{r} \square \\ \times\ 2 \\ \hline 14 \end{array}$
17. $\begin{array}{r} 8 \\ \times\ \square \\ \hline 24 \end{array}$
18. $\begin{array}{r} \square \\ \times\ 5 \\ \hline 35 \end{array}$
19. $\begin{array}{r} \square \\ \times\ 4 \\ \hline 160 \end{array}$
20. $\begin{array}{r} \square \\ \times\ 5 \\ \hline 500 \end{array}$

Copy and complete. Draw an array.

21. $3 \times 5 = \square$ $5 \times 3 = \square$ $15 \div 3 = \square$ $15 \div 5 = \square$

Write the family of facts for the set of numbers.

22. 8, 7, 56   23. 9, 3, 27   24. 5, 20, 4   25. 6, 18, 3

Solve.

26. A classroom has 28 chairs. They are in 4 equal rows. How many chairs are in a row?

27. Sarah placed 14 books in 2 equal stacks. How many were in each stack?

28. 24 children divide into 4 teams for art. How many children are on each team?

29. A book has 40 pages. Each story takes 5 pages. How many stories are in the book?

30. Each stick of chalk was broken into 3 pieces. I have 27 pieces. How many sticks of chalk were there?

31. A class writes 32 letters to 4 authors. Each author is sent the same number of letters. How many letters go to each author?

Computers in Supermarkets

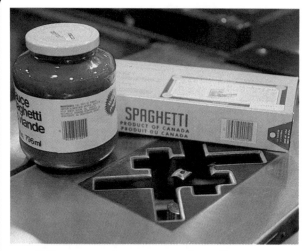

Most grocery packages have dark bars printed on them. The pattern of the bars is the **Universal Product Code (UPC)**.

Every product has its own code. Look at several UPC symbols.

1. How are they alike?

2. How are they different?

When you buy groceries, the clerk at the checkout counter uses the UPC symbols.

3. What does the clerk do?

Each UPC symbol tells the store's computer what the product is. Special input equipment is needed to read the bars. A **bar code reader** is built into the checkout counter.

When the store's computer gets the input, it looks up each code in its **memory**. It finds the name and price of the product. Then it prints this on the cash register tape.

Discuss.

4. Why is the bar code useful in supermarkets?

5. How else might computers be used in supermarkets?

153

Basic Division Facts, Divisors to 9

Jean has made 6 boxes for her 18 animals.
She puts the same number of animals
into each box.
How many animals are in each box?

Divide.   18 ÷ 6

$6 \times$ **3** $= 18 \longrightarrow 18 \div 6 =$ **3**   or $6\overline{)18}$ with **3** above

3 animals are in each box.

WORKING TOGETHER

Copy and complete.

1. $7 \times \square = 56$ **2.** $9 \times \square = 36$ **3.** $8 \times \square = 64$ **4.** $6 \times \square = 42$

$7\overline{)56}$ with $\square$ above $9\overline{)36}$ with $\square$ above $64 \div 8 = \square$ $42 \div 6 = \square$

Give a multiplication fact that can be used for the division.
Then complete the division fact.

5. $\square \times \square = 32$ $8\overline{)32}$ **6.** $\square \times \square = 63$ $63 \div 7 = \square$

7. $\square \times \square = 18$ $6\overline{)18}$ **8.** $\square \times \square = 40$ $8\overline{)40}$

EXERCISES

Find the quotient.

1. $9\overline{)27}$ 2. $7\overline{)35}$ 3. $6\overline{)42}$ 4. $8\overline{)40}$ 5. $6\overline{)24}$

6. $7\overline{)49}$ 7. $9\overline{)45}$ 8. $6\overline{)54}$ 9. $7\overline{)28}$ 10. $8\overline{)48}$

11. $56 \div 8$ 12. $12 \div 6$ 13. $81 \div 9$ 14. $36 \div 6$ 15. $18 \div 9$

16. $64 \div 8$ 17. $27 \div 9$ 18. $14 \div 7$ 19. $72 \div 8$ 20. $54 \div 9$

Solve.

21. Six students have the same number of coins. They have 24 coins in all. How many coins does each have?

22. Jean's 18 animals have 4 legs each. How many legs do they have altogether?

23. Jean buys 12 more animals and divides them evenly among her 6 boxes. How many in all are now in each box?

24. Ivana has 72 football cards. She has the same number of cards for each of 9 teams. How many cards does she have for each team?

Try This

A number greater than 1 is a **prime number** if it has only two factors, 1 and itself.

Example: 5 is a prime number. Its only factors are 1 and 5.

Show why these are not prime numbers.

1. 6 2. 15 3. 16 4. 20 5. 42 6. 22

Which of these are prime numbers?

7. 11 8. 7 9. 35 10. 17 11. 9 12. 2

155

1 and 0 in Division

Mark gave away 3 marbles.
He gave 1 to each friend.
How many friends got a marble?

Mark has 0 goldfish to share
among 4 friends. How many
goldfish does each friend get?

$1 \times 3 = 3$, so $3 \div 1 = 3$ or $1\overline{)3}$

$4 \times 0 = 0$, so $0 \div 4 = 0$ or $4\overline{)0}$

Three friends each got a marble.

Each friend gets 0 goldfish.

WORKING TOGETHER

Copy and complete.

1. $1 \times 8 = 8$
$8 \div 1 = \square$

2. $1 \times 9 = 9$
$9 \div 1 = \square$

3. $5 \times 0 = 0$
$0 \div 5 = \square$

4. $2 \times 0 = 0$
$0 \div 2 = \square$

Divide.

5. $4 \div 1$

6. $5 \div 1$

7. $0 \div 9$

8. $0 \div 7$

9. $1\overline{)5}$

10. $1\overline{)6}$

11. $3\overline{)0}$

12. $1\overline{)0}$

156

Find the quotient.

1. $1\overline{)4}$ 2. $1\overline{)7}$ 3. $9\overline{)0}$ 4. $1\overline{)2}$ 5. $6\overline{)0}$ 6. $4\overline{)0}$

7. $1\overline{)3}$ 8. $2\overline{)0}$ 9. $7\overline{)0}$ 10. $8\overline{)0}$ 11. $1\overline{)5}$ 12. $1\overline{)8}$

Divide.

13. $6 \div 1$ 14. $9 \div 1$ 15. $0 \div 3$ 16. $0 \div 5$ 17. $8 \div 1$

18. $0 \div 7$ 19. $0 \div 1$ 20. $7 \div 1$ 21. $1 \div 1$ 22. $0 \div 4$

Solve.

23. Rhonda found 3 conch shells and 2 sundial shells. She gave them all away. How many people could get 1 shell each?

24. George shared his lunch with Kit. He had 0 apples in his lunch. How many apples did they each have for lunch?

25. Roger has 8 markers in one box and 0 markers in another. How many markers does he have?

26. Steve and his friends have 4 model cars to play with. Each person uses 1 car. How many people can play?

27. The store has 0 apples. How many people can buy 6 apples?

Copy and complete the pyramid.
Each number is the product of the two numbers below it.

1.
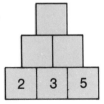

2.
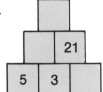

3.
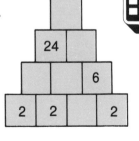

4. Make up a pyramid of your own. Ask a friend to complete it.

Remainders

Geoffrey wants to place the same
number of rocks in each box.
How many should he put in each box?
How many rocks will be left over?

Divide. $4\overline{)27}$

Choose the fact that is not too great.	Multiply.	Subtract.	Show the **remainder**.
$\begin{array}{c\|c\|c\|c} \times & 5 & 6 & 7 \\ \hline 4 & 20 & 24 & 28 \end{array}$	$\begin{array}{r} 6 \\ 4\overline{)27} \\ 24 \end{array}$	$\begin{array}{r} 6 \\ 4\overline{)27} \\ -24 \\ \hline 3 \end{array}$	$\begin{array}{r} 6\ \text{R3} \\ 4\overline{)27} \\ -24 \\ \hline 3 \end{array}$

He should put 6 rocks in each box.
There will be 3 rocks left over.

WORKING TOGETHER

Which multiplication fact would you use?

1. $3\overline{)8}$ $\begin{array}{c\|c\|c\|c} \times & 1 & 2 & 3 \\ \hline 3 & 3 & 6 & 9 \end{array}$ **2.** $5\overline{)37}$ $\begin{array}{c\|c\|c\|c\|c} \times & 5 & 6 & 7 & 8 \\ \hline 5 & 25 & 30 & 35 & 40 \end{array}$

Copy and complete. Draw an array.

3. $\begin{array}{r} 4\ \text{R}\square \\ 2\overline{)9} \\ -\square \\ \hline \square \end{array}$ **4.** $\begin{array}{r} \square\ \text{R}\square \\ 6\overline{)32} \\ -\square \\ \hline \square \end{array}$ **5.** $\begin{array}{r} \square\ \text{R}\square \\ 9\overline{)33} \\ -\square \\ \hline \square \end{array}$

158

Find the quotient and the remainder.

1. $4\overline{)9}$ 2. $7\overline{)24}$ 3. $3\overline{)10}$ 4. $5\overline{)35}$ 5. $4\overline{)38}$

6. $8\overline{)23}$ 7. $6\overline{)47}$ 8. $5\overline{)24}$ 9. $4\overline{)32}$ 10. $3\overline{)20}$

11. $7\overline{)57}$ 12. $8\overline{)11}$ 13. $9\overline{)43}$ 14. $6\overline{)42}$ 15. $2\overline{)19}$

16. $44 \div 7$ 17. $34 \div 6$ 18. $61 \div 8$ 19. $54 \div 9$ 20. $55 \div 7$

Solve.

21. Susan has 55 photos. She puts 8 on each page. How many pages does she fill? How many photos are left over?

22. Harold has 15 stamps to share equally with Kate. How many do they each get? How many stamps are left over?

23. 4 friends share 38 hockey cards equally. How many does each person get? How many are left over?

24. Geoffrey has 27 rocks and 4 boxes. He wants to put 8 rocks in each box. How many more rocks does he need?

KEEPING SHARP

Give the product.

1. 6×2 2. 4×7 3. 9×5 4. 3×3 5. 7×6 6. 9×3

7. 4×9 8. 5×0 9. 6×8 10. 4×2 11. 7×1 12. 8×4

Multiply.

13. 5×1 14. 6×5 15. 0×9 16. 4×2 17. 7×8

18. 9×2 19. 5×7 20. 3×8 21. 7×3 22. 5×5

Find the quotient.

1. 9) 36
2. 6) 30
3. 7) 56
4. 7) 42
5. 6) 48

6. 56 ÷ 8
7. 18 ÷ 6
8. 72 ÷ 9
9. 54 ÷ 9
10. 35 ÷ 7

11. 7 ÷ 1
12. 0 ÷ 8
13. 0 ÷ 9
14. 4 ÷ 1
15. 3 ÷ 1

Find the quotient and the remainder.

16. 5) 11
17. 6) 39
18. 8) 42
19. 7) 9
20. 6) 54

21. 7) 16
22. 8) 18
23. 5) 17
24. 8) 24
25. 9) 64

26. 9) 45
27. 5) 28
28. 7) 31
29. 6) 45
30. 6) 14

31. Laurie shows her collection of 48 rings. She puts 8 rings in each row. How many rows are there?

32. Helen sets up 72 stamps in groups of 8. How many groups of stamps are there?

33. Scott arranges his 21 Cub badges in 7 rows. How many badges are in each row?

34. 54 displays take 9 tables. There are the same number of displays on each table. How many displays are on a table?

35. Janet puts 5 dolls on each shelf. She has 23 dolls and 4 shelves. How many dolls are left over?

36. Harold puts 7 puppets on each stand. How many stands does he need for 28 puppets?

Facts Challenge

How well do you know your facts?
Use a calculator to check.

8 × 7 (Think the answer.)   =   (Check with the display.)

Key in. Answer mentally. Press = to check.
Keep track of your score.

Set I.			
	4 + 7	16 − 7	17 − 8
	9 + 5	14 − 8	15 + 7
	9 − 2	15 + 9	19 + 6
	8 + 9	15 − 6	23 + 9
	6 + 7	17 − 9	34 − 7
	8 − 5	18 + 6	42 + 8
	9 + 4	12 − 3	63 − 7
	5 + 8	13 + 7	51 − 9
	6 + 9	16 − 8	35 + 8

Set II.			
	8 × 5	49 ÷ 7	5 × 5 + 6
	9 × 3	54 ÷ 6	4 × 8 + 7
	7 × 5	56 ÷ 8	3 × 9 + 4
	6 × 7	45 ÷ 5	8 × 6 + 3
	5 × 4	36 ÷ 9	6 × 9 − 8
	3 × 8	63 ÷ 7	7 × 9 − 5
	9 × 9	42 ÷ 6	9 × 8 + 8
	7 × 8	64 ÷ 8	4 × 9 + 7
	5 × 6	72 ÷ 9	8 × 7 − 9

Score: 25 − 27 correct   22 − 24 correct   0 − 21 correct

Facts Master
Award

Nice Going
Award

Keep Trying
Award

Choose the Operation

A picture can help you check your number sentence for a problem.

Brenda has 3 colors of paint. She needs 12 colors to make a poster. How many more colors does she need? $$12 - 3 = 9$$  has Brenda needs 9 more colors.	Brenda has 12 pots of paint. 3 pots of paint fit into a box. How many boxes does she need? $$12 \div 3 = 4$$  Brenda needs 4 boxes.
Ken puts his markers into 3 boxes. He puts 12 markers into each box. How many markers does he have? $$3 \times 12 = 36$$  Ken has 36 markers.	Brenda had some paint brushes. She gave 3 to Ken. She has 12 left. How many did she have to start with? $$3 + 12 = 15$$  gave Brenda had 15 paint brushes.

WORKING TOGETHER

How many stickers are in Grant's album?
He put the same number on each of 8 pages.

1. How many stickers fit on 1 page?
2. How many pages are there?
3. Should you add, subtract, multiply,
   or divide to find the total?
4. Find the answer. Check it.
5. Give the answer in a sentence.

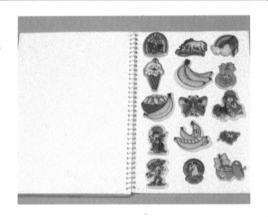

PROBLEMS

Solve. Draw a picture to check your answer.

1. A box holds 18 cough drops. Each day I have 2 cough drops. How many days will it take me to finish the box?

2. Scott collected 2 eggs. He plans to give me 1 dozen eggs. How many more eggs must he collect?

3. Hope School has 7 classrooms. Each classroom has 21 students. How many students go to Hope School?

4. 24 crates of nails are sent to Kingston. 6 crates are returned. How many crates are not returned?

5. A parking lot can hold 36 cars. There are 12 cars in the lot. How many empty parking spaces are there?

6. In a bike-a-thon Carlos rode 4 km. Nicole rode 3 km more than Carlos. How many kilometres did they ride in all?

Should you add, subtract, multiply, or divide?

7. There are □ students in a class. Each student has 5 pencils. What is the total number of pencils?

8. There are □ envelopes. They are put in packages of 8. How many packages are there?

9. The temperature this morning was □°C. It rose 3°C. What is the temperature now?

10. Jules is 92 cm tall. His little sister is □ cm tall. How much taller is Jules?

Make up a problem. Then have a classmate solve it.

11. 15 buttons
    3 coats

12. 96 balloons
    54 float away
    15 break

13.

    20¢ each,   7¢ each

163

Problem Solving Review

Solve.

1. Eric had 1 dollar, 3 quarters, 4 dimes, 2 nickels, and 6 pennies in his pocket. He bought lunch for $2.04. What coins does Eric have left?

2. Two students stood back to back. One student walked 39 paces forward. The other walked 46 paces forward. How far apart were they then?

3. How many invitations are in 7 packs?

12 party invitations

4. Which coin is older? How much older is it?

5. Copy and continue this pattern for two more rows. Then copy and complete the table below.

    ➡   A
            BBB
           CCCCC
       DDDDDDD

Letter	A	B	C	D	E	F	G	H	I	J	K	L
Number of letters in row	1	3										

6. How many letters are in the M row?

7. How many letters are in the P row?

8. Which row has exactly 33 letters?

9. Which row has exactly 45 letters?

10. The class bought Mrs. Long a charm bracelet. The bracelet cost $7. The charms cost $5 each. How much did the charm bracelet cost in all?

164

Chapter Checkup

Copy and complete.

1. $7 \times \square = 63$ 2. $5 \times \square = 50$ 3. $\square \times 6 = 54$ 4. $\square \times 7 = 35$

5. $\square \times 5 = 0$ 6. $8 \times \square = 48$ 7. $1 \times \square = 9$ 8. $\square \times 9 = 81$

Divide.

9. $25 \div 5$ 10. $28 \div 4$ 11. $18 \div 6$ 12. $36 \div 4$ 13. $54 \div 9$

14. $0 \div 2$ 15. $9 \div 9$ 16. $8 \div 1$ 17. $5 \div 1$ 18. $30 \div 6$

19. $8 \overline{)40}$ 20. $9 \overline{)72}$ 21. $4 \overline{)16}$ 22. $6 \overline{)42}$ 23. $7 \overline{)63}$

24. $5 \overline{)29}$ 25. $4 \overline{)18}$ 26. $8 \overline{)35}$ 27. $7 \overline{)49}$ 28. $6 \overline{)30}$

Copy and complete. Draw an array.

29.
$$
\begin{array}{c} 4 \\ \times \square \\ \hline 24 \end{array}
\qquad
\begin{array}{c} 6 \\ \times \square \\ \hline 24 \end{array}
\qquad 24 \div 4 = \square \qquad 24 \div 6 = \square
$$

Write the family of facts for the set of numbers.

30. 4, 32, 8   31. 3, 7, 21   32. 5, 40, 8   33. 9, 7, 63

Solve.

34. Twenty oranges were in the bag. 6 children each eat 3. How many oranges are not eaten?

35. Six girls share 50 seashells equally. How many shells does each girl get? How many extra shells are there?

36. Forty children sign up for floor hockey. There are 5 teams. How many children are on each team?

37. Each car can carry 6 people. There are 54 people. How many cars are needed?

Cumulative Checkup

Subtract.

1. 936
  − 585

2. 620
  − 483

3. 700
  − 539

4. 462
  − 281

5. 305
  − 90

6. $25.64
  − 8.25

7. $94.00
  − 17.29

8. 5300
  − 4236

9. 4708
  − 899

Multiply.

10. 4 × 60

11. 3 × 900

12. 9 × 37

13. 6 × 349

14. 6 × 8 × 4

15. 3 × 7 × 9

16. 4 × 8 × 7

17. 5 × 9 × 3

18. 430
  × 4

19. 675
  × 6

20. 378
  × 7

21. 802
  × 8

22. 800
  × 9

23. 246
  × 9

24. 408
  × 5

25. 535
  × 3

How many?

26. vertices

27. edges

28. faces

29. lines

30. line segments

31. right angles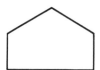

Does the picture suggest a slide, flip, or turn?

32.

33.

34.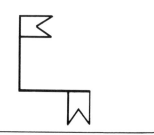

166

7/Measurement

In this chapter,
you will measure lengths,
areas, volumes, masses,
and capacities.

Centimetres and Millimetres

The **centimetre (cm)** and **millimetre (mm)** are used
to measure the length of a small object.

The butterfly has a wingspan
of **about 7 cm**.

The width of the butterfly's body
is less than 1 cm.

The width of the body is **4 mm**.

1 cm = 10 mm

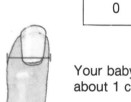

Your baby finger is
about 1 cm wide.

A paper clip and a dime
are about 1 mm thick.

WORKING TOGETHER

Write the length to the nearest centimetre.

1. 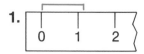   **2.**   **3.**

Write the length in millimetres.

4.   **5.**   **6.**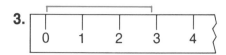

Measure in millimetres.

7.    **8.**    **9.**

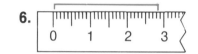

168

EXERCISES

Write the length to the nearest centimetre.

1.
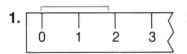

2.

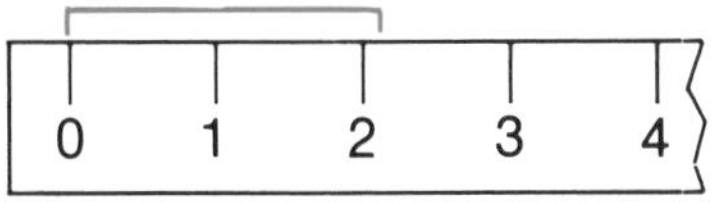

| 0 | 1 | 2 | 3 | 4 |

3.

| 0 | 1 | 2 | 3 | 4 |

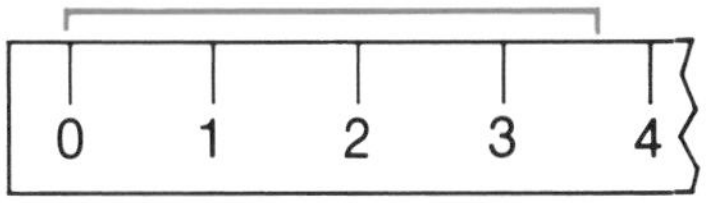

Write the length in millimetres.

4.

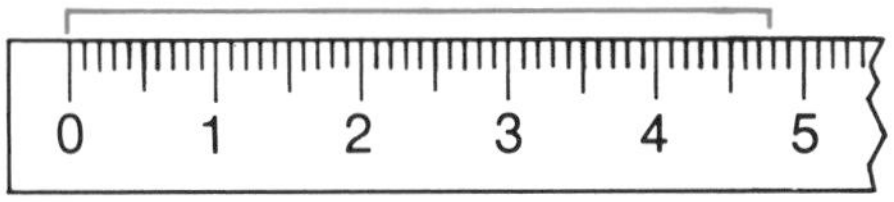

| 0 | 1 | 2 | 3 | 4 | 5 |

5.

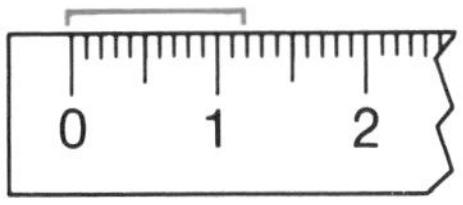

| 0 | 1 | 2 |

6.

| 0 | 1 | 2 |

Estimate in centimetres.

Measure to the nearest centimetre.

7.

8.

9.

10. the length of this page

11. the length of your pencil

12. The length of your hand

Measure in millimetres.

13.

14.

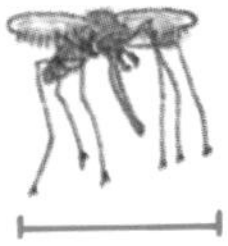

15.

16. the thickness of this book

17. the width of an eraser

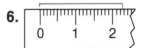

KEEPING SHARP

Find the sum.

1. 42 + 13 + 2

2. 36 + 59 + 21

3. 321 + 546 + 32

4. 516 + 231 + 451

5. 412 + 213 + 589

6. 317 + 408 + 127

7. 428 + 32 + 50

8. 508 + 47 + 60

9. 217 + 20 + 8

169

Metres and Kilometres

The **metre (m)** is used to measure long lengths.

    The length of the space shuttle is measured in metres.

The **kilometre (km)** is used to measure very long distances.

    The distance that the shuttle travels is measured in kilometres.

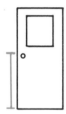
The door knob is about **1 m** high.

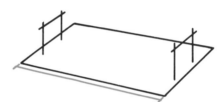
Ten times the length of a soccer field is about **1 km**.

> **1 m = 100 cm**
> **1 km = 1000 m**

WORKING TOGETHER

Which unit, metre or kilometre, is better for measuring this?

1.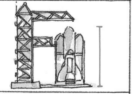

2.

3.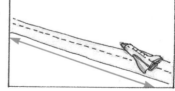

Estimate in metres. Measure to the nearest metre.

4. the height of the chalkboard ledge

5. the height of the chalkboard

6. the length of the bulletin board

EXERCISES

Which unit, metre or kilometre, is better for measuring this?

1.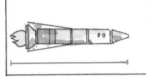

2.

3.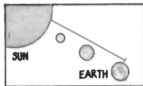

Estimate in metres. Measure to the nearest metre.

4. the length of the chalkboard

5. the height of the door

6. the width of the classroom

7. the height of a friend

8. the height of the bulletin board

9. the width of the hall

Choose the best estimate.

10.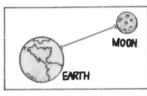

380 m   38 km   380 000 km

11.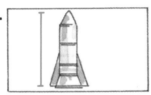

300 cm   30 m   3 km

12.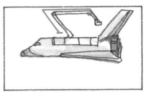

15 cm   15 m   15 km

13.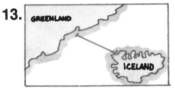

500 m   5 km   500 km

14.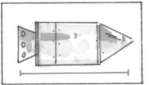

15 cm   15 m   15 km

15.

38 m   38 km   38 000 km

Try This

The ladder of an anchored ship has 6 m above the water and 5 m below the water. During the evening, the tide comes in to raise the water level by 2 m. How much of the ladder is above the water now?

171

Perimeter

Chad jogs around the schoolyard.
How far does he jog?

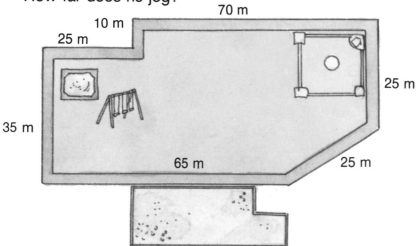

Perimeter is the distance around a shape.

To find how far Chad jogs,
add the lengths of the sides.

The perimeter of the schoolyard is 255 m.

$$
\begin{array}{r}
35 \\
25 \\
10 \\
70 \\
25 \\
25 \\
+\ 65 \\
\hline
255
\end{array}
$$

WORKING TOGETHER

Find the perimeter.

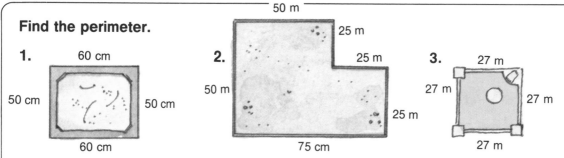

1. 60 cm / 50 cm / 50 cm / 60 cm

2. 50 m / 25 m / 25 m / 50 m / 25 m / 75 cm

3. 27 m / 27 m / 27 m / 27 m

Measure the sides to the nearest centimetre. Find the perimeter.

4. the front cover of this book

5. the top of your desk

172

EXERCISES

Find the perimeter.

1.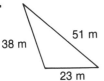
24 mm, 21 mm, 25 mm

2.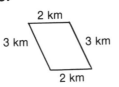
42 cm, 32 cm, 39 cm, 43 cm

3.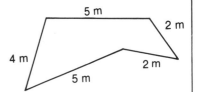
5 m, 2 m, 4 m, 5 m, 2 m

4.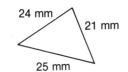
51 m, 38 m, 23 m

5.
2 km, 3 km, 3 km, 2 km

6.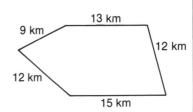
13 km, 9 km, 12 km, 12 km, 15 km

Measure the sides in centimetres. Find the perimeter.

7.

8.

9. the cover of a reader

10. a pencil case

11. the chalkboard

12. the classroom door

Solve.

13. The kindergarten playground is 25 m wide and 25 m long. What is its perimeter?

14. The parking lot is 24 m long and 21 m wide. What is its perimeter?

15. The soccer field is 91 m long and 54 m wide. What is its perimeter?

16. How much fencing is needed to go around a school garden 3 m wide and 6 m long?

Try This

Find the perimeter of the circle.

1.

2.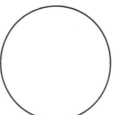

173

Area

Area is the amount of surface covered by a shape.

1 cm The area of this square is **one square centimetre (1 cm^2).**
1 cm

The area of the label is the number of square centimetres that it covers.

In the first row, 8 squares are covered.
5 rows are covered.

5 rows of 8
5×8
$= 40$

The area of the label is 40 cm^2.

WORKING TOGETHER

Find the area of the label in square centimetres.

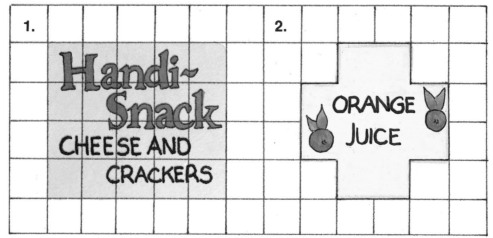

Find the area of the label in square centimetres.

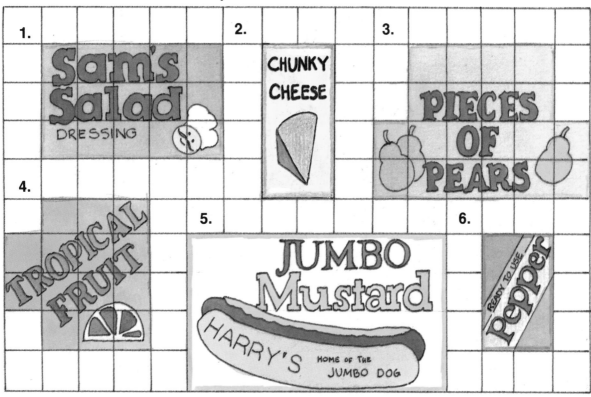

1.
2.
3.
4.
5.
6.

Use square centimetres. Make a shape with the area.

7. 10 cm^2

8. 21 cm^2

9. 25 cm^2

Try This

Find the area
of this label.

Units of Area

The area of a computer key
is about **one square centimetre (1 cm²)**.

The area of the computer table
is about **one square metre (1 m²)**.

Small areas are measured in square centimetres.
Large areas are measured in square metres.

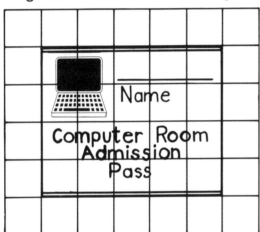

The area of the pass card is the
number of square centimetres that it covers.

4 rows of 5	5 columns of 4
4 × 5	5 × 4
= 20	= 20

The area of the pass card is 20 cm².

WORKING TOGETHER

**Which unit, square centimetre or square metre, is better
for measuring the area?**

1. a carpet

2. a ceiling tile

3. a lawn

Find the area.

4.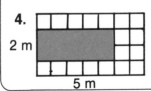
2 m
5 m

5.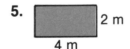
2 m
4 m

6.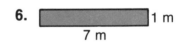
1 m
7 m

EXERCISES

Which unit, square centimetre or square metre, is better for measuring the area?

1. a pillow

2. a wall

3. a computer keyboard

4. a monitor screen

5. a floor

6. a computer manual

Find the area.

7.
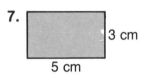
3 cm

5 cm

8.
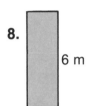
6 m

2 m

9.
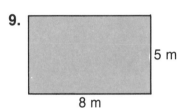
5 m

8 m

Measure the sides. Find the area.

10.

11.

12.

Solve.

13. A cassette has a length of 10 cm and a width of 6 cm. What is the area of the cassette?

14. The floor of a computer room has a length of 6 m and a width of 5 m. What is its area?

After a computer is switched on, the **cursor** flashes on the screen. This shows where the next typed character goes.

1. Type on the **keyboard** what a classmate reads to you. To correct a mistake, press ⬅, then retype the character.

177

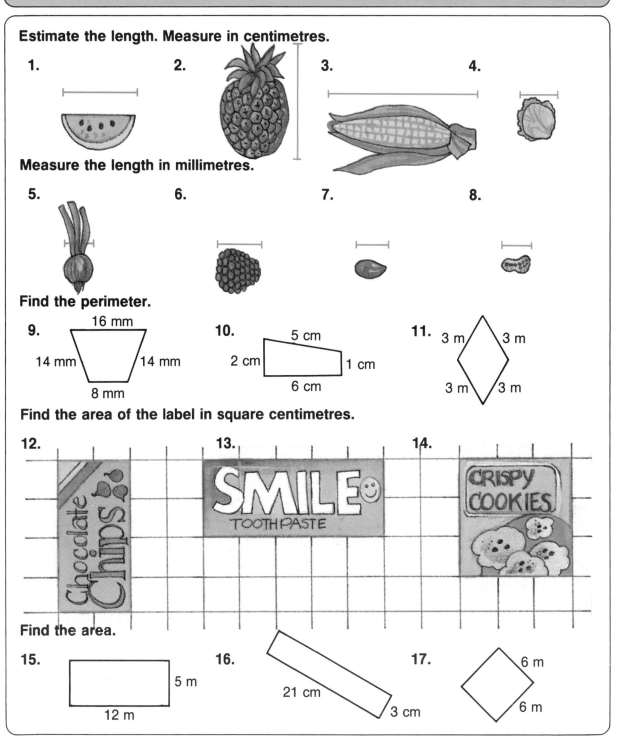

PRACTICE

Estimate the length. Measure in centimetres.

1.

2.

3.

4.

Measure the length in millimetres.

5.

6.

7.

8.

Find the perimeter.

9. 16 mm
14 mm   14 mm
8 mm

10. 5 cm
2 cm   1 cm
6 cm

11. 3 m   3 m
3 m   3 m

Find the area of the label in square centimetres.

12.

13.

14.

Find the area.

15. 5 m
12 m

16. 21 cm   3 cm

17. 6 m
6 m

Turtle Graphics

Logo is a computer language. It lets you move a turtle (▲) on the screen. HOME position is the centre of the screen with the turtle pointing up.

The commands
    FD 100
    RT 75
    FD 150
    HOME
tell the turtle to draw this.→

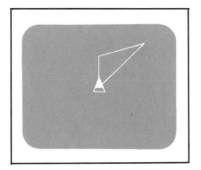

Logo Commands	
FORWARD	FD
BACK	BK
RIGHT	RT
LEFT	LT
PENUP	PU
PENDOWN	PD
HIDETURTLE	HT
SHOWTURTLE	ST
HOME	
*DRAW	
*CLEARSCREEN	CS

(* for MIT Logo)

1. Play Turtle with a classmate. First mark a path on the floor. Then walk along the path and call out your moves. The other person writes down the commands.

Draw a picture for the commands or type them on a computer. Compare the results with your floor path.

2. Experiment with your own designs. Can you make the turtle draw these?

Volume

What is the volume of Sean's box?

Volume is the amount of space occupied by an object.

The volume of each cube is **one cubic centimetre (1 cm^3)**.

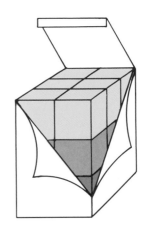

Sean fills the box with cubes.
He has 6 cubes on the top layer.
He has 3 layers of 6 cubes.

The volume of Sean's box is 18 cm^3.

WORKING TOGETHER

Build the shape with centimetre cubes. Find the volume.

1.
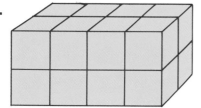

2.
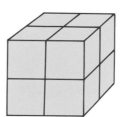

3.
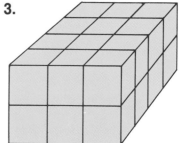

4.
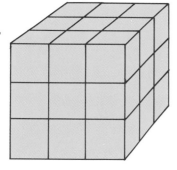

5.
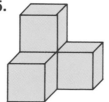

6.
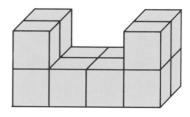

Build the shape with centimetre cubes. Find the volume.

1.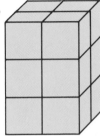

2.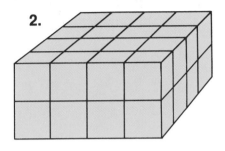

3.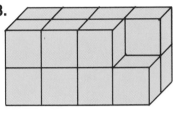

4.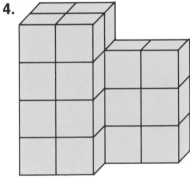

5.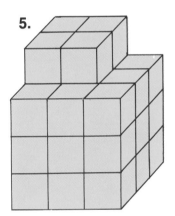

6.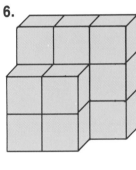

Use centimetre cubes. Build a shape with the volume.

7. 6 cm³

8. 14 cm³

9. 20 cm³

Try This

How many blocks were needed to build the pyramid?

181

Litres and Millilitres

Cory used a one-**litre (L)** container to fill Brig's water bowl. Cory used a **millilitre (mL)** eyedropper to put some liquid vitamins into the water.

1 L = 1000 mL

The litre is used to measure how much a large container holds.	The millilitre is used to measure how much a small container holds.

WORKING TOGETHER

Which unit, litre or millilitre, is better for measuring this?

1.   2.    3.

Choose the best estimate.

4.   5.   6.

5 mL 500 mL 5 L	10 mL 1 L 10 L	500 mL 5 L 50 L

EXERCISES

Which unit, litre or millilitre, is better for measuring this?

1.

2.

3.

Choose the best estimate.

4.

| 35 mL | 350 mL | 35 L |

5.

| 40 mL | 4 L | 40 L |

6.

| 2 mL | 200 mL | 2L |

7.

| 25 mL | 250 mL | 1 L |

8.

| 28 mL | 280 mL | 28 L |

9.

| 1 mL | 10 mL | 100 mL |

Solve.

10. A restaurant has 9 cream jugs. Each one contains 125 mL of cream. How many millilitres of cream are there?

11. 50 L of lemonade were made for the party. The children drank 39 L. How many litres were left over?

 KEEPING SHARP

Multiply or divide.

1. 6 × 4   2. 9 × 3   3. 32 ÷ 4   4. 42 ÷ 7   5. 6 × 8   6. 9 × 7

7. 36 ÷ 9   8. 8 × 7   9. 28 ÷ 7   10. 48 ÷ 6   11. 56 ÷ 7   12. 63 ÷ 9

13. 45 ÷ 5   14. 3 × 8   15. 8 × 9   16. 81 ÷ 9   17. 35 ÷ 5   18. 70 ÷ 7

Kilograms and Grams

Some groceries are priced according to their **mass**.

Kilograms (kg) are used to measure the mass of heavy objects.
Each of these has a mass of about 1 kg.

Grams (g) are used to measure the mass of light objects.
Each of these has a mass of about 1 g.

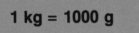

1 kg = 1000 g

 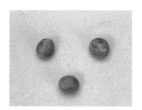

WORKING TOGETHER

Which unit, kilogram or gram, is better for measuring this?

1.
2.
3.

Choose the best estimate.

4.

| 300 g | 1 kg | 3 kg |

5.

| 4 g | 400 g | 1 kg |

6.

| 6 g | 60 g | 6 kg |

184

List three objects in the classroom with a mass measured in this unit.

1. kilograms

2. grams

Which unit, kilogram or gram, is better for measuring this?

3.

4.

5.

Choose the best estimate.

6.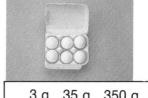

| 45 g | 450 g | 4 kg |

7.

| 10 g | 100 g | 1 kg |

8.

| 3 g | 300 g | 3 kg |

9.

| 3 g | 35 g | 350 g |

10.

| 600 g | 6 kg | 60 kg |

11.

| 3 g | 300 g | 3 kg |

Solve.

12. A small loaf of bread with a mass of 225 g is cut into 9 slices. What is the mass of each slice?

13. A nut mixture had 340 g of peanuts, 170 g of cashews, and 85 g of walnuts. How many grams of nuts were there in the mixture?

Use these pictures to find the mass of the cat.

Try This

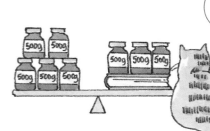

Reading Time

Cione is the timekeeper at the finish line of a bicycle race.
She records the finishing time to the nearest minute.

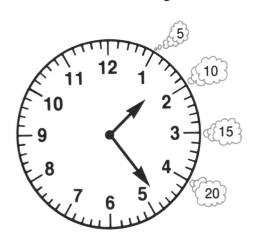

The **hour hand** has just passed 1.

From 12, count forward by fives, then by ones,
to read the **minute hand**.

Cione records the winner's finishing time as **1:24 p.m.**

After midnight but before noon is **a.m.**
After noon but before midnight is **p.m.**

WORKING TOGETHER

Write the time.

1.

afternoon

2.

morning

3.

evening

4.

morning

Write the time.

1.
morning

2.
evening

3.
morning

4.
afternoon

5.
morning

6.
afternoon

7.
afternoon

8.
evening

Draw a circular clock. Show the time.

9. `12:38` 10. `9:43` 11. `10:02` 12. `2:27` 13. `11:16`

Use a clock face to help find the total time taken by each racer.

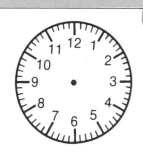

Racer	Starting Time	Finishing Time
14. A	7:20 a.m.	9:20 a.m.
15. B	9:30 a.m.	10:40 a.m.
16. C	8:40 a.m.	11:55 a.m.
17. D	11:30 a.m.	1:40 p.m.
18. E	10:20 a.m.	1:25 p.m.

Try This

Copy the clock face. Draw two straight lines to divide the clock face into three parts. The sum of the numbers in each part must be the same.

Now try six parts.

187

Units of Time

Marni's class is invited to watch a space movie Friday morning. There are 3 h of school in the morning. The movie lasts 150 min. Do they have enough time to watch the movie?

1 h = 60 min

$$3 \text{ h} = 3 \times 60 \text{ min}$$
$$= 180 \text{ min}$$

The movie lasts only 150 min.
There is more than enough time to watch the movie.

1 year = 12 months	1 d = 24 h (hours)
1 year = 52 weeks	1 h = 60 min (minutes)
1 week = 7 d (days)	1 min = 60 s (seconds)

WORKING TOGETHER

Copy and complete.

1.

min	s
1	60
2	
3	
4	

2.

h	min
1	60
2	
3	
4	

3.

d	h
1	24
2	
3	
4	

4.

weeks	d
1	7
2	
3	
4	

5.

years	months
1	12
2	
3	
4	

Copy and complete.

6. 2 weeks 3 d = ☐ d   **7.** 4 d 5 h = ☐ h   **8.** 6 h 2 min = ☐ min

EXERCISES

Which unit of time is best to complete the sentence?

1. It took the class 10 ☐ to ride on the bus to the movie.

2. The class took 3 ☐ to complete an assignment about the movie.

3. The space movie for another Friday is 2 ☐ long.

4. In 15 ☐, some students may become astronauts.

Copy and complete.

5. 5 min = ☐ s

6. 9 min = ☐ s

7. 4 h = ☐ min

8. 7 h = ☐ min

9. 6 d = ☐ h

10. 2 d = ☐ h

11. 4 weeks = ☐ d

12. 3 years = ☐ months

13. 7 years = ☐ months

14. 3 years = ☐ weeks

15. 8 years = ☐ weeks

16. 9 weeks = ☐ d

17. 3 min 4 s = ☐ s

18. 2 h 5 min = ☐ min

19. 7 d 10 h = ☐ h

20. 3 d 5 h = ☐ h

21. 5 weeks 1 d = ☐ d

22. 2 weeks 3 d = ☐ d

Solve.

23. The class spent 5 h 20 min at the Science Centre. How many minutes did they spend there?

24. It took 45 min 10 s for the bus to travel to the Science Centre. How many seconds did the bus take?

Do you remember what to do if you press the wrong number key?
Press [Cl] or [CE] once. Repeat the number you are entering.

Write the key presses that correct the mistakes.

1. 69 + 47   [6] [9] [+] [4] [8] ☐ ☐ ☐ ☐ [=] (116.)

2. 684 − 392   [6] [8] [4] [−] [3] [6] [2] ☐ ☐ ☐ ☐ ☐ [=] (292.)

3. 456 − 89   [4] [6] ☐ ☐ ☐ ☐ ☐ [−] [8] [9] [=] (369.)

189

Build the shape with centimetre cubes. Find the volume.

1.
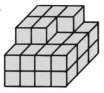

2.
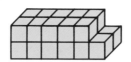

3.

Choose the best estimate.

4.

| 35 mL | 350 mL | 3 L |

5.

| 6 mL | 600 mL | 6 L |

6.
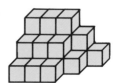

| 1 mL | 100 mL | 1 L |

7.

| 20 g | 200 g | 2 kg |

8.

| 3 g | 300 g | 3 kg |

9.

| 2 g | 200 g | 2 Kg |

Write the time.

10.

morning

11.

evening

12.

evening

13.

afternoon

Copy and complete.

14. 6 min = ☐ s

15. 5 h = ☐ min

16. 2 d = ☐ h

17. 3 min 5 s = ☐ s

18. 4 years = ☐ months

19. 2 years = ☐ weeks

Calculate with Measures

Dad	Mom	Greg	Arlene	Katie
183 cm	164 cm	172 cm	122 cm	107 cm
79 kg	52 kg	66 kg	23 kg	18 kg

Calculate.

1. How much taller is Greg than Katie?

2. What is the mass of Dad and Mom together?

3. Suppose the family lay head-to-foot in a line. Find the total length.

4. A small elevator will hold 500 kg. Can the whole family get in at one time?

5. Who has the greater mass, Mom, or Arlene and Katie together?

6. Who has the greater mass, Dad and Katie together, or Greg and Arlene together?

Calculate the area.

7.

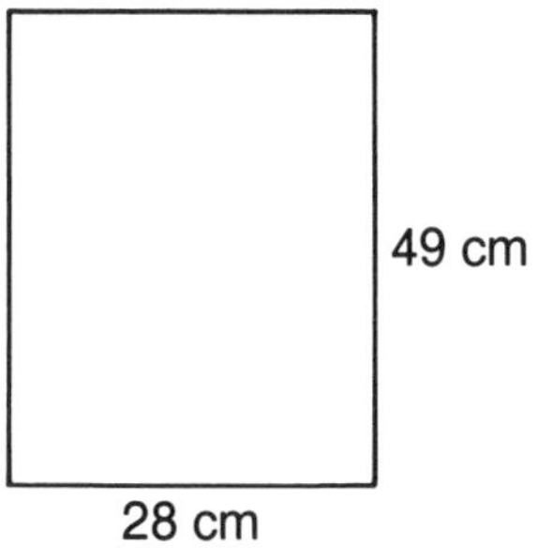

49 cm

28 cm

	Length	Width	Area
8.	35 m	22 m	
9.	24 cm	24 cm	
10.	125 m	55 m	
11.	29 km	29 km	
12.	76 m	34 m	

Choose the Information

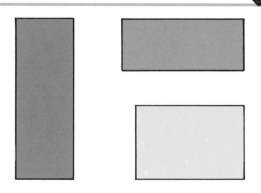

Lloyd has some colored papers to make a sign. The red paper is 58 cm long and 20 cm wide. The yellow paper is 39 cm long. The orange paper is 45 cm long. How long is the longest sign he can make using the red and orange papers?

Think. What information is needed?
- red paper, 58 cm long
- orange paper, 45 cm long

What information is not needed?
- yellow paper, 39 cm long
- red paper, 20 cm wide

Plan and do. Find the total.

```
    1
    5 8
  + 4 5
  -----
  1 0 3
```

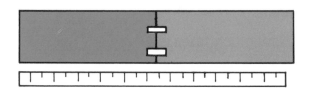

Look back. Lloyd checks his answer by measuring. The longest sign is 103 cm.

WORKING TOGETHER

In a parade, the marching band formed 8 rows. 4 players marched in each row. Policemen riding on horses formed 6 rows. 3 horses were in each row. How many players were in the marching band?

1. What information is needed?

2. What information is not needed?

3. Solve the problem.

4. Give the answer in a sentence.

5. What other questions could be asked about the same information?

PROBLEMS

1. What does the driver need to drive a taxi?

a.   b.   c.   d.   e.

Tell what information is not needed.

2. 5 vans came to the school. Each van had 2 headlights. 3 people sat in each front seat. 11 people were in each van. How many people were there in all?

3. 10 cars are in a used car lot. $\frac{1}{2}$ of them are two-door cars. $\frac{3}{10}$ of them are sports cars. How many are not sports cars?

Choose the information needed. Solve the problem.

4. How much ribbon is needed for first prize? Each ribbon is 15 cm long.

1st   2nd   3rd

5. 9 kites are flying. Each kite has 4 stars and 6 stripes. Each star has 5 points. How many stars are there in all?

6. The zoo had 375 birds. 227 of them were songbirds. A shipment of 38 birds came. 29 of them were songbirds. Now how many songbirds are at the zoo?

7. Rhoda bought a T-shirt for $2.95 and a wallet for $2.49. She spent 80¢ for a milkshake. Then she bought some socks for $1.95. What is the total she spent on clothes?

8. 400 people were at the concert. 286 people came by car. The rest came in 3 buses. 38 people were on each bus. How many people came by bus?

Problem Solving Review

Solve.

1. Four girls and 3 boys sit at each table. There are 21 children in all. How many tables are there? What is the total number of girls?

2. Sherry and Jeff played table tennis. Sherry won with a score of 15. She won by 5 points. What was Jeff's score?

3. Leo wants to give a gift to his cousin. He bought a bicycle horn and wrapping paper. How much did he pay?

4. How much more did the gift cost than the paper?

> *February 5*
>
> *bicycle horn* $5.00
> *wrapping paper* $1.25

5. Gina has 3 more records than Rose. Rose has 12 fewer records than Chris. Chris has 23 records. How many records does Gina have?

6. A string of lights has 18 bulbs. Every third bulb is yellow. How many bulbs are yellow? How many are not yellow?

7. Kate had 4 nickels, 2 dimes, and 6 quarters. She spent 1 quarter, 1 dime, and 3 nickels. How much money does she have left?

8. Darcy has 3 sisters. 2 sisters are younger. He is 2 years older than his sister Maude. Maude is 8 years old. How old is Darcy?

The numbers on the T-shirts form a pattern. Which number belongs on the last shirt?

9.

10.

194

Chapter Checkup

Estimate the length. Measure to the nearest centimetre.

1. _____

2. _____

3. _____

Measure in millimetres.

4. _____

5. _____

6. _____

Which length unit is best for measuring this?

7. the length of a car

8. the width of a steering wheel

9. a highway distance

Choose the best estimate.

10.

| 12 g   120 g   12 kg |

11.

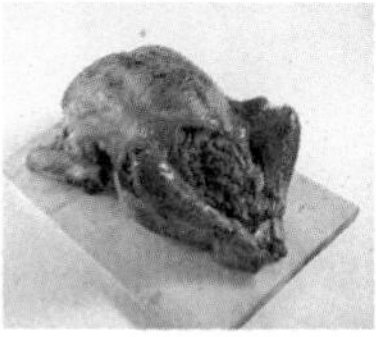

| 70 g   7 kg   70 kg |

12.

| 2 mL   200 mL   2 L |

Solve.

13. A book cover is 18 cm long and 8 cm wide. What is the area of the cover?

14. A carpet is 6 m long and 9 m wide. What is the area of the carpet?

15. A lawn is 21 m long and 33 m wide. How much fencing is needed to fence in the lawn?

16. A square room is 10 m by 10 m. How much ceiling molding is needed to go around the room?

Build the shape with centimetre cubes. Find the volume.

17.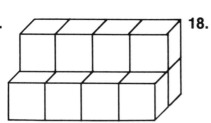

18.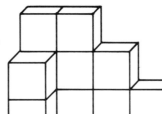

19.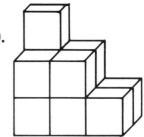

Cumulative Checkup

Add.

1. 540
  + 380

2. 457
  + 285

3. 109
  + 797

4. 490
  + 629

5. 153
  + 458

6. 2068
  + 1973

7. 4050
  + 3950

8. 2975
  + 2897

9. 3569
  + 1567

10. 32 + 45 + 62 + 90

11. 28 + 17 + 43 + 9

12. 325 + 140 + 279 + 85

13. 77 + 8 + 45 + 7

Subtract.

14. 8720
  − 2853

15. 6300
  − 2975

16. 7004
  − 5725

17. 3709
  − 1480

18. 600
  − 473

19. 597
  − 486

20. 327
  − 48

21. 705
  − 90

22. 380
  − 295

Multiply.

23. 600
  × 8

24. 40
  × 9

25. 372
  × 9

26. 105
  × 9

27. 638
  × 7

28. 295
  × 7

29. 643
  × 4

30. 227
  × 5

31. 800
  × 8

32. 27
  × 8

33. 6 × 5 × 7

34. 8 × 2 × 7

35. 6 × 7 × 8

36. 4 × 7 × 5

Divide.

37. $7\overline{)40}$

38. $6\overline{)26}$

39. $8\overline{)72}$

40. $7\overline{)56}$

41. $9\overline{)84}$

42. $8\overline{)0}$

43. $9\overline{)75}$

44. $6\overline{)51}$

45. $1\overline{)9}$

46. $5\overline{)45}$

8/Fractions and Decimals

In this chapter you will learn how to use fractions and decimals to talk about part of a whole or a set. You will learn how to add and subtract decimals to tenths.

Fractions

Jill's sandwich was in 4 equal parts.
She ate 1 part at recess and kept
3 parts for her lunch. What fraction
of the sandwich did she keep for lunch?

4 equal parts   Jill kept 3 parts.

$\dfrac{3}{4}$ ← numerator
      ← denominator

three-fourths

Jill kept three-fourths of her sandwich for lunch.

WORKING TOGETHER

Does the drawing show equal parts?

1.   2.   3.   4.

How many equal parts are there?

5.   6.   7.   8.

What fraction of the whole is colored?

9.   10.   11.   12.

198

What fraction of the whole is colored?

1.
2.
3.
4.

5.
6.
7.
8.

9.
10.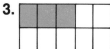
11.
12.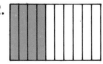

Draw a picture. Color the fraction named.

13. $\frac{1}{2}$ of an apple

14. $\frac{2}{3}$ of a glass of juice

15. seven-eighths of a pizza

16. $\frac{3}{10}$ of a cake

17. three-fifths of a garden

18. one-sixth of a flag

Try
This

Copy and continue the pattern.

1.

2.

3.

4.

199

Part of a Set

Here are the flags for each
of the 10 digits. What fraction
tells how many flags show
a circle?

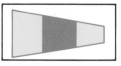
zero

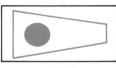
one

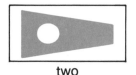
two

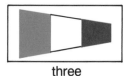
three

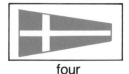
four

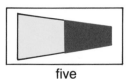
five

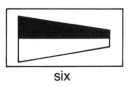
six

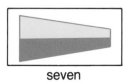
seven

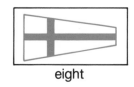
eight

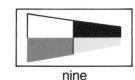
nine

2 flags show a circle.
10 flags in all.

$\dfrac{2}{10}$ ← number talked about
← number in all

$\frac{2}{10}$ of the flags show a circle.

WORKING TOGETHER

Give a fraction to complete the sentence. Use the pictures of the flags.

1. $\frac{\square}{\square}$ have red.

2. $\frac{\square}{\square}$ have black.

3. $\frac{\square}{\square}$ have blue.

4. $\frac{\square}{\square}$ have white.

5. $\frac{\square}{\square}$ have a cross.

6. $\frac{\square}{\square}$ have 4 colors.

Use the picture of the shapes.

7. How many shapes in all?

8. What fraction are squares?

What fraction of the set is colored?

1.

2.

3. ◯ ◯ ◯ ◯

4. ▽ ▼ ▽ ▽ ▽

5. □ ■ ■ ■ ■

6. ⬡ ⬢ ⬡ ⬡ ⬢

7.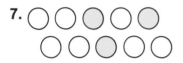

8. ◡ ◡ ◡ ◡ ◡
   ◡ ◡ ◡ ◡ ◡

9.

Show the fraction.

10. Draw 4 flags. Color $\frac{1}{4}$ of them blue.

11. Draw 5 flags. Color $\frac{3}{5}$ of them red.

Solve.

12. Three of the 10 provinces are Prairie Provinces. What fraction is that?

13. Each of the 10 provinces has a flag. 5 of them show an animal. What fraction is that?

14. There are 2 flags for the Territories. Both of them show animals. What fraction is that?

15. One of the 4 flags of the Atlantic Provinces shows an island. What fraction is that?

Take turns playing Turtle Target Practice with a classmate.

1. One player places a sticker or a piece of Plasticine on the screen to be a target.

2. The other player types two commands. How close is the turtle to the target?

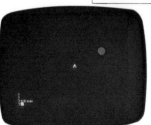

Fractions Greater Than One

How many circles?

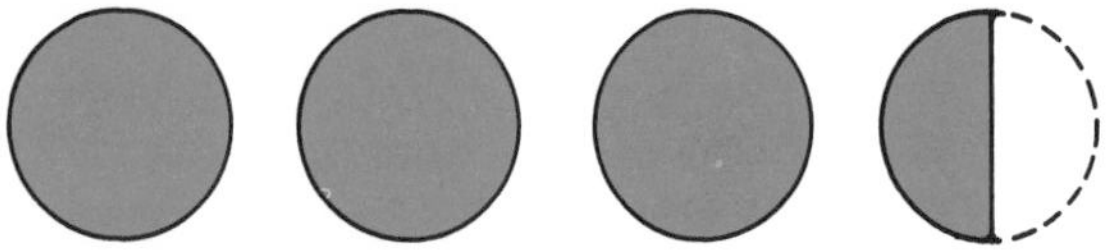

three **and** one-half circles

$3\frac{1}{2}$

How many squares?

two **and** four-tenths squares

$2\frac{4}{10}$

Three balls in a package. How many packages?

 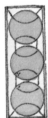 

two **and** one-third packages

$2\frac{1}{3}$

WORKING TOGETHER

How much is colored?

1.

2.

3.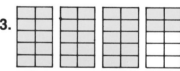

4.

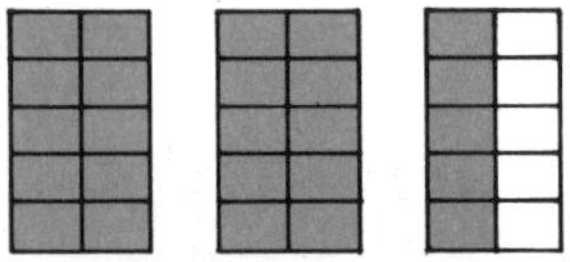

5.

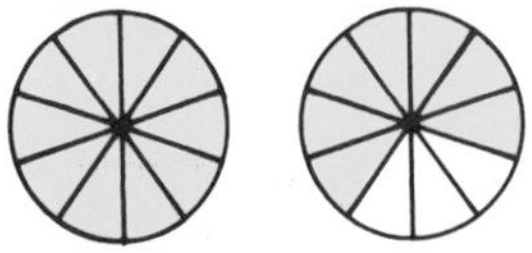

6.

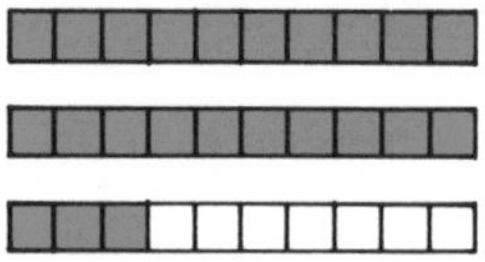

How many sets are there?

7.

8.

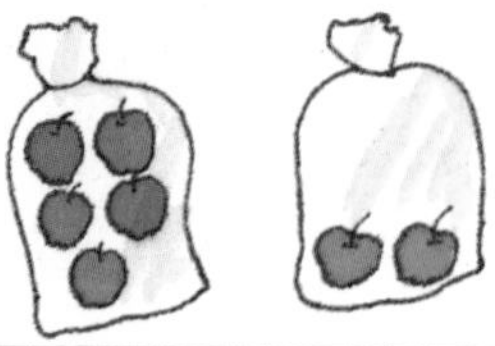

9.

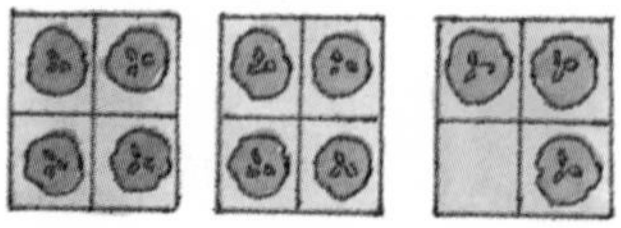

202

EXERCISES

How much is colored?

1.

2. △ △ △ △

3.

How many sets are there?

4.

5.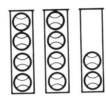

6.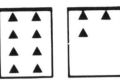

Draw a picture.

7. $1\frac{1}{4}$

8. $2\frac{1}{2}$

9. $2\frac{3}{5}$

10. $1\frac{7}{10}$

Solve. Draw a picture to help you.

11. Anna puts 10 stamps on a page in her album. She has 25 stamps. How many pages will that fill?

12. Carol puts 5 beads on each friendship pin. She has 15 beads. How many pins can she make?

13. Roy uses 10 sheets of paper to make a booklet. He has 14 sheets. How many booklets will that make?

14. There are 10 jacks in a set. Ted has only 8. What fraction is that?

Try This

Sam has 8 large pies for dessert for 76 people.
He can cut the pies into eighths or tenths.
How can he do this so there is no pie left over?

203

Equivalent Fractions

Gus and Sam ate 5 of the
10 pieces of cake. Their sister
said, ''You ate one-half
of the cake!'' Was she right?

 $\frac{5}{10}$ $\frac{1}{2}$ $\frac{5}{10} = \frac{1}{2}$

She was right. $\frac{5}{10}$ and $\frac{1}{2}$ name the same amount.

WORKING TOGETHER

Copy and complete the fractions.

1.

$\frac{1}{2} = \frac{\square}{4}$

2.

$\frac{1}{2} = \frac{\square}{6}$

3.

$\frac{2}{5} = \frac{\square}{10}$

4.

$\frac{1}{2} = \frac{5}{\square}$

5.

$\frac{3}{4} = \frac{6}{\square}$

6.

$\frac{4}{\square} = \frac{8}{\square}$

Draw a picture to help answer the question.

7. Does $\frac{1}{4}$ equal $\frac{2}{8}$?

8. Does $\frac{3}{5}$ equal $\frac{9}{10}$?

204

EXERCISES

Copy and complete the fractions.

1.

$$\frac{1}{2} = \frac{\square}{6}$$

2.

$$\frac{3}{5} = \frac{\square}{10}$$

3.

$$\frac{1}{2} = \frac{\square}{10}$$

4.

$$\frac{3}{\square} = \frac{6}{\square}$$

5.

$$\frac{1}{\square} = \frac{2}{\square}$$

6.

$$\frac{2}{\square} = \frac{1}{\square}$$

Write two fractions for the colored part.

7.

8.

9.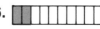

Draw a picture to help answer the question.

10. Does $\frac{4}{5}$ equal $\frac{7}{10}$?

11. Does $\frac{2}{8}$ equal $\frac{1}{4}$?

12. Jack and Loni each had a mini pizza. Jack ate $\frac{5}{8}$ of his. Loni ate $\frac{3}{4}$ of hers. Who ate more?

13. Sara may have either $\frac{1}{2}$ or $\frac{3}{6}$ of a container of lemonade. She likes lemonade. Which should she choose?

KEEPING SHARP

Copy and complete the chart.

		Round to the nearest		
		thousand	hundred	ten
1.	8471			
2.	2816			
3.	7235			
4.	5950			

Write a fraction for the shaded part.

1.   **2.** 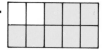 **3.**   **4.**

Copy and complete the fractions.

5.

$$\frac{4}{10} = \frac{\square}{5}$$

6.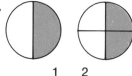

$$\frac{1}{2} = \frac{2}{\square}$$

7.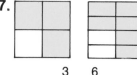

$$\frac{3}{\square} = \frac{6}{\square}$$

Show the fraction.

8. Draw 4 circles. Color $\frac{1}{4}$ of them blue.

9. Draw 5 squares. Color $\frac{3}{5}$ of them red.

How much is colored?

10.   **11.**   **12.**

Draw a picture to help answer the question.

13. Does $\frac{2}{5}$ equal $\frac{5}{10}$?

14. Does $\frac{1}{2}$ equal $\frac{4}{8}$?

15. Paul puts 6 muffins in each package. He has 19 muffins. How many packages can he make?

16. Ray puts 8 stamps on a page. He has 16 stamps. How many pages will they fill?

Solve.

17. A cake was cut into 10 pieces. $\frac{3}{10}$ of the cake was eaten. What fraction was left?

18. Marie's family will be on holiday for 1 of the 4 weeks in February. What fraction is that?

Patterns and Turtle Graphics

Events that repeat make a pattern.

1. Act out the pattern.

REPEAT 5 [SNAP FINGERS, CLAP HANDS, CLAP HANDS]

2. Complete the statement that describes this pattern.

REPEAT ☐ [V]

3. Complete the statement that describes this pattern.

REPEAT 5 [☐]

Repeat statements are also useful in turtle graphics.

4. Complete the statement that describes
these commands.   LT 75 LT 75 LT 75

REPEAT ☐ [LT 75]

5. Complete the statement that describes
these commands.   FD 20 BK 20 RT 120
FD 20 BK 20 RT 120
FD 20 BK 20 RT 120

REPEAT 3 [☐]

Draw the pattern.
Change the commands to make the pattern larger.

Experiment with your own patterns.
Try these.

6. REPEAT 5 [FD 15 PU FD 5 PD]   **7.** REPEAT 12 [RT 10 FD 30 LT 40 BK 45]

Decimal Tenths

Numbers in tenths can be written as **decimals**.

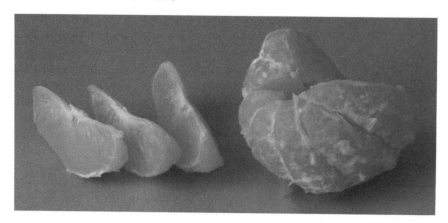

three-tenths

fraction

$\frac{3}{10}$

place value chart

ones	tenths
0	3

decimal

0.3

WORKING TOGETHER

How much is colored? Give a fraction and a decimal.

1.

2.

3.

4.

Draw a picture. Write the decimal.

5.
ones	tenths
0	4

6.
ones	tenths
0	8

7.
ones	tenths
1	0

8. two-tenths   **9.** six-tenths   **10.** $\frac{7}{10}$ **11.** $\frac{5}{10}$ **12.** $\frac{10}{10}$

Complete the counting by tenths.

13. 0.1, 0.2, ☐, ☐, 0.5, ☐, ☐, ☐, 0.9, ☐

EXERCISES

How much is colored? Write a fraction and a decimal.

1.

2.

3.

4.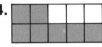

5.

6.

7.

8.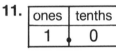

Write the decimal.

9.

ones	tenths
0	9

10.

ones	tenths
0	2

11.

ones	tenths
1	0

12. five-tenths   **13.** six-tenths   **14.** $\frac{8}{10}$ **15.** $\frac{10}{10}$ **16.** $\frac{4}{10}$

17. Chang ran four-tenths of a kilometre.

18. Diana swam five of the ten laps.

19. Effie can jump one-tenth of a metre higher.

20. Tim read $\frac{7}{10}$ of his book in one day.

Use as few key presses as you can.

1. Use only the keys ☐2 , ☐+ , ☐− , ☐× , ☐÷ , and ☐= . Make the display show 9.

2. Use only ☐5 , ☐+ , ☐− , ☐× , ☐÷ , and ☐= to get 11 in the display.

3. Use only ☐4 , ☐+ , ☐− , ☐× , ☐÷ , and ☐= to get 6 in the display.

209

Decimals Greater Than 1.0

Jenny and Beth need 2.5 m of cloth.

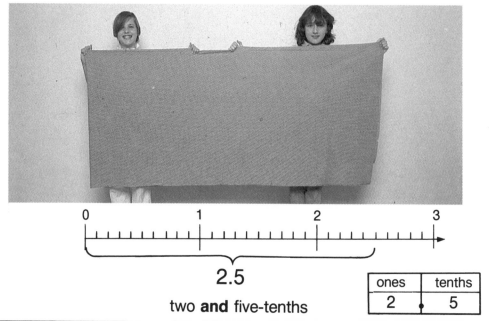

2.5

two **and** five-tenths

ones	tenths
2	5

How much is colored? Give a fraction and a decimal.

1. 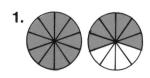 **2.**   **3.**   **4.**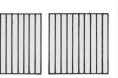

Count by tenths.

5. from 0.7 to 1.6   **6.** from 1.7 to 2.5   **7.** from 3.5 to 4.4

Draw a picture. Write the decimal.

8. 2 ones 8 tenths   **9.** two and one-tenth   **10.** 3   **11.** $4\frac{5}{10}$

How many ones can you make? How many tenths are left over?

12. 13 tenths   **13.** 30 tenths   **14.** 26 tenths

How much is colored? Write the decimal.

1.

2.

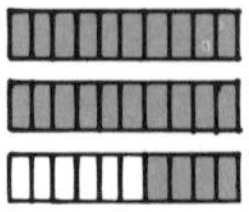

3.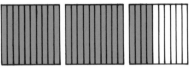

4.

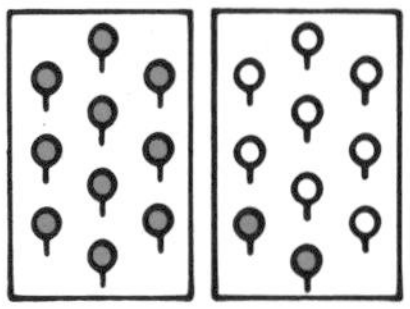

5.

6.

7.

Count by tenths.

8. from 0.8 to 1.4

9. from 1.7 to 2.3

10. from 14.6 to 15.2

How many ones can you make? How many tenths are left over?

11. 15 tenths

12. 20 tenths

13. 11 tenths

14. 34 tenths

Solve.

15. Maya jumped a distance of one and eight-tenths metres. Write the decimal.

16. Peter finished the race in nine and four-tenths seconds. Write the decimal.

17. Is 2 the same as 2.0?

18. Is 0.3 the same as 3.0?

19. Give the decimal name for A.

20. Give the decimal name for B.

KEEPING SHARP

Add or subtract.

1.   734
   + 189

2.   921
   − 345

3.   607
   − 289

4.   543
   + 267

5.   624
   + 158

Comparing and Ordering Decimals

Which is less, 1.8 or 1.3?

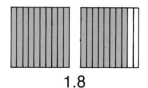
1.8

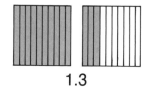
1.3

Compare the ones.

If the ones are the same, compare the tenths.

1.3 is less than 1.8.   1.3 < 1.8

Which is greater, 2.7 or 3.1?

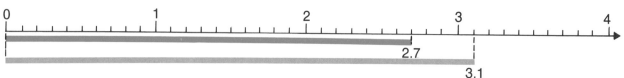

3.1 is greater than 2.7.   3.1 > 2.7

WORKING TOGETHER

Use >, <, or = to make a true statement.

1.

0.5 ◯ 0.7

2.

1.6 ◯ 1.3

3.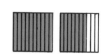

2.0 ◯ 1.7

4. 0.9 ◯ 0.6   **5.** 1.0 ◯ 0.8   **6.** 3.8 ◯ 4.1   **7.** 8.5 ◯ 5.8

Order from least to greatest.

8. 0.3, 0.7, 0.1, 0.5

9. 1.3, 4.7, 7.2, 2.6

10. 3.5, 3.9, 3.1, 3.0

11. 2.6, 2.4, 1.4

12. 1.6, 2.0, 1.7, 2.5

13. 5.6, 6.1, 4.8, 5.3

EXERCISES

Use >, <, or = to make a true statement.

1.

$$0.3 \bigcirc 0.6$$

2.

$$1.1 \bigcirc 1.0$$

3.

$$0.5 \bigcirc 1.2$$

4. $0.5 \bigcirc 0.8$ **5.** $3.7 \bigcirc 7.3$ **6.** $4.2 \bigcirc 4.0$ **7.** $6.1 \bigcirc 5.9$

8. $2 \bigcirc 2.0$ **9.** $4.8 \bigcirc 5.2$ **10.** $8.0 \bigcirc 0.8$ **11.** $5.3 \bigcirc 5.5$

Order from least to greatest.

12. 1.3, 1.7, 1.1, 1.2

13. 2.5, 0.5, 1.5, 3.5

14. 6.3, 1.9, 4.1, 3.6

15. 3.7, 4.1, 3.5, 4.3

Solve.

16. Marcie ran the 100 m race in 24.6 s. Karl ran it in 23.8 s. Who was faster?

18. Bob needs 2.9 m of cloth. He has 3.0 m. Does he have enough?

17. Copy this line. Write the numbers 3.3, 2.5, and 4.2 by the correct dots.

Try This

The new library book goes between books numbered B275 and B276. What number could it be given?

Adding Decimals

The recipe for Rocket Punch calls for 1.5 L of ginger ale and 2.5 L of cranberry cocktail. How much liquid does the recipe call for?

Add.   1.5 + 2.5

Line up the places.	Write the decimal point in the answer.	Add tenths. Regroup.	Add ones.
1 . 5 + 2 . 5	1 . 5 + 2 . 5 .	1 1 . 5 + 2 . 5 . 0	1 1 . 5 + 2 . 5 4 . 0

The recipe calls for 4.0 L of liquid.

WORKING TOGETHER

Add.

1. 0.4
    + 0.2

2. 0.1
    + 0.7

3. 3.4
    + 1.5

4. 2.6
    + 5.1

5. 7.0
    + 1.9

6. 0.8
    + 0.6

7. 4.5
    + 3.9

8. 23.7
    + 53.4

9. 16.9
    + 5.2

10. 391.2
    + 86.8

Line up the places. Add.

11. 0.5 + 0.3

12. 4.7 + 2.7

13. 63.4 + 9.6

EXERCISES

Find the sum.

1. 0.6 + 0.3	2. 1.5 + 4.4	3. 8.3 + 2.7	4. 13.6 + 42.9	5. 378.4 + 527.1
6. 82.4 + 3.6	7. 97.1 + 40.5	8. 258.4 + 48.7	9. 851.2 + 7.8	10. 4.3 + 66.9

11. 1.6 + 2.4   **12.** 32.9 + 47.4   **13.** 6.5 + 0.8

14. 324.8 + 8.1   **15.** 7.2 + 20.5   **16.** 453.1 + 27.0

Solve.

17. Fred's score was 8.4. His partner's score was 5.8. What was their total score?

18. Marcy's scores were 4.3 and 3.6. What was her total score?

19. Ann's costume needs 1.6 m of cloth. Nina's needs 2.5 m. How much cloth do they need altogether?

20. The distance from Jean's house to Ray's is 1.8 km. Betty lives 0.6 km beyond Ray. How far is it from Jean's house to Betty's?

KEEPING SHARP

Multiply.

1. 40 × 6	2. 50 × 3	3. 80 × 5	4. 90 × 7	5. 60 × 8
6. 200 × 9	7. 700 × 4	8. 300 × 2	9. 500 × 4	10. 900 × 8

Subtracting Decimals

Sy's Restaurant had 3.5 apple pies.
2.7 of them were served at lunch.
How much apple pie was left?

Subtract.   3.5 − 2.7

 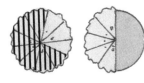

Line up the places.

Write the decimal point in the answer.	Not enough tenths. Regroup.	Subtract tenths.	Subtract ones.
3 . 5 − 2 . 7 .	2 15 3̶ . 5̶ − 2 . 7 .	2 15 3̶ . 5̶ − 2 . 7 . 8	2 15 3̶ . 5̶ − 2 . 7 0 . 8

0.8 of an apple pie was left.

WORKING TOGETHER

Copy and complete.

	1.	2.	3.	4.	5.
			7 12	4 10	11 3 1̶ 16
	4 . 7	1 9 . 5	8̶ . 2̶	5̶ . 0̶	4̶ 2̶ . 6̶
	− 2 . 6	− 1 2 . 3	− 4 . 7	− 2 . 8	− 1 8 . 9
	□ . □	□ . □	□ . □	□ . □	□ . □

Subtract.

6.	7.	8.	9.	10.
0.7	7.4	8.1	63.0	53.2
− 0.2	− 5.1	− 3.6	− 21.8	− 18.7

11. 4.8 − 2.5   **12.** 8.5 − 2.9   **13.** 45.6 − 8.7

EXERCISES

Find the difference.

1.   0.5
   − 0.4

2.   4.2
   − 0.9

3.   8.5
   − 1.8

4.   0.6
   − 0.6

5.   83.4
   − 56.1

6.   3.8
   − 2.9

7.   92.6
   − 77.1

8.   43.2
   − 15.8

9.   735.4
   − 129.3

10.   85.2
   − 7.4

11. 0.7 − 0.3

12. 42.6 − 18.3

13. 28.7 − 3.5

14. 35.2 − 16.8

15. 938.7 − 2.4

16. 371.0 − 24.3

Solve.

17. Rob had 8.6 pages filled in his stamp book. He took the stamps off 2.4 pages. How many pages were filled then?

18. Julie ran the 50 m race in 10.4 s. Nicole ran it in 9.7 s. How much faster was Nicole?

19. Ying lives 3.7 km from town. Tom lives 1.9 km from town. How much farther does Ying live?

20. Beth had a mass of 31.4 kg last year. She gained 2.7 kg. What is her mass now?

Try This

Forgetful Franny is telling a pen pal about herself. She has forgotten to put in the decimal points. Copy the numbers and place the decimal points for her.

Dear Clara,
My name is Frances.
I am 95 years old.
I am 1368 cm tall
and have a mass
of 314 kg.

PRACTICE

How much is colored? Write a fraction and a decimal.

1.

2.

3.

4.   **5.**   **6.**

Use >, <, or = to make a true statement.

7. 0.7 ◯ 7   **8.** 0.2 ◯ 0.3   **9.** 0.4 ◯ 1   **10.** 4 ◯ 0.6

11. 0.5 ◯ 5.0   **12.** 8.3 ◯ 3.8   **13.** 2.7 ◯ 0.9   **14.** 0.7 ◯ 4.0

Add or subtract.

15.   0.1   **16.**   0.9   **17.**   1.7   **18.**   72.3
    + 0.7   + 0.6   + 5.8   + 19.8

19.   0.8   **20.**   3.9   **21.**   9.2   **22.**   84.5
    − 0.5   − 1.6   − 6.6   − 17.9

Solve.

23. Marvin is 139.6 cm tall. Hannah is 136.9 cm tall. How much taller is Marvin?

24. A practice run is 10 laps around the gym. Willie has done 9 laps. What decimal is this?

25. In a relay race, Harold's time was 4.3 s, Zoe's was 4.1 s, and Pete's was 3.9 s. What was their total time?

26. Sylvia can do the shuttle run in 14.7 s. Alice can do it in 13.6 s. How much faster is Alice?

Add or Subtract Decimals

Remember how to enter decimal numbers.

       0.7   Press ⬚ 7 .

       3.5   Press 3 ⬚ 5 .

You can program a calculator to add
or subtract decimals.

6.4 6 ⬚ 4 + ⬚ 9 = (7.3)
+ 0.9

9.3 9 ⬚ 3 − 4 ⬚ 7 = (4.6)
− 4.7

**Add or subtract. Locate the answers on the
number line. What do the letters spell?**

1.
  2.9   8.4   3.6
 + 1.5   − 2.8   + 1.7
   [S]   [P]   [R]

          7.2   1.1
       − 2.5   + 3.9
        [H]   [A]

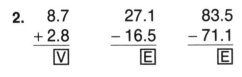

2.
  8.7   27.1   83.5
 + 2.8 − 16.5 − 71.1
   [V]   [E]   [E]

  3.6   7.4   12.6
 + 6.1   + 5.9   − 3.8
   [L]   [R]   [C]

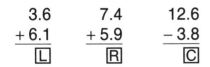

3. Make up a number line puzzle of your own.

Find a Reasonable Answer

Plums are 3 for 25¢. About how much will 5 plums cost?

Nadia's estimate was about 45¢. Is her answer reasonable? 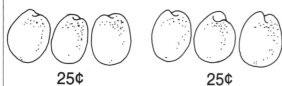 25¢　　　25¢ Yes. 6 plums cost 50¢, so 5 plums will cost less than 50¢.	Jim's estimate was about 40¢. His answer is reasonable too. 1 plum costs about 8¢.　$\begin{array}{r} 8 \\ 3)\overline{25} \\ -24 \\ \hline 1 \end{array}$ 5 plums cost about 40¢.　　$5 \times 8 = 40$

A moose can hear a man 2 km away.
How far away can 2 moose hear a man?

Jim's answer was 4 km. $2 \times 2 = 4$ Is his answer reasonable?	Nadia's answer was 2 km. Her answer makes sense because it does not matter how many moose there are.

WORKING TOGETHER

Is the answer reasonable? Use the picture to help you explain.

1. 50 candles were on the cake. George blew out all but 14. How many candles were still lit?

Kyle's answer was 14 candles.

2. How many heels are there in 26 pairs of socks?

Sharon's answer was 26 heels.

PROBLEMS

Which answer is correct? Explain.

1. Heather and Todd are playing on the beach. Heather made 5 sand piles and Todd made 3. How many sand piles would there be if they piled them together?

   | 1 pile | 2 piles | 8 piles |

2. How many 3¢ stamps are there in a dozen?

   | 9 stamps | 12 stamps | 36 stamps |

3. How many hours are there from 5:00 in the morning to 2:00 in the afternoon?

   | 3 hours | 7 hours | 9 hours |

4. You pick 9 apples from a tree with 17 apples. How many apples do you have?

   | 8 apples | 9 apples | 26 apples |

Is the student's answer reasonable? Explain.

5. A telephone book has about 92 names on each page. How many names will there be on 89 pages?
   Mario's answer was 181 names.

6. Gwen has 60 peanuts to share equally among 5 friends and herself. How many will each person get?
   Gwen's answer was 10 peanuts.

7. A tree stump shows 153 rings in the wood. Each ring stands for 1 year of the tree's life. One branch of the tree shows 47 rings. How old is the tree?
   Linden's answer was 200 years.

8. In spring, the temperature of the lake was 7°C. In summer, the lake's temperature was 19°C. How much did the temperature rise?
   Adele's answer was 26°C.

9. Which is the better buy?
   Ann's answer was 3 bars for 89¢.

   1 bar of soap, 43¢   3 bars of soap, 89¢

Problem Solving Review

Solve.

1. A carpenter had 52 nails and 28 screws. She used 25 screws and 19 nails to build a bookcase. How many nails and how many screws are left?

2. Mr. Calkin's mustache measures 8 cm on one side but only 7 cm on the other side. There is a 1 cm space under his nose. How far is it from one tip of his mustache to the other?

3. What are the two middle letters in the alphabet?

4. It takes 1 day for 4 men to dig 1 hole. How long will it take them to dig 3 holes?

5. Jill cuts a 7 m log into 7 equal pieces. It takes her 1 min to cut 1 piece. How long does it take to cut the 7 pieces?

 6. Suppose you have 1 min of recess on the first day of school. You have 2 min of recess on the second day, 4 min on the third day, 8 min on the fourth day, and so on. How long would recess be at the end of 10 school days?

Day of school	1	2	3	4	5	
Minutes of recess	1	2	4			

7. 35 Canada geese were on the pond. All but 19 flew away. How many geese flew away? How many were left on the pond?

8. Rae has 3 quarters and 2 dimes. Mandy has 7 dimes and 6 nickels. Who has more money? How much more?

Chapter Checkup

How much is colored? Write a fraction.

1.

2.

3.

4.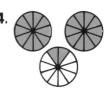

What fraction of the set is colored?

5.

6.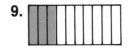

7.

8.

How much is colored? Write a decimal.

9.

10.

11.

12.

Copy and complete the fractions.

13. $\frac{1}{2} = \frac{\Box}{\Box}$

14. $\frac{3}{5} = \frac{\Box}{\Box}$

Add or subtract.

15. $\begin{array}{r} 0.2 \\ +\,0.7 \end{array}$	**16.** $\begin{array}{r} 0.8 \\ +\,0.6 \end{array}$	**17.** $\begin{array}{r} 0.8 \\ -\,0.6 \end{array}$	**18.** $\begin{array}{r} 18.3 \\ +\,32.7 \end{array}$	**19.** $\begin{array}{r} 8.7 \\ -\,1.5 \end{array}$
20. $\begin{array}{r} 5.6 \\ +\,2.9 \end{array}$	**21.** $\begin{array}{r} 4.2 \\ -\,1.4 \end{array}$	**22.** $\begin{array}{r} 9.7 \\ +\,42.5 \end{array}$	**23.** $\begin{array}{r} 46.0 \\ -\,21.6 \end{array}$	**24.** $\begin{array}{r} 93.4 \\ -\,6.8 \end{array}$

Solve.

25. Kay walked 1.2 km to her friend's house. Then she walked 0.4 km to the store. How far did she walk?

26. Yuri lives 3.4 km from school. Tanya lives 2.9 km from school. How much farther does Yuri live?

27. A storybook has 10 chapters. Betty has read 7 of them. What fraction of the book is that?

28. Draw a picture to show an equivalent fraction for $\frac{2}{8}$.

Cumulative Checkup

Write the standard form.

1. 2 hundred thousands 5 thousands 6 tens 3 ones

2. 7 ten thousands 6 hundreds 8 tens

3. four hundred thousand eight hundred ninety-two

4. seventy thousand six hundred seventy-six

5. 100 000 + 50 000 + 4000 + 300 + 80

6. 700 000 + 7000 + 10 + 8   **7.** 30 000 + 600 + 20 + 9

8. 5000 + 9   **9.** 8000 + 200 + 6

Divide.

10. 81 ÷ 9   **11.** 64 ÷ 8   **12.** 0 ÷ 7   **13.** 56 ÷ 9   **14.** 63 ÷ 7

15. 30 ÷ 4   **16.** 36 ÷ 9   **17.** 42 ÷ 6   **18.** 9 ÷ 1   **19.** 72 ÷ 8

20. 8)‾45   **21.** 7)‾56   **22.** 3)‾17   **23.** 9)‾0   **24.** 5)‾36

Measure the sides in centimetres.
Then find the perimeter and the area.

25.

26.

27.

Find the volume.

28.

29.

30.

224

9/Multiplication

In this chapter you will learn
to multiply larger numbers.

Multiplying a Two-Digit Number

A school bus can seat 48 students.
How many students can 3 buses seat?

Multiply.   3 × 48

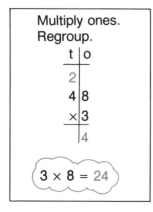

Multiply ones. Regroup.	Multiply tens. Add the extra tens.
t o 2 4 8 × 3 4	t o 2 4 8 × 3 1 4 4
3 × 8 = 24	3 × 4 = 12 12 + 2 = 14

3 buses can seat 144 students.

WORKING TOGETHER

Copy and complete.

   2
1. 2 4
   × 7
  ☐ 8

2. 3 5
  × 6
 ☐ 0

3. 7 3
  × 3
 ☐ 9

    ☐
4. 4 9
  × 6
 ☐ ☐

5. 2 6
  × 4
 ☐

Write in vertical form. Multiply.

6. 8 × 61

7. 5 × 87

8. 73 × 4

9. 46 × 3

Find the product.

1. 64
   × 3

2. 81
   × 7

3. 29
   × 5

4. 38
   × 6

5. 98
   × 2

6. 75
   × 4

7. 54
   × 6

8. 30
   × 7

9. 52
   × 3

10. 72
    × 7

11. 67
    × 6

12. 91
    × 8

Write in vertical form. Multiply.

13. 2 × 46

14. 37 × 9

15. 4 × 14

16. 80 × 5

17. 8 × 42

Solve.

18. Nella travels 27 km a day on the school bus. How far does she travel on the bus in 5 d?

19. There are 6 wheels on a school bus. How many wheels are there on 36 school buses?

20. Guy's class has 29 students. Guy and 7 others take the bus to school. How many do not come by bus?

21. There are 28 students in each of 3 classes. Their 3 teachers take them on a trip. How many bus seats are needed?

Try This

Why was the school bus afraid of the sports car?

448 156 384 234 406 232 156   348 273
576 234 232   522 156 351 351 256 576

Use this table to help you answer the riddle.

×	4	6	7	9
39	E	A	T	L
64	O	C	B	W
58	S	I	U	Y

227

Multiplying a Three-Digit Number

The ferry between Newfoundland and Nova Scotia can carry 345 vehicles on each trip. How many vehicles can it carry in 4 trips?

Multiply. 4 × 345

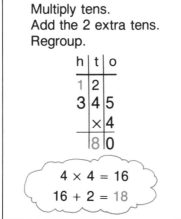

Multiply ones.
Regroup.

```
    h | t | o
        2
    3 | 4 | 5
  ×       | 4
        |   | 0
```

4 × 5 = 20

Multiply tens.
Add the 2 extra tens.
Regroup.

```
    h | t | o
    1   2
    3 | 4 | 5
  ×       | 4
        8 | 0
```

4 × 4 = 16
16 + 2 = 18

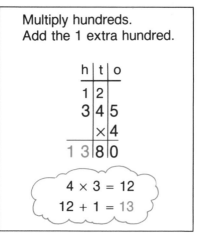

Multiply hundreds.
Add the 1 extra hundred.

```
    h | t | o
    1   2
    3 | 4 | 5
  ×       | 4
  1 3 | 8 | 0
```

4 × 3 = 12
12 + 1 = 13

The ferry can carry 1380 vehicles in 4 trips.

WORKING TOGETHER

Copy and complete.

1.
```
   □ 3
   6 3 7
 ×     5
 □ 1 8 □
```

2.
```
   □ 2
   4 3 6
 ×     4
 1 7 □ □
```

3.
```
   1
   7 6 2
 ×     3
 2 □ □ □
```

4.
```
   □
   3 0 8
 ×     7
 □ 5 □
```

5.
```
   □ □
   6 4 9
 ×     6
 3 □ □ □
```

EXERCISES

Multiply.

1. $\begin{array}{r} 377 \\ \times 3 \\ \hline \end{array}$	**2.** $\begin{array}{r} 571 \\ \times 2 \\ \hline \end{array}$	**3.** $\begin{array}{r} 980 \\ \times 2 \\ \hline \end{array}$	**4.** $\begin{array}{r} 204 \\ \times 5 \\ \hline \end{array}$	**5.** $\begin{array}{r} 969 \\ \times 6 \\ \hline \end{array}$
6. $\begin{array}{r} 623 \\ \times 9 \\ \hline \end{array}$	**7.** $\begin{array}{r} 743 \\ \times 4 \\ \hline \end{array}$	**8.** $\begin{array}{r} 502 \\ \times 6 \\ \hline \end{array}$	**9.** $\begin{array}{r} 970 \\ \times 8 \\ \hline \end{array}$	**10.** $\begin{array}{r} 513 \\ \times 5 \\ \hline \end{array}$

11. 4×528 **12.** 863×7 **13.** 609×3 **14.** 147×6 **15.** 524×3

16. 8×865 **17.** 961×4 **18.** 9×854 **19.** 403×8 **20.** 7×752

Solve.

21. A jumbo jet airliner holds 442 passengers. How many passengers can 7 jumbo jets hold?

22. An airplane can fly 885 km in 1 h. How many kilometres can it fly in 4 h?

23. The Toronto Transit Commission has 632 subway cars. Mechanics have 8 of them in the repair shop. How many subway cars are fit for use?

24. It is 760 km from Calgary to Regina. Val drives from Calgary to Regina and back 3 times each year. How many kilometres is that in a year?

KEEPING SHARP

Use >, <, or = to make a true statement.

1. $328 + 823 \bigcirc 823 + 328$

2. $963 - 369 \bigcirc 936 - 396$

3. $234 + 567 \bigcirc 987 - 123$

4. $1402 - 899 \bigcirc 402 + 128$

5. $\$309 + \$949 \bigcirc \$1567 - \$309$

6. $3206 - 1957 \bigcirc 2206 - 957$

7. $1338 - 446 \bigcirc 446 + 446$

8. $8642 - 1357 \bigcirc 1234 + 5678$

9. $555 + 777 \bigcirc 2222 - 999$

10. $6314 - 3641 \bigcirc 4136 - 1364$

11. $4638 + 2785 \bigcirc 2688 + 4735$

12. $2222 - 888 \bigcirc 666 + 666$

Multiplying Dollars and Cents

How much do 3 children's tickets cost?

Multiply. 3 × $2.75

$2.75 = 275 cents

```
2 1                    2  1
2 7 5 cents         $ 2 . 7 5
  × 3        or         × 3
8 2 5 cents         $ 8 . 2 5
```

825 cents = $8.25

3 children's tickets cost $8.25.

WORKING TOGETHER

Multiply the whole numbers.
Use the product to help you
multiply the dollars and cents.

This product can be shown
in dollars and cents.

1. 129	$1.29	**2.** 295	$2.95	**3.** 55	55¢
× 2	× 2	× 5	× 5	× 7	× 7

Multiply.

4. $5.38	**5.** $2.05	**6.** $4.40	**7.** 75¢	**8.** $0.75
× 7	× 6	× 5	× 4	× 4

EXERCISES

Multiply.

1. $3.27
   × 2

2. $8.24
   × 5

3. $6.91
   × 7

4. $5.75
   × 8

5. $2.67
   × 2

6. $9.07
   × 4

7. 62¢
   × 8

8. $5.63
   × 4

9. $2.90
   × 9

10. $0.49
    × 6

11. $7.65
    × 3

12. $0.38
    × 9

13. $5.98
    × 6

14. 27¢
    × 5

15. $2.10
    × 7

16. 3 × $5.77

17. 8 × $4.44

18. 9 × 45¢

19. 5 × $3.08

20. 4 × $5.42

21. 7 × $0.31

22. 6 × $8.09

23. 2 × $9.29

24. 3 × $1.63

25. 8 × $2.07

26. 2 × 15¢

27. 5 × $6.35

Solve. Use the information on the opposite page.

28. What is the cost of 6 adult tickets to the movies?

29. Can 7 children buy movie tickets for $20.00?

30. A family buys 2 adult tickets, 1 student ticket, and 2 children's tickets. What is the total cost?

31. Popcorn costs 75¢. Soft drinks cost 85¢. What does it cost 1 child to go to the movies and buy popcorn and a drink?

Discover the rule for the number square. Copy and complete the square.

(Hint: The rule works for horizontal and vertical rows, but not diagonals.)

8		96
3	2	
24		576

231

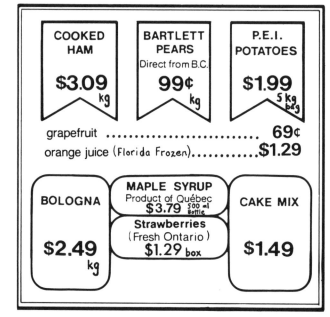

PRACTICE

Find the product.

1. 76
   × 5

2. 81
   × 4

3. 37
   × 2

4. 86
   × 8

5. 50
   × 9

6. $0.37
   × 7

7. 45¢
   × 6

8. 92
   × 4

9. 27
   × 8

10. $0.43
    × 5

11. 5 × 72

12. 18 × 7

13. 5 × 40¢

14. 6 × $0.93

15. 65 × 4

16. 28 × 7

17. 8 × 36

18. 87 × 4

19. 146
    × 7

20. 872
    × 4

21. 508
    × 8

22. $5.92
    × 2

23. $2.68
    × 3

24. 830
    × 5

25. 478
    × 9

26. 318
    × 6

27. 453
    × 3

28. 694
    × 4

Use information from the advertisement to find the cost.

29. 3 kg cooked ham

30. 2 kg Bartlett pears

31. 4 kg bologna

32. 6 boxes strawberries

33. 5 bags P.E.I. potatoes

34. 4 bottles maple syrup

35. 7 cans orange juice

36. 3 grapefruit

37. 5 boxes cake mix

COOKED HAM
$3.09 kg

BARTLETT PEARS
Direct from B.C.
99¢ kg

P.E.I. POTATOES
$1.99 5 kg bag

grapefruit .... 69¢
orange juice (Florida Frozen)...........$1.29

BOLOGNA
$2.49 kg

MAPLE SYRUP
Product of Québec
$3.79 500 ml bottle

Strawberries
(Fresh Ontario)
$1.29 box

CAKE MIX
$1.49

232

How Much Will That Cost?

track pants $19.95

Shorts $10.98

T-Shirt $12.29

running shoes $21.98

Socks $3.59

Jacket $24.87

The Sports Wear Shop had a sale.
Find the total bill for each customer.

1.

Name *Carl*

Article	Number bought	Price for 1	Cost ☒
shorts	2	$10.98	
running shoes	1 pr	$21.98	
track pants	2	$19.95	
		Total ⊞	

2.

Name *Joe*

Article	Number bought	Price for 1	Cost ☒
socks	4 pr.		
running shoes	2 pr.		
jacket	1		
		Total ⊞	

3.

Name *Ravinder*

Article	Number bought	Price for 1	Cost ☒
track pants	1		
T-shirts	3		
socks	2 pr		
		Total ⊞	

4.

Name *Les*

Article	Number bought	Price for 1	Cost ☒
T-shirts	2		
socks	3 pr.		
shorts	1		
track pants	2		
		Total ⊞	

Estimating Products

Pam has $40.00.
Can she buy 7 tapes?

Round dollars and cents
to the nearest dollar.
Estimate the product.

$4.88 rounds to $5.00.

$$\begin{array}{r} \$5.00 \\ \times\,7 \\ \hline \$35.00 \end{array}$$

The price is about $35.00.

Because the number was rounded upwards,
the estimate is higher than the exact product.

Pam can buy 7 tapes.

WORKING TOGETHER

Round to the nearest dollar or the nearest hundred.

1. $4.61   **2.** $9.29   **3.** 538   **4.** $2.52   **5.** 43

Round to the nearest ten cents or the nearest ten.

6. $4.61   **7.** $9.29   **8.** 538   **9.** $2.52   **10.** 43

Estimate the product.
Is the estimate high or low? Why?

11. $\begin{array}{r} 57\cent \\ \times\,6 \\ \hline \end{array}$ **12.** $\begin{array}{r} 57 \\ \times\,6 \\ \hline \end{array}$ **13.** $3 \times \$4.28$ **14.** 3×428

234

Round to the nearest dollar or the nearest ten cents.
Then estimate the product. Is the estimate high or low?

1. 44¢
   × 6

2. $3.28
   × 2

3. $5.62
   × 3

4. $0.67
   × 5

5. $9.72
   × 7

6. 9 × $6.26   7. 4 × 88¢   8. $9.14 × 6   9. 35¢ × 8   10. 3 × $4.93

Round to the nearest hundred or the nearest ten.
Then estimate the product. Is the estimate high or low?

11. 23
    × 8

12. 662
    × 4

13. 71
    × 2

14. 38
    × 6

15. 519
    × 8

Estimate. Then solve.

16. Posters cost $3.19. What is the price of 4 posters?

17. A bus seats 48 students. How many students do 5 buses seat?

18. A puzzle costs $3.37. Joe has $10.00. Can he buy 3 puzzles?

19. A class of 28 students is arranged in 4 equal teams for gym. How many are on each team?

Try This

Be a detective!
Find the missing numerals.

1. ☐ 6
   × ☐
   ─────
   7 ☐ 4

2. ☐ ☐ ☐
   × 7
   ─────
   3 ☐ 4 2

3.   4
    2 6 ☐
    × ☐
   ─────
   1 ☐ ☐ 5

4.   2
    6 ☐
   × ☐
   ─────
   2 ☐ 0

5. ☐ 6 6
   × ☐
   ─────
   7 ☐ ☐ 8

6. ☐ 5 ☐
   × 3
   ─────
   ☐ 3 ☐ 7

 7. ☐ ☐ ☐
   × ☐
   ─────
   2 5 3 8

235

Multiplying by a Multiple of 10

There are 30 cases of dog food in the store. Each case has 24 cans. How many cans of dog food are in the store?

Multiply. 30 × 24

Write in vertical form.	Multiply. 0 × 24	Multiply. 3 tens × 24
| ```
  t o
  2 4
× 3 0
``` | ```
  t o
  2 4
× 3 0
    0
``` | ```
h t o
  2 4
× 3 0
7 2 0
``` |

There are 720 cans of dog food in the store.

WORKING TOGETHER

Copy and complete.

1. 7 4
    × 2 0
    ▭ 0

2. 5 3
    × 4 0
    ▭ 0

3. 6 8
    × 7 0
    ▭ ▢

4. 8 0
    × 5 0
    ▭ ▢

5. 1 9
    × 3 0

Write in vertical form. Multiply.

6. 70 × 31   7. 30 × 46   8. 20 × 60   9. 93 × 80
```

EXERCISES

Find the product.

1.	74 × 60	**2.**	53 × 90	**3.**	86 × 20	**4.**	40 × 70	**5.**	38 × 40	**6.**	41 × 10
7.	63 × 80	**8.**	60 × 30	**9.**	38 × 70	**10.**	67 × 40	**11.**	84 × 90	**12.**	20 × 50

Write in vertical form. Multiply.

13. 80 × 28   **14.** 30 × 74   **15.** 10 × 65   **16.** 50 × 94   **17.** 60 × 86

18. 20 × 30   **19.** 70 × 61   **20.** 40 × 54   **21.** 90 × 20   **22.** 20 × 47

Solve.

23. A fish tank holds 36 L of water. How many litres of water do 20 tanks hold?

24. The pet store has 26 budgies and 30 canaries. How many of these birds do they have in all?

25. A package of fish food contains 65 mL. How many millilitres of fish food are in 50 packages?

26. A large lizard can eat 35 flies in 1 d. How many flies can it eat in 60 d?

KEEPING SHARP

Add.

1.	324 + 2360	**2.**	315 + 900	**3.**	56 + 1680	**4.**	456 + 2280	**5.**	639 + 2130
6.	522 + 2610	**7.**	384 + 1440	**8.**	132 + 3300	**9.**	470 + 5640	**10.**	114 + 1520

11. 112 + 640   **12.** 343 + 2940   **13.** 602 + 2580   **14.** 414 + 6210

15. 170 + 2040   **16.** 74 + 2960   **17.** 186 + 2480   **18.** 56 + 1680

Multiplying by a Two-Digit Number

Gunther can take 36 pictures with 1 roll of film.
How many pictures can he take with 24 rolls of film?

Multiply. 24 × 36

Estimate.	Multiply. 4 × 36	Multiply. 2 tens × 36	Add.
$36 \longrightarrow 40$ $\times 24 \longrightarrow \times 20$ $ 800$	h t o $3\,6$ $\times 2\,4$ $1\,4\,4$	h t o $3\,6$ $\times 2\,4$ $1\,4\,4$ $7\,2\,0$	h t o $3\,6$ $\times 2\,4$ $1\,4\,4$ $7\,2\,0$ $8\,6\,4$

864 is close to 800. The product is reasonable.

Gunther can take 864 pictures with 24 rolls of film.

WORKING TOGETHER

Copy and complete the exercise. Follow the steps.

1.
$$\begin{array}{r} 14 \\ \times 32 \end{array}$$
Multiply. 2 × 14 ⟶ ☐
Multiply. 3 tens × 14 → ☐0
Add. ⟶ ☐

2.
$$\begin{array}{r} 87 \\ \times 54 \end{array}$$
Multiply. 4 × 87 ⟶ ☐
Multiply. 5 tens × 87 → ☐
Add. ⟶ ☐

Find the product.

3. $\begin{array}{r} 68 \\ \times 7 \end{array}$
4. $\begin{array}{r} 68 \\ \times 20 \end{array}$
5. $\begin{array}{r} 68 \\ \times 27 \end{array}$
6. $\begin{array}{r} 17 \\ \times 23 \end{array}$

Estimate the product. Tell if the estimate is high or low.

1. 14 × 12	2. 22 × 33	3. 76 × 25	4. $47 × 18	5. 80 × 19	6. 67 × 51

Multiply.

7. 44 × 62	8. 68 × 14	9. 81 × 18	10. 56 × 15	11. 45 × 42	12. 33 × 48

13. 71 × 69   **14.** $29 × 31   **15.** 75 × 34   **16.** 15 × 32   **17.** 69 × 44

18. 37 × 17   **19.** 25 × 28   **20.** 49 × 53   **21.** 76 × 76¢   **22.** 89 × 98

Solve.

23. A camera sells for $59. Last year a store sold 32 of them. How much did the store receive for the cameras?

24. There are 12 flash bulbs in a box. How many bulbs are in 25 boxes?

25. Gunther takes 19 min to photograph 1 class. Can he photograph 14 classes in 4 h? (1 h = 60 min)

26. Jered's class has 29 students. 27 of them bought the class picture. How many did not buy the picture?

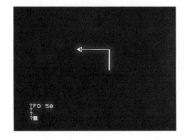  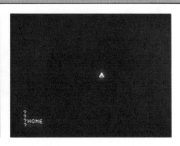

1. What turn does the turtle need to make a square corner?

2. What turn makes the turtle face in the opposite direction?

3. What turn makes the turtle turn all the way around?

Round to the nearest hundred or the nearest ten.
Estimate the product. Is the estimate high or low?

1. 91 $\times 4$	**2.** 467 $\times 2$	**3.** 112 $\times 9$	**4.** 159 $\times 6$	**5.** 32 $\times 8$
6. 215 $\times 4$	**7.** 49 $\times 2$	**8.** 576 $\times 5$	**9.** 43 $\times 7$	**10.** 99 $\times 3$

11. 752 × 6   **12.** 5 × 806   **13.** 7 × 82   **14.** 329 × 4

Multiply.

15. 14 $\times 20$	**16.** 23 $\times 80$	**17.** 34 $\times 10$	**18.** 29 $\times 40$	**19.** 44 $\times 50$
20. 89 $\times 32$	**21.** 62 $\times 45$	**22.** 17 $\times 73$	**23.** 36 $\times 98$	**24.** 56 $\times 39$
25. 45 $\times 81$	**26.** 52 $\times 74$	**27.** 37 $\times 57$	**28.** 83 $\times 64$	**29.** 57 $\times 26$

Solve.

30. How far does a car travel in 13 h? It goes 95 km each hour.

31. A car passes 8 telephone poles each minute. How many poles does it pass in 45 min?

32. It is 1050 km across Manitoba and Saskatchewan. Can a car travelling 85 km each hour make the trip in 13 h?

33. A small plane flies 185 km each hour. Can it cross Manitoba and Saskatchewan in 5 h?

34. It is 571 km from Winnipeg to Regina. Can a car travelling 90 km each hour make the trip in 6 h?

35. Ingrid flies 205 km each hour for 3 h. Ian drives 78 km each hour for 8 h. Who goes farther?

Curves and Turtle Graphics

1. How can you make a circle using Logo?
   Try playing Turtle and acting it out.
   Use heel-to-toe steps. Each footstep
   suggests a line segment.

You can draw curves on the screen using a
REPEAT command. A REPEAT command makes
the turtle do the same thing many times.

2. Type. REPEAT IO [FD 5 RT 9]

3. What part of a circle was drawn?

4. How much did the turtle turn?

5. Change the number of repeats to make
   the turtle draw a half circle.

6. How much did the turtle turn?

7. Change the number of repeats to make
   the turtle draw a whole circle.

8. How much did the turtle turn?

9. Make the turtle draw a larger circle.

10. Experiment with your own designs.
    Can you make the turtle draw these?

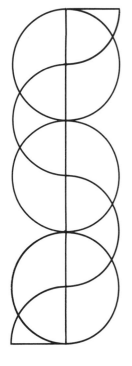

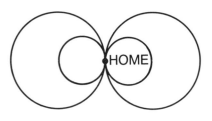

Guess and Test

I am thinking of two numbers.
Their product is 36.
Their quotient is 4.
What are the two numbers?

Think. A product is the answer when you multiply.

A quotient is the answer when you divide.

Plan and do. Guess an answer. Test to see if it is correct.

It is helpful to use a system for guesses.

Factors of 36	Do they give quotient 4?
1 × 36 = 36	36 ÷ 1 = ?
2 × 18 = 36	18 ÷ 2 = ?
3 × 12 = 36	12 ÷ 3 = 4 ✓

Try again.

Look back. The two numbers are 3 and 12.

Are other numbers possible? Continue the chart to find out.

WORKING TOGETHER

Three numbers, next to each other, add up to 18.

1. What is the pattern?

0 + 1 + 2 = 3
1 + 2 + 3 = 6
2 + 3 + 4 = ?

2. Copy and continue the pattern of the sums. 3, 6, □, □, □, □, □
Is 18 in the pattern?

3. Guess and test some numbers.

4. What are the three numbers?

Three numbers, next to each other, add up to 35.

5. Continue the pattern of the sums. Is 35 in the pattern?

6. Guess and test some numbers. What are the three numbers?

PROBLEMS

Use the chart. Guess and test to solve the problem.

1. Pierre has three more nickels than quarters. How many nickels does he have if he has $1.65 in all?

Quarters	Nickels	Amount
1	4	25¢ + 20¢ = 45¢
2	5	50¢ + 25¢ = 75¢

2. Marge counted 6 cows and chickens. They had a total of 20 legs. How many cows were there?

Cows	Chickens	Number of legs
1	5	4 + 10 = 14
2	4	8 + 8 = 16

What are the numbers?

3. The sum of two numbers is 13. Their product is 40.

4. The product of two numbers is 12. Their difference is 1.

5. The quotient of two numbers is 5. Their sum is 18.

Guess and test to solve.

6. Move one block to another pile so that the sums of the piles are equal.

2	5	8
3	6	9
4	7	10

7. In a game at the fair, balls are thrown into these baskets. What is the least number of balls needed to score exactly 34?

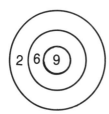

8. Arrange the eight dominos below to match this number pattern.⟶

6	4	2	0
3	4	1	5
3	4	6	3
2	5	5	0

243

Problem Solving Review

Solve.

1. Sheets of paper are 4 for 19¢.
   About how much will 1 sheet cost?
   About how much will 6 sheets
   cost?

2. The temperature outside is 13°C.
   The temperature inside is 21°C.
   What is the difference
   in temperature?

3. Omar grew 48 pumpkins. He gave
   8 neighbors 4 pumpkins each. How
   many pumpkins does he have left?

4. An elevator went from the ground
   floor to the 15th floor. Then it went
   down 8, up 6, down 3, and up 1.
   What floor was it at then?

5. How many 4's are needed
   to number all the houses on a
   street from 1 to 50?

6. The product of two numbers is 24.
   Their sum is 11. What are the two
   numbers?

7. Estimate. How much does the
   dog weigh?

8. Tahnee's answer was 35 kg.
   Is her answer reasonable?

9. **Think**. How would you find
   out how much the dog weighs?

244

Chapter Checkup

Solve.

1. An elevator in the CN Tower in Toronto can carry 22 passengers each trip. How many passengers can it carry in 25 trips?

2. An elevator can make 27 trips to the Space Deck in 1 h. How many trips can it make in 16 h?

3. The Sky Pod on the CN Tower is 350 m above the ground. An elevator travels 6 m each second. Can it reach the Sky Pod in 57 s?

4. The CN Tower is open for visitors 13 h each day. How many hours is it open for visitors in March?

5. It costs $4.50 for an adult ticket for the Space Deck. How much will 6 adult tickets cost?

6. Postcards of the CN Tower cost 49¢ each. How much will 28 postcards cost?

Round. Estimate the product.
Is the estimate high or low?
Find the exact product for exercises 12-16.

7. 32	8. 427	9. 18	10. 22	11. 468
×3	×2	×6	×48	×7

12. $1.84	13. 78¢	14. $7.28	15. 36	16. 844
×4	×6	×3	×51	×5

Cumulative Checkup

Add or subtract.

1. $\begin{array}{r} 7.0 \\ +\,3.6 \\ \hline \end{array}$ 2. $\begin{array}{r} 0.4 \\ +\,0.7 \\ \hline \end{array}$ 3. $\begin{array}{r} 9.2 \\ -\,7.3 \\ \hline \end{array}$ 4. $\begin{array}{r} 8.2 \\ +\,0.4 \\ \hline \end{array}$ 5. $\begin{array}{r} 6.0 \\ -\,3.5 \\ \hline \end{array}$

6. $\begin{array}{r} 35.4 \\ +\,27.8 \\ \hline \end{array}$ 7. $\begin{array}{r} 14.1 \\ -\,7.8 \\ \hline \end{array}$ 8. $\begin{array}{r} 40.6 \\ -\,15.5 \\ \hline \end{array}$ 9. $\begin{array}{r} 26.3 \\ +\,14.7 \\ \hline \end{array}$ 10. $\begin{array}{r} 37.2 \\ -\,18.4 \\ \hline \end{array}$

11. $75.6 - 24.7$ 12. $1.7 + 0.9$ 13. $82.4 - 1.8$

Multiply or divide.

14. 28×7 15. $27 \div 9$ 16. $72 \div 9$ 17. 16×9 18. 9×50

19. 3×60 20. $50 \div 6$ 21. $0 \div 6$ 22. 8×40 23. 6×500

Find the missing factor.

24. $7 \times \square = 49$ 25. $\square \times 9 = 81$ 26. $\square \times 8 = 0$ 27. $5 \times \square = 40$

28. $7 \times \square = 63$ 29. $9 \times \square = 36$ 30. $\square \times 6 = 36$ 31. $9 \times \square = 9$

Order from least to greatest.

32. 2.4, 2.8, 2.0, 2.5   33. 1.2, 0.7, 0.5, 1.4

34. 3.6, 6.5, 4.2, 3.8   35. 4.6, 3.8, 4.0, 3.9

Copy and complete.

36. 3 h = $\square$ min   37. 3 d = $\square$ h   38. 5 weeks = $\square$ d

39. 6 min = $\square$ s   40. 8 d = $\square$ h   41. 8 min = $\square$ s

42. 5 years = $\square$ months   43. 2 years = $\square$ weeks

44. 6 min 8 s = $\square$ s   45. 9 d 4 h = $\square$ h

46. 8 weeks 3 d = $\square$ d   47. 3 h 10 min = $\square$ min

10/Division

In this chapter you will learn
to do divisions like 347 ÷ 5.

Sharing Tens and Ones

Three sisters had a garage sale.
They made $69. What was
each sister's share?

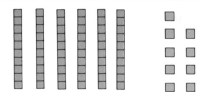

Divide. 3) $69

Share 6 tens first.

 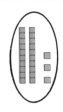

6 tens shared. 9 ones still to share.

```
        t|o
      $2
  3) $6|9
    - 6|↓   3 × 2
     0|9
```

Share 9 ones.

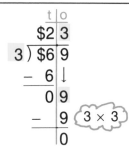

9 ones shared. 0 ones left.

```
        t|o
      $2|3
  3) $6|9
    - 6|↓
     0|9
       |
      -|9   3 × 3
       |0
```

Each sister's share was $23.

WORKING TOGETHER

Copy and complete.

```
       3□              3□              2□
1. 2) 6 2       2. 3) 9 6       3. 4) 8 0       4. 2) 24        5. 46 ÷ 2
   - 6 ↓           - 9 ↓           -□ ↓
    0 2             0 □            □ □
   -□              -□
    □               □
```

248

EXERCISES

Find the quotient.

1. 3) 36
2. 2) 64
3. 4) 44
4. 3) 99
5. 8) 80

6. 1) 59
7. 2) 28
8. 3) 63
9. 2) 42
10. 2) 68

11. 82 ÷ 2
12. 33 ÷ 3
13. 26 ÷ 2
14. 87 ÷ 1
15. 36 ÷ 3

16. 84 ÷ 4
17. 60 ÷ 6
18. 48 ÷ 4
19. 84 ÷ 2
20. 88 ÷ 8

Solve.

21. Susan sorted 96 marbles into 3 equal groups. How many marbles were in each group?

22. Nicki sold 4 spools of thread and 40 needles. How many sewing items did she sell?

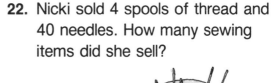

23. Pat had 66 books and 4 scarves to sell. She put the books in 3 equal piles. How many books were in each pile?

24. 28 children came to the sale. An equal number of boys and girls came. How many girls came?

> **Try This**

You can use multiplication to check division.

```
    2 2
3 ) 6 6
   -6 ↓
    6
   - 6
    0
```

22 ← quotient
× 3 ← divisor
66 ← dividend

The product matches the dividend.
Your division is correct.

Use multiplication to check your division in exercises 1 to 5 above.

Regrouping Tens

Marcel has 72 plants. He wants to divide
them evenly among 3 flower beds.
How many plants should he put in each bed?

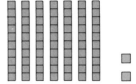

Divide. $3\overline{)72}$

Share tens.
Each group has 2 tens.

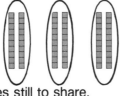

6 tens shared. 1 ten 2 ones still to share.

```
    t|o
    2|
 3)7|2
  -6|↓
   1|2
```
3×2

Regroup 1 ten 2 ones as 12 ones.
Share ones.

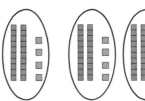

12 ones shared.

```
    t|o
    2|4
 3)7|2
  -6|↓
   1|2
  -1|2
    |0
```
3×4

Marcel should put 24 plants in each bed.

WORKING TOGETHER

Copy and complete.

1.
```
    1□
 5)6 5
  -5 ↓
   1 5
  -□
   □
```

2.
```
    3□
 2)7 4
  -6 ↓
  □□
  -□
   □
```

3.
```
    1□
 3)4 5
  -□ ↓
  □□
  -□
   □
```

4. $4\overline{)60}$

5. $57 \div 3$

EXERCISES

Find the quotient.

1. 4)64　　2. 5)75　　3. 4)84　　4. 2)54　　5. 2)38

6. 7)91　　7. 4)92　　8. 6)84　　9. 3)69　　10. 3)84

11. 8)96　　12. 5)90　　13. 2)78　　14. 2)48　　15. 3)48

Divide.

16. 70 ÷ 5　　17. 72 ÷ 6　　18. 76 ÷ 4　　19. 57 ÷ 3　　20. 26 ÷ 2

21. 56 ÷ 4　　22. 98 ÷ 7　　23. 42 ÷ 3　　24. 55 ÷ 5　　25. 78 ÷ 3

26. 36 ÷ 2　　27. 80 ÷ 4　　28. 51 ÷ 3　　29. 90 ÷ 6　　30. 52 ÷ 4

Solve.

31. Kim has 42 plants in all. She has the same number of each of 3 kinds. How many of each kind does she have?

32. Russell divides 65 plants evenly among 5 window boxes. How many plants does he put in each box?

33. Four friends picked 56 boxes of berries. Each picked the same number of boxes. How many boxes of berries did each pick?

34. In the orchard there are 2 kinds of fruit trees. There are 36 of each kind of tree. How many fruit trees are in the orchard?

KEEPING SHARP

Write the numeral in expanded form.

1. 38　　　　2. 465

3. 902　　　　4. 2746

5. 3580　　　　6. 6001

7. 48 327　　　8. 50 092

Regrouping with Remainders

Game tickets at the fair cost 7¢.
How many tickets can Mario buy with 87¢?
How much will he have left over?

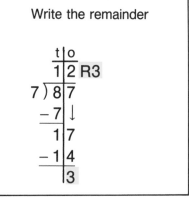

Divide. 7$\overline{)87}$

Share 8 tens.	Regroup. Share ones.	Write the remainder
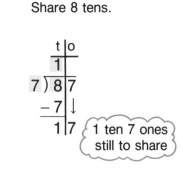	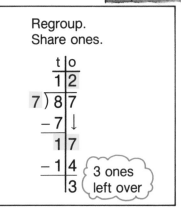	

Mario can buy 12 tickets.
He will have 3¢ left over.

To check the division, multiply.

12 ← quotient
× 7 ← divisor
————
84
+ 3   Add the remainder.
————
87 ← dividend

WORKING TOGETHER

Copy and complete. Check exercise 4 by multiplying and adding.

1. $\begin{array}{r} 1\,\square \\ 3\overline{)57} \\ -3\downarrow \\ \hline 27 \\ -\square \\ \hline \square \end{array}$

2. $\begin{array}{r} 1\,\square\,R\square \\ 6\overline{)93} \\ -6\downarrow \\ \hline 33 \\ -\square \\ \hline \square \end{array}$

3. $\begin{array}{r} 1\,\square\,R\square \\ 7\overline{)99} \\ -7\downarrow \\ \hline \square\square \\ -\square \\ \hline \square \end{array}$

4. 4$\overline{)78}$

5. 35 ÷ 2

252

EXERCISES

Divide. Check exercises 3 and 18 by multiplying and adding.

1. $3 \overline{)49}$ 2. $5 \overline{)63}$ 3. $6 \overline{)86}$ 4. $4 \overline{)97}$ 5. $7 \overline{)73}$

6. $5 \overline{)68}$ 7. $6 \overline{)99}$ 8. $3 \overline{)87}$ 9. $2 \overline{)59}$ 10. $8 \overline{)93}$

11. $67 \div 4$ 12. $56 \div 3$ 13. $96 \div 8$ 14. $93 \div 7$ 15. $75 \div 6$

16. $69 \div 5$ 17. $89 \div 6$ 18. $90 \div 4$ 19. $87 \div 3$ 20. $84 \div 5$

Solve.

21. Earl made 50 throws at the Ring Toss. How many tickets did he have to buy?

22. There are 4 students on each team for the egg and spoon relay race. How many teams can be made from 75 students?

23. Mario has 87¢. What is the greatest number of nickels he can have? How many pennies would he have?

24. 92 people had their fortune told. Only 7 people had their mass guessed. How many more had their fortune told?

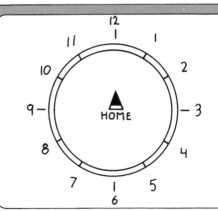

Pretend that HOME for the turtle is at the centre of a clock face.

What turn does the turtle make from HOME to point to the time?

1. 3 o'clock   2. 1 o'clock

3. 9 o'clock   4. 8 o'clock

Find the quotient. Use multiplication to check the first exercise of each row.

1. $2\overline{)46}$ 　　2. $4\overline{)84}$ 　　3. $2\overline{)\$68}$ 　　4. $3\overline{)93}$ 　　5. $7\overline{)77}$

6. $4\overline{)72}$ 　　7. $5\overline{)65}$ 　　8. $3\overline{)87}$ 　　9. $8\overline{)96}$ 　　10. $6\overline{)96}$

11. $3\overline{)\$51}$ 　　12. $2\overline{)76}$ 　　13. $5\overline{)68}$ 　　14. $8\overline{)89}$ 　　15. $7\overline{)94}$

16. $4\overline{)99}$ 　　17. $3\overline{)76}$ 　　18. $2\overline{)53}$ 　　19. $8\overline{)93}$ 　　20. $6\overline{)85}$

21. $66 \div 3$ 　　22. $62 \div 2$ 　　23. $48 \div 4$ 　　24. $\$96 \div 3$ 　　25. $88 \div 4$

26. $64 \div 4$ 　　27. $\$56 \div 2$ 　　28. $84 \div 7$ 　　29. $84 \div 6$ 　　30. $75 \div 5$

31. $78 \div 3$ 　　32. $96 \div 4$ 　　33. $86 \div 3$ 　　34. $58 \div 5$ 　　35. $92 \div 7$

36. $93 \div 6$ 　　37. $81 \div 5$ 　　38. $97 \div 8$ 　　39. $88 \div 7$ 　　40. $69 \div 5$

Solve.

41. When Mrs. Taylor preserves peaches, she puts 6 in each jar. How many jars can she fill with 87 peaches?

42. Mrs. Taylor uses 5 apples for each pie. How many pies could she make with 63 apples?

43. Ted and Eric earn a total of $38 with a yard sale. How much is each boy's share?

44. Ron has 48 refrigerator magnets. He sells them in sets of 3. How many sets can he sell?

45. Sal uses the telephone in her work. She spends about 3 min on each call and about 2 min between calls. How many calls can she make in 1 h?

254

Logo Procedures

You can teach the turtle new commands.

1. Play Turtle.
   - First mark a figure like this on the floor. →
   - Show the person playing Turtle where the shapes of a hat, a flag, and a box are in the figure.
   - Say the command HAT or FLAG or BOX. The Turtle walks out the path of the shape.
   - Decide on the FD, BK, RT, and LT commands used to make the shape.

You can teach the computer turtle a new command.
You write a **procedure**.

TO tells the computer that you are going to write a procedure.
END tells the computer that you are finished.

```
TO STAR
REPEAT 5 [FD 40 RT 144]
END
```

```
TO TRIANGLE
REPEAT 3 [FD 40 RT 120]
END
```

2. Type in the procedure called STAR. After that, what happens when you type STAR?

3. Type in the procedure called TRIANGLE. After that, what happens when you type TRIANGLE?

4. Use STAR to draw stars anywhere on the screen. Remember to use PU.

5. Draw triangles anywhere on the screen.

6. Write a procedure to draw a square. Call it SQ.

7. Try typing this command.
   REPEAT 12 [SQ RT 30]

Experiment with your own procedures.
Can you write a procedure to draw a circle?

What Does the Remainder Mean?

A remainder may make the answer 1 greater.
- 4 photos on a page
- 5 photos in all
- How many pages used?
- The remaining photo needs a page.
- 2 pages are used.

$$\begin{array}{r} 1\text{ R}1 \quad \text{or} \quad 2 \\ 4\overline{)5} \\ -4 \\ \hline 1 \end{array}$$

A remainder may be ignored.
- A pencil costs 4¢.
- I have 5¢.
- How many pencils can I buy?
- The remaining 1¢ is not enough to buy another pencil.
- I can buy only 1 pencil.

$$\begin{array}{r} 1\text{ R}1 \quad \text{or} \quad 1 \\ 4\overline{)5} \\ -4 \\ \hline 1 \end{array}$$

A remainder may be shared to make a **mixed-number** answer.
- 5 apples to share
- 4 people
- How many apples each?
- The remaining apple can be shared.
- Each person gets $1\frac{1}{4}$ apples.

$$\begin{array}{r} 1\text{ R}1 \quad \text{or} \quad 1\frac{1}{4} \\ 4\overline{)5} \\ -4 \\ \hline 1 \end{array}$$

WORKING TOGETHER

Tell what to do with the remainder.

1. I spend 39¢.
   I have only nickels.
   How many nickels do I use?

2. Sam worked 5 h. He spent the same amount of time on each of 2 jobs. How long did he spend on each?

Divide. Show the remainder.

1. $3\overline{)20}$ 2. $4\overline{)27}$ 3. $7\overline{)40}$ 4. $9\overline{)54}$ 5. $5\overline{)36}$

6. $2\overline{)13}$ 7. $8\overline{)43}$ 8. $6\overline{)36}$ 9. $4\overline{)38}$ 10. $9\overline{)61}$

Solve. Decide how to use the remainder.

11. 7 people
    4 in each car
    How many cars are needed?

12. 17 wheels
    4 for each car
    How many cars can be made?

13. How many cards each?
    5 players
    36 cards

14. 30 stories
    6 stories in each book
    How many books?

15. 8 tomatoes in a package
    20 packages
    How many tomatoes?

16. How many problems can I finish?
    30 min working time
    7 min needed for each problem

17. 34¢ in nickels and pennies
    How many nickels?
    How many pennies?

18. 6 eggs fill a small carton.
    33 eggs in all
    How many small cartons needed?

19. 2 children
    5 crackers
    How many crackers each?

20. How many teams?
    27 children in all
    6 children on a team

KEEPING SHARP

Multiply.

1. 5×4 2. 3×6 3. 2×3 4. 6×6 5. 8×5

6. 4×3 7. 6×2 8. 9×0 9. 7×4 10. 5×7

11. 9×3 12. 3×7 13. 8×7 14. 4×8 15. 2×9

16. 8×6 17. 6×7 18. 7×1 19. 9×6 20. 7×3

Regrouping Hundreds

For school sports, 276 students
are placed in 3 groups.
The groups are equal in size.
How many are in each group?

Divide. 3) 276

Can't share 2 hundreds among 3.	Regroup 2 hundreds 7 tens as 27 tens. Share tens.	Share ones.
h | t | o 3) 2 | 7 | 6	h | t | o 　9 3) 2 | 7 | 6 − 2 | 7 ↓ 　0 | 6	h | t | o 　9 | 2 3) 2 | 7 | 6 − 2 | 7 ↓ 　　　6 −　　6 　　　0

6 ones still to share.

0 ones left.

There are 92 students in each group.

WORKING TOGETHER

Copy and complete.

1. 159 = ☐ hundred ☐ tens ☐ ones

2. 405 = ☐ hundreds 5 ones
or ☐ tens 5 ones

3. For 8) 248, share ☐ tens first.

4. For 3) 159, share ☐ tens first.

5. ☐
　4) 248

6. ☐
　5) 250

258

Divide.

1. 3)189
2. 5)155
3. 4)168
4. 2)140
5. 4)84

6. 6)426
7. 3)279
8. 5)100
9. 8)568
10. 7)357

Do the quotients make a Magic Square?

11.

2)162	9)99	4)244
7)217	5)255	3)213
6)246	1)91	8)168

12.

4)248	5)205	6)486
9)729	7)427	3)126
9)369	3)246	8)488

Solve.

13. There are 156 students in Grades 3, 4, and 5. Each grade has the same number of students. How many are in Grade 4?

14. The 200 m relay race starts at 2:00 p.m. The track is marked off in 4 equal parts. How long is each part?

Try This

1. A Thrift Pack has 5 pencils. A Bargain Pack has 7 pencils. How much are you paying for each pencil when you buy a Thrift Pack?

2. 3 single pencils sell for 24¢. How much would 5 single pencils sell for?

3. How could you buy 5 pencils and spend the least amount of money?

4. How could you buy 10 pencils for the least amount of money?

Finding an Average

A total of $368 was spent on 4 field trips. What was the **average** cost of a trip?

If a number is thought of as being shared equally, the result is an average.

Divide. $368 ÷ 4

```
     $ 92
4 ) $368
   − 36↓
     08
    − 8
      0
```

The average cost of a field trip was $92.

WORKING TOGETHER

What division can be used to find the average?

1. Three snacks cost 96¢.

2. Five students have 105 colored pencils.

Write a sentence about the average.

3. Five magazines cost $10.
```
     $ 2
5 ) $10
```

4. There are 124 students in 4 classes.
```
      31
4 ) 124
```

EXERCISES

Divide to find the average.

1. A total of 96 students went on 4 field trips.

2. 120 counters were placed in 6 packages.

3. The school spent $355 on 5 films.

4. 3 pencils cost 45¢.

5. Marta earned $56 in 8 weeks on her paper route.

6. 217 students rode on 7 buses.

7. In 5 school days, 200 cartons of milk were bought.

8. René had 7 d to collect 21 insects.

9. There are 96 beads in 3 bags.

10. 8 clubs have 240 members.

11. 115 berries are in 5 baskets.

12. 6 classes have 180 students.

13. In a mathematics class, 7 students complete 86 exercises.

14. In the pet store there are 19 mice in 3 cages.

Divide.

15. 168 ÷ 4   16. 78 ÷ 3   17. 180 ÷ 6   18. 159 ÷ 3   19. 427 ÷ 7

20. 459 ÷ 9   21. 400 ÷ 5   22. 92 ÷ 7   23. 568 ÷ 8   24. 110 ÷ 9

Use a calculator to find the missing numbers.

1. 5)620̄ (□ above)

2. □)504 (84 above)

3. 3)□ (295 above)

4. 4)912 (□ above)

5. □)1148 (164 above)

6. 5)□ (348 above)

7. □)4146 (691 above)

8. 26)□ (309 above)

261

PRACTICE

Divide.

1. $3\overline{)156}$ 2. $6\overline{)186}$ 3. $5\overline{)355}$ 4. $7\overline{)\$427}$ 5. $4\overline{)248}$

6. $9\overline{)639}$ 7. $6\overline{)\$546}$ 8. $3\overline{)210}$ 9. $8\overline{)488}$ 10. $2\overline{)164}$

11. $208 \div 4$ 12. $189 \div 3$ 13. $\$360 \div 6$ 14. $405 \div 5$ 15. $357 \div 7$

16. $148 \div 2$ 17. $369 \div 9$ 18. $328 \div 8$ 19. $140 \div 7$ 20. $300 \div 5$

Solve. Decide how to use the remainder.

21. Mark has 86¢. How many stickers can he buy?

22. Each box can hold 6 golf balls. There are 20 golf balls. How many boxes are needed?

23. Vic has 3 dimes, 4 nickels, and 7 pennies. How many markers can he buy?

24. Mark and Vic have 3 sandwiches to share. How many sandwiches does each receive?

Find the average.

25. Four stamp collectors have a total of 328 stamps.

26. Iris earns a total of 350 marks on 5 tests.

27. Seven students get a total of $567 in pledges in a bike-a-thon for a new hospital.

28. The reading corner in Reggie's classroom has 8 shelves. They hold a total of 168 books.

Remainders

When you divide on a calculator, sometimes you get a decimal number.

2 6 ÷ 4 = (6.5)

This means that there is a remainder.

$$
\begin{array}{r}
6 \text{ R2} \\
4\overline{)26}
\end{array}
$$

Both of these answers mean 6 whole units and something left over.

Divide. How many whole units are in the answer?

1. 97 ÷ 2   **2.** 783 ÷ 5   **3.** 516 ÷ 8   **4.** 498 ÷ 4

When you solve word problems, you must decide what to do with the remainder.

Solve.

5. 4 people share 38 books equally.
3 8 ÷ 4 = (9.5)
How many books will each get?

6. Carlo can spend 36 h on 5 jobs.
3 6 ÷ 5 = (7.2)
How much time can he spend on each job?

7. 212 students are to sit in rows. There are 8 seats in each row.
2 1 2 ÷ 8 = ( )
How many rows are needed?

8. 100 stamps are to be shared equally by 8 people.
1 0 0 ÷ 8 = ( )
How many stamps will each get?

9. The elevator to the tower holds 22 people. 121 people are waiting.
1 2 1 ÷ 2 2 = ( )
How many trips are needed?

10. Lance can read 3 lines in 4.5 s.
4 · 5 ÷ 3 = ( )
How long does it take him to read 1 line?

263

Find the Missing Information

Greg Woods is counting the items in his storeroom. What does he need to know before he can list the number of items on this shelf?

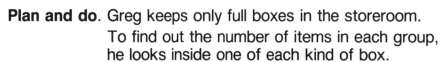

Think. What information is missing?

Plan and do. Greg keeps only full boxes in the storeroom. To find out the number of items in each group, he looks inside one of each kind of box.

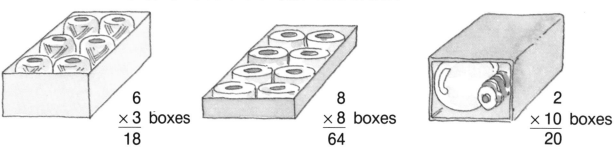

$$\begin{array}{r} 6 \\ \times 3 \text{ boxes} \\ \hline 18 \end{array}$$

$$\begin{array}{r} 8 \\ \times 8 \text{ boxes} \\ \hline 64 \end{array}$$

$$\begin{array}{r} 2 \\ \times 10 \text{ boxes} \\ \hline 20 \end{array}$$

Look back. Greg lists 18 balls of string, 64 rolls of tape, and 20 light bulbs
Does he have enough light bulbs?
What else do you need to know?

WORKING TOGETHER

Choose the information you need. Then solve the problem.

1. A full package contains 30 sheets of construction paper. I used almost half the sheets in my package. How many sheets have I used?

   a. There are 5 colors in a package.
   b. 7 sheets are blue and 8 are red.
   c. 6 sheets are green and 3 are yellow.
   d. 16 sheets are left in the package.

PROBLEMS

What other information do you have to know before you can solve the problem?

1. A garter snake is 30 cm long. A python at the zoo is 3 m long. How much longer is the python?

2. I bought a muffin for 30¢. I gave the clerk a $2 bill. How much change did I receive?

Make up numbers for the missing information. Then solve the problem.

3. Pears cost 55¢ for 5. Apples cost □¢ each. How much do 1 apple and 1 pear cost?

4. There are □ students in the class. Each student gets ○ textbooks. How many textbooks are needed?

5. Each side of a square room is □ m. What is the perimeter of the room?

6. A rectangular room is □ m long and ○ m wide. What is the area of the room?

Make up a problem for the numbers. Then solve it.

7. 31
   × 8
   ___

8. 14
   27
   + 83
   ___

9. $1.09
   − 0.56
   _____

10. 48 ÷ 12

What information is missing? Tell how you would solve the problem.

11. The baseball team won half its games. How many games was that?

12. Six players on the team were boys. How many were girls?

13. 24 students went on a field trip. The same number went in each car. How many cars were there?

14. Annette baked a pie. She served some to her grandfather. How much of the pie was left?

265

Problem Solving Review

Solve.

1. How can you arrange 8 chairs in a square room so that there are 3 chairs along every wall? Peter said it could not be done. Is his answer reasonable? Explain.

2. Miranda mailed letters to 8 friends. $\frac{2}{8}$ of the letters went air mail. $\frac{5}{8}$ of the letters contained photos. How many letters contained photos?

3. Where would you open your book so that the sum of the two facing pages is 21?

4. Karl worked for 17 d. Nicole worked 5 d a week for 3 weeks. Who worked more days? How many more?

5. The bird in the clock cuckoos on the hour. It cuckoos once at 1 o'clock, twice at 2 o'clock, and so on. How many times does it cuckoo at 12:45?

6. How many times does the bird cuckoo in a day?

Tell what other information is needed to solve the problem. Make up numbers for the missing information. Solve.

7. The temperature is 11°C. One hour ago it was colder. How much warmer is it now?

8. Teresa left the room. She came back at 2:45 p.m. How long was she gone?

9. Sophie had $5.00. She bought a yellow scarf. How much money does she have left?

10. Jack had some money. He bought a belt for $1.67. How much money does he have left?

Chapter Checkup

Find the quotient. Use multiplication to check the first exercise of each row.

1. $2\overline{)42}$ 2. $3\overline{)90}$ 3. $4\overline{)84}$ 4. $2\overline{)68}$ 5. $3\overline{)63}$

6. $5\overline{)85}$ 7. $6\overline{)90}$ 8. $4\overline{)\$72}$ 9. $8\overline{)96}$ 10. $7\overline{)91}$

11. $6\overline{)75}$ 12. $5\overline{)76}$ 13. $8\overline{)99}$ 14. $7\overline{)73}$ 15. $4\overline{)63}$

16. $3\overline{)186}$ 17. $7\overline{)490}$ 18. $6\overline{)\$306}$ 19. $5\overline{)255}$ 20. $4\overline{)284}$

21. $93 \div 3$ 22. $86 \div 2$ 23. $60 \div 2$ 24. $66 \div 6$ 25. $88 \div 4$

26. $68 \div 4$ 27. $\$54 \div 3$ 28. $98 \div 7$ 29. $84 \div 6$ 30. $95 \div 5$

31. $95 \div 8$ 32. $57 \div 2$ 33. $81 \div 5$ 34. $90 \div 7$ 35. $63 \div 4$

36. $355 \div 5$ 37. $\$480 \div 6$ 38. $324 \div 4$ 39. $287 \div 7$ 40. $400 \div 8$

Solve.

41. A ticket costs $7. Sid spent $84. How many tickets did he buy?

42. There are 28 desks in a classroom. How many rows of 5 can be made?

43. A hotel has 217 rooms. There are 7 floors. How many rooms are there on each floor?

44. There are 69 people. A van holds 8 people. How many vans are needed?

Find the average.

45. Five dairy farms have a total of 205 cows.

46. Maria answers 4 problems in 17 min.

47. Three friends meet for lunch. The restaurant bill is $21.

48. A baseball team scores 30 runs in 9 games.

Cumulative Checkup

Measure to the nearest centimetre.

1. 2. 3.

Measure to the nearest millimetre.

4. 5. 6.

Which unit, metre, centimetre, or millimetre, is best for measuring this?

7. length of an ant   8. width of a book   9. length of a room

Which unit, gram or kilogram, is better for measuring this?

10.    11.    12.

Which unit, litre or millilitre, is better for measuring this?

13.    14.    15.

How much is colored?

16. 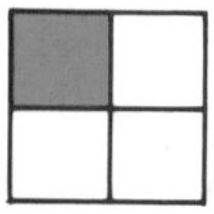   17. 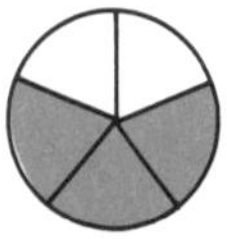   18. 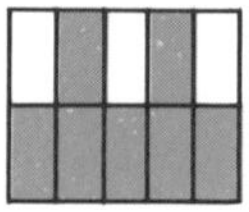   19.

20.    21. 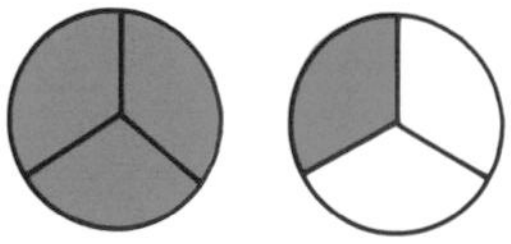   22.

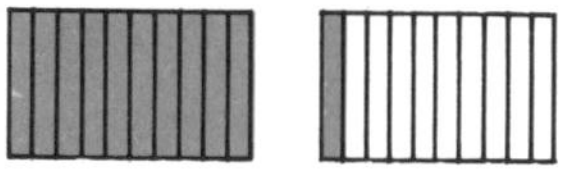

Copy and complete the fractions.

23.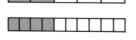

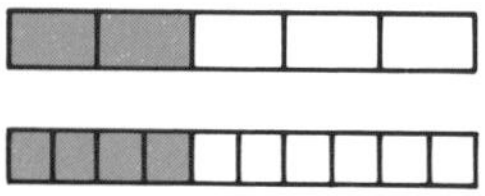

$$\frac{2}{5} = \frac{\square}{10}$$

24.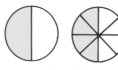

$$\frac{1}{2} = \frac{\square}{8}$$

25.

$$\frac{2}{\square} = \frac{4}{\square}$$

268

11/Graphing

In this chapter you will collect information and then display it on graphs.

Organizing Information

Kyle took a **survey** to find his friends' favorite fruits.
He made a **tally sheet** to record the information.

Fruit	Tally
Apple			
Orange	++++
Pear				
Banana	++++		
Peach		

++++ means 5.

WORKING TOGETHER

How many friends prefer this fruit?

1. apple   **2.** orange   **3.** pear   **4.** banana   **5.** peach

6. How many friends did Kyle survey?

7. How many friends prefer apples or oranges?

8. How many more friends prefer bananas than prefer pears?

9. How many friends prefer juicy fruits?

Take a survey to find your classmates' favorite popsicles.

10. Draw this tally sheet.

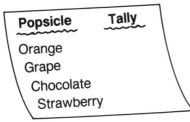

Popsicle	Tally
Orange
Grape
Chocolate
Strawberry

11. Record the survey results on the tally sheet.

12. What popsicle do most classmates prefer?

13. What is the least favorite popsicle?

Jane took a survey to find her classmates' favorite fruit drinks.

Fruit Drink	Tally
Apple	++++ II
Orange	III
Grape	++++ ++++
Pineapple	IIII
Other	III

1. How many students are in the class?

2. Which fruit drink is the favorite?

3. How many more students prefer grape drink than prefer orange drink?

4. How many students do not prefer apple drink?

Joe gathered vegetables to make a salad.

5. Make a tally sheet to show the information.

6. How many more mushrooms than radishes are there?

7. How many vegetables are there in all?

8. How many more radishes and onions are there than tomatoes?

Make a tally sheet to show the information.

9. Take a survey of 10 students to find out how many prefer cereal, eggs, toast, or waffles for breakfast.

10. Take a survey of 15 students to find out how many prefer chicken, fish, steak, or spaghetti.

Try This

Check labels in your kitchen. Where was the food packed? Make a tally chart.

Reading Pictographs

Tina counted the ice cream cones she sold today.

Tina drew this **pictograph** to show the information.

Title →	Ice Cream Cones Sold	
Labels →	Vanilla	🍦 🍦
	Chocolate	🍦 🍦 🍦 🍦
	Banana	🍦
	Orange	◗
	Butter Pecan	🍦 🍦 ◗
	Chocolate Chip	🍦 🍦 🍦
Key →	🍦 means 4 cones	

Chocolate chip has 3 symbols. This means **3 × 4**, or **12** cones sold.
Orange has half a symbol. This means **half of 4**, or **2** cones sold.

WORKING TOGETHER

How many of this flavor were sold?

1. vanilla
2. butter pecan
3. banana
4. chocolate

5. How many more chocolate cones were sold than butter pecan cones?

6. How many cones were sold in all?

How many cones do these symbols mean?

7.

8.

9.

272

Lemonade Sold	
Saturday	🥤🥤🥤🥤🥤
Sunday	🥤🥤🥤🥤🥤🥤
Monday	🥤🥤
Tuesday	🥤🥤🥤
Wednesday	🥤
🥤 means 10 glasses	

How many glasses were sold?

1. Saturday   2. Sunday

3. Wednesday   4. Tuesday

5. How many more glasses were sold on Sunday than on Tuesday?

6. How many glasses were sold in all on Saturday and Sunday?

How many cookies were sold?

7. chocolate chip   8. lemon

9. date and nut   10. peanut butter

11. How many more cream-filled cookies were sold than lemon?

12. How many more peanut butter cookies were sold than date and nut?

13. How many chocolate chip and peanut butter cookies were sold in all?

Homemade Cookies Sold	
Chocolate chip	🍪🍪🍪🍪🍪
Date and nut	🍪🍪🍪🍪
Peanut butter	🍪🍪🍪🍪🍪🍪🍪
Cream-filled	🍪🍪🍪
Lemon	🍪🍪
🍪 means 2 cookies	

14. Why do you think lemon cookies had the least sales?

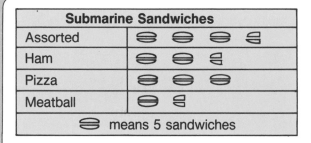

Submarine Sandwiches	
Assorted	🥪🥪🥪🥪
Ham	🥪🥪🥪
Pizza	🥪🥪🥪
Meatball	🥪🥪
🥪 means 5 sandwiches	

Try This

How many sandwiches were eaten?

1. assorted   2. ham   3. pizza

4. How many more assorted than ham sandwiches were eaten?

Drawing Pictographs

Keith was taking a survey to find the most popular paint color for cars.

Keith made a **tally sheet**.

Color	Tally
Blue	₮₮₮ ₮₮₮ ‖
Red	₮₮₮ ₮₮₮ ₮₮₮ ‖
Gray	₮₮₮ ‖
White	‖‖
Yellow	‖

Keith drew a **pictograph**.
He chose ⌐o‾‾o to mean 4 cars.

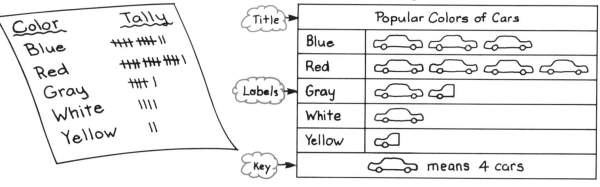

WORKING TOGETHER

1. Why do you think 4 was chosen as the meaning of ⌐o‾‾o ?

Take a survey to find how many classmates come to school by bicycle, bus, car, or walking.

2. Make a tally sheet.

3. Take the survey and record the results on the tally sheet.

4. Choose a symbol and its meaning.

5. Draw the pictograph frame with title, labels, and key. Draw the symbols.

Draw a pictograph using the information from the tally sheet.

1. Cars Sold

Day	Tally
Tues.	‖‖ ‖
Wed.	‖‖
Thurs.	‖‖ ‖‖
Fri.	‖‖ ‖‖
Sat.	‖

2. Trucks Seen

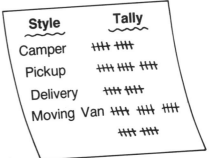

Style	Tally
Camper	‖‖ ‖‖
Pickup	‖‖ ‖‖ ‖‖
Delivery	‖‖ ‖‖
Moving Van	‖‖ ‖‖ ‖‖ ‖‖ ‖‖

3. Make a tally sheet and draw a pictograph to show this information.

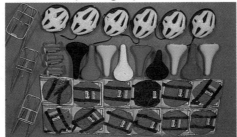

4. Take a survey to find out the kinds of bicycles your classmates have. Make a tally sheet and draw a pictograph to show how many classmates have standard, 3-speed, 5-speed, or 10-speed bicycles.

A computer can do arithmetic. The instructions must be given in a computer language like Logo or BASIC.

Give the output.

1. PRINT 576 − 27

2. PRINT 5 * 8

3. PRINT 27/ 3

4. PRINT 418 + 376

5. PRINTT 7 * 7

6. FIND 987 + 654

> In Logo and BASIC
> * means multiply,
> / means divide.

Reading Bar Graphs

The camp counsellor takes a survey of the campers
to find their favorite activities.

This **horizontal bar graph** shows the information.

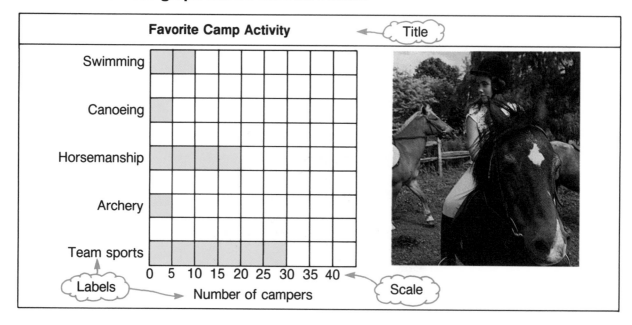

WORKING TOGETHER

How many campers prefer this activity?

1. horsemanship 2. archery 3. team sports 4. canoeing

5. How many more campers prefer team sports than prefer swimming?

6. How many campers do not prefer team sports?

7. How many more campers prefer horsemanship than prefer water sports?

8. How would you arrange the labels to make a vertical bar graph?

EXERCISES

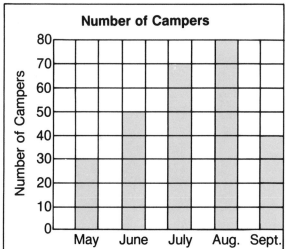

Number of Campers

How many camped in this month?

1. May   **2.** July

3. August   **4.** September

5. How many more camped in June than in September?

6. How many more camped in July and August than in the other months?

7. How would you arrange the labels to make a horizontal bar graph?

---

8. Which bird was seen most often?

9. Which bird was seen least often?

10. Which bird was seen 25 times?

11. How many times were goldfinches seen?

12. How many more chickadees were seen than robins?

13. Why do you think more chickadees and robins were seen than other birds?

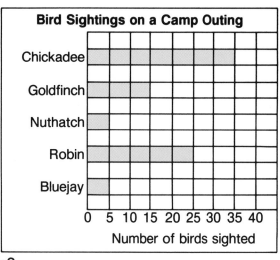

Bird Sightings on a Camp Outing

Number of birds sighted

KEEPING SHARP

Multiply or divide.

1. 4×6 **2.** 5×8 **3.** 9×3 **4.** $20 \div 4$ **5.** $30 \div 6$ **6.** $42 \div 7$

7. 6×8 **8.** $45 \div 9$ **9.** $32 \div 8$ **10.** $56 \div 8$ **11.** 7×4 **12.** 9×6

The students in Ricardo's class gave their shoe size.

Shoe Size								
5	4	4	3	3	2	3	4	5
2	3	3	2	4	3	2	4	3
3	4	4	3	3	2	2	3	2

1. Make a tally chart to show this information.

How many students prefer this type of program?

2. cartoons   **3.** comedy

4. adventure   **5.** sports

6. How many more students prefer cartoons than prefer sports?

7. What is the most popular type of program?

8. How many students were surveyed?

Favorite TV Shows	
Cartoons	👤 👤 👤
Comedy	👤 👤 👤 ⸮
Adventure	👤 👤 👤
Sports	👤 👤 ⸮
Other	👤
👤 stands for 4 students	

Take a survey of your classmates to find their favorite fast food restaurant.

9. Make a tally sheet and draw a pictograph.

Use the bar graph.

10. Which piece of playground equipment is the most popular?

11. Which piece of playground equipment is the least popular?

12. How many more children play with a soccer ball than with a frisbee?

13. Why do you think more children play with a soccer ball than with a frisbee?

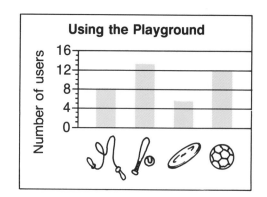

Using the Playground

278

Word Processing

A computer cannot think of a story, but it can help you as you write one. A special program called **word processing** helps you change, or **edit**, what you write. You can **take out** words you don't want. You can **put in extra** words. You can **move** sentences or paragraphs from place to place.

1. How would you change the story below?

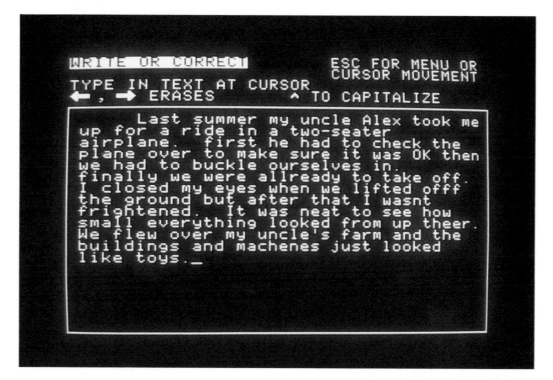

```
WRITE OR CORRECT          ESC FOR MENU OR
                          CURSOR MOVEMENT
TYPE IN TEXT AT CURSOR
←, → ERASES          ^ TO CAPITALIZE

        Last summer my uncle Alex took me
up for a ride in a two-seater
airplane.  first he had to check the
plane over to make sure it was OK then
we had to buckle ourselves in.
finally we were allready to take off.
I closed my eyes when we lifted offf
the ground but after that I wasnt
frightened.   It was neat to see how
small everything looked from up theer.
We flew over my uncle's farm and the
buildings and machenes just looked
like toys._
```

The computer does not care how many times you make changes. It will print a copy of your story as often as you wish.

2. Write a story. Mark any changes you want. Then give it to your teacher. Make more changes if necessary. Make a final copy to keep.

Drawing Bar Graphs

Tracey asked her classmates their birthplaces.
She recorded the information on a tally sheet.

Tracey chose a scale of 2.

She drew a **horizontal bar graph** to show the information.

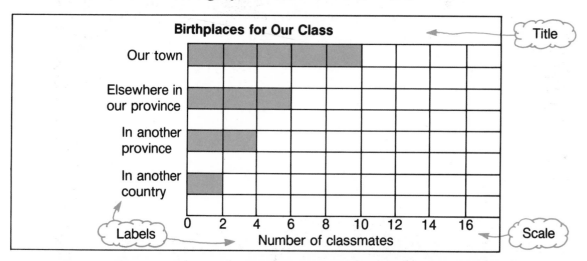

WORKING TOGETHER

Take a survey of your classmates to find their favorite season.
Draw a horizontal bar graph.

1. Make a tally sheet.

2. Take the survey and record the results on the tally sheet.

3. Choose a scale.

4. Draw the bar graph frame with title, labels, and scale. Draw the bars.

EXERCISES

Draw a horizontal bar graph to show the information in the tally sheet.

1. Types of Homes

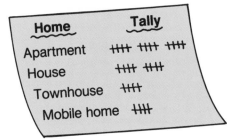

Home	Tally
Apartment	ʜʜʜ ʜʜʜ ʜʜʜ
House	ʜʜʜ ʜʜʜ
Townhouse	ʜʜʜ
Mobile home	ʜʜʜ

2. Customers on Paper Routes

Name	Tally
Tracey	10
Anne	30
Jeff	20
Rob	50

Make a tally sheet and draw a vertical bar graph.

3. The students in Brian's class said how many hours of TV they watched on Saturday.

Hours of TV Watched							
0	2	2	3	1	2	0	1
1	6	1	3	1	2	0	3
2	3	0	1	2	0	1	0
1	0	4	1	0	4	6	1

Make a tally sheet and draw a horizontal bar graph.

4. the number of children in each classmate's family

5. the month of each classmate's birthday

Make a tally sheet and draw a vertical bar graph.

6. the hair color of each classmate

7. the eye color of each classmate

Add or subtract. Then turn the calculator upside down. Match the word in the display to one of the pictures.

1.	**2.**	**3.**	**4.**	**5.**
859	9825	757	1065	45 230
− 555	− 2087	− 419	+ 1980	+ 32 115

Make up some problems with these answers. What are the words?

907   345   3704   918   5537   3215   993

281

Places on a Map

The map shows part of Ottawa, the capital of Canada.
The numbers and letters along the edges help locate
places on the map.

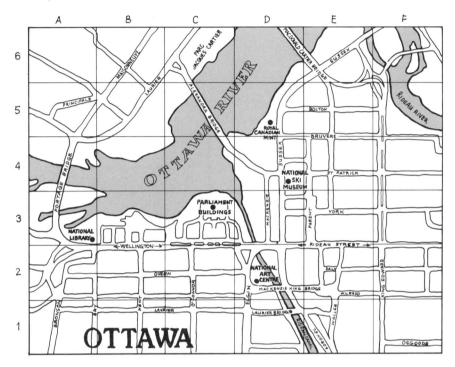

The **region** for the Parliament Buildings is **(C,3)**.

WORKING TOGETHER

Name.

1. a building in region (A,3)

2. a building in region (D,2)

3. two streets that meet in region (C,2)

Name the region.

4. National Ski Museum

5. Royal Canadian Mint

282

Name.

1. a bridge in region (D,1)

2. two streets in region (B,2)

3. a bridge in region (C,5)

4. a curved road in region (D,5)

5. two streets that meet in region (A,1)

6. two streets that meet in region (F,2)

Write the region.

7. Parc Jacques Cartier

8. MacKenzie King Bridge

9. where Sussex Drive meets York Street

10. where Elgin Street meets Wellington Street

11. where the Rideau Canal meets the Ottawa River

12. where the Rideau Canal meets Wellington Street

13. Osgoode Street

14. Macdonald-Cartier Bridge

Write as many regions as possible for this.

15. Bolton Street

16. Bay Street

17. Rideau River

18. Portage Bridge

Copy the grid. Make a map by showing this place in its region.

19. city hall in (E,5)

20. cinema in (B,2)

21. fire hall in (D,4)

22. school in (A,6)

Using a map of your own city or a city nearby, locate 10 different places. List each place and its region. Include important parks, buildings, and relatives' homes.

Try This

Positions on a Grid

In each balloon is a piece of paper that tells the position of a prize.

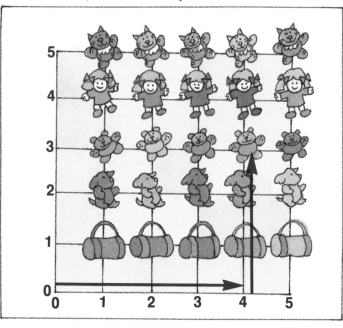

The **ordered pair** was (**4,3**) or 4 units over, 3 units up.

WORKING TOGETHER

What prize is at this position?

1. (3,2)   **2.** (5,4)   **3.** (4,5)   **4.** (1,4)

What is the ordered pair of this prize?

		Units over	Units up	Ordered pair
5.				
6.				
7.				

EXERCISES

What prize is at this position?

1. (1, 4)   2. (3, 6)   3. (5, 2)

4. (2, 1)   5. (4, 3)   6. (3, 4)

Copy and complete the ordered pair.

7. is at (2,□). 8. is at (□,1).

9. is at (□,5). 10. is at (1,□).

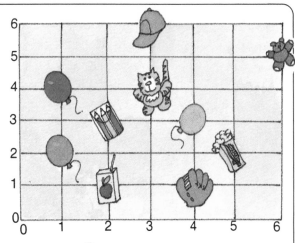

Write the letter at this position.
Find the message.

11. (2, 4)   12. (1, 2)   13. (4, 1)

14. (6, 5)   15. (5, 4)   16. (6, 2)

17. (3, 3)   18. (2, 6)   19. (1, 5)

20. (2, 1)   21. (3, 0)   22. (5, 4)

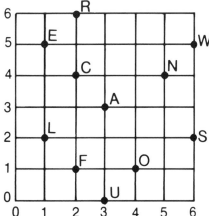

Plot the points on a 10 by 10 grid. Join the points in order. What is the figure?

23. (5, 9)   24. (6, 9)   25. (6, 10)   26. (5, 10)   27. (5, 8)

28. (3, 6)   29. (1, 4)   30. (1, 1)   31. (3, 1)   32. (5, 5)

33. (7, 1)   34. (9, 1)   35. (9, 4)   36. (7, 6)   37. (5, 8)

KEEPING SHARP

Subtract.

1. 58
   − 25

2. 85
   − 38

3. 156
   − 47

4. 241
   − 159

5. 326
   − 158

285

The campers kept a record of the number of each kind
of owl that they saw during one week.

Owl	Tally
Saw-whet	II
Great Horned	ﬁﬁ I
Screech	ﬁﬁ
Barn	ﬁﬁ

1. Choose a scale.

2. Draw a horizontal bar graph.

3. Which owl was seen most often?

4. Which owl was seen least often?

5. How many more screech owls were
   seen than saw-whet owls?

A record was kept of the attendance of the campers.

6. Choose a scale.

7. Draw a vertical bar graph.

8. On which day was attendance highest?

9. How many more children attended
   on Monday than on Thursday?

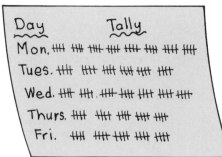

Day	Tally
Mon.	ﬁﬁ ﬁﬁ ﬁﬁ ﬁﬁ ﬁﬁ ﬁﬁ ﬁﬁ ﬁﬁ
Tues.	ﬁﬁ ﬁﬁ ﬁﬁ ﬁﬁ ﬁﬁ ﬁﬁ
Wed.	ﬁﬁ ﬁﬁ ﬁﬁ ﬁﬁ ﬁﬁ ﬁﬁ ﬁﬁ
Thurs.	ﬁﬁ ﬁﬁ ﬁﬁ ﬁﬁ ﬁﬁ
Fri.	ﬁﬁ ﬁﬁ ﬁﬁ ﬁﬁ ﬁﬁ

Write the ordered pair.

10. fox   11. skunk

12. hawk   13. raccoon

14. woodpecker   15. squirrel

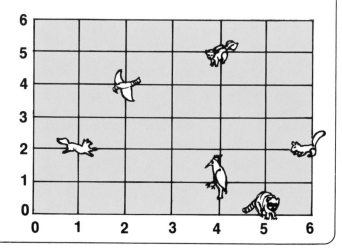

Air Travel

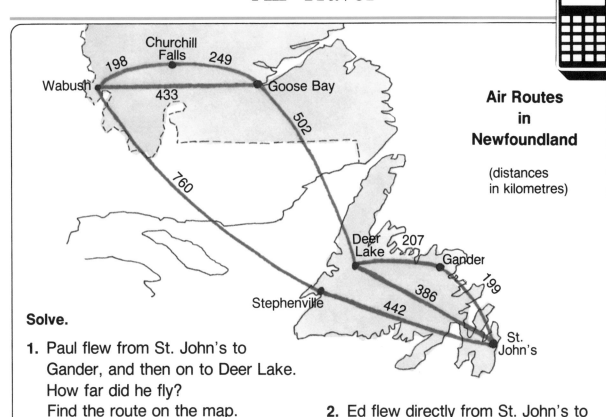

**Air Routes
in
Newfoundland**

(distances
in kilometres)

Churchill Falls
198
249
Wabush
433
Goose Bay
502
760
Deer Lake
207
Gander
199
386
Stephenville
442
St. John's

Solve.

1. Paul flew from St. John's to
   Gander, and then on to Deer Lake.
   How far did he fly?
   Find the route on the map.
   Add the numbers shown along it.

   1 9 9 + 2 0 7 = ⟨   ⟩

2. Ed flew directly from St. John's to
   Deer Lake. How much shorter was
   his route than Paul's?

3. How much farther is it from
   Stephenville to St. John's than from
   Deer Lake to St. John's?

4. Janice flew from Deer Lake and got
   off at the second stop. She had
   gone 751 km. Where was she?

5. Ed flew from Goose Bay to
   Wabush, and then back by way of
   Churchill Falls. How far did he fly?

6. What is the shortest trip by air from
   Gander to Wabush? How far is it?

7. Paul flew 908 km from Goose Bay.
   What city was he in? What route
   did he take?

8. Plan a trip that starts and ends in
   Deer Lake. Take in each city on the
   map. Tell what the route is. How
   long is it?

Use a Model

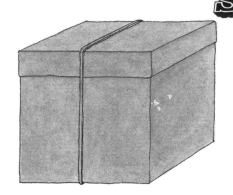

Joe uses a rubber band to keep the lid on a square box. Each side of the box is 10 cm. How far does the rubber band stretch around the box?

Think.   The rubber band goes around a square.

Plan and do.   Joe traced around the bottom of the box. Then he measured the distance around the square.

Joe gave this solution. *The rubber band stretches 40 cm around the box.*

Look back.   Use a different way to solve the problem. Does Joe's solution make sense?

WORKING TOGETHER

1. Which figures cover 12 square units?

2. The distance around figure c is 16 units. Find the distances around figure a, figure b, and figure d.

3. Make different figures that have an area of 12 square units. Find the one with the shortest perimeter.

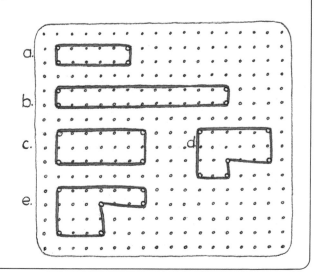

PROBLEMS

Act out the problem or use a model to solve it.

1. Erica's class made a human pyramid. 4 students were on the bottom layer, 3 students were on the next layer, and one student less was on each layer above that. How many students were in the pyramid?

2. Five friends sat on one side of the lunch table. Minta sat next to Bruce. Sally sat next to Paul. Ruth sat in the third seat from Bruce. Minta sat in the third seat from Sally. Who sat on the other side of Paul?

3. Five soccer teams play during the season. Each team plays every other team once each month. How many soccer games are there during the months of May, June, July, and August?

4. I counted 7 cycle riders and 19 cycle wheels in the children's parade. How many bicycles and tricycles were in the parade?

5. At what time between 11 and 1 o'clock is the minute hand exactly over the hour hand?

6. How many blocks are needed to surround one block? All sides and all corners must be covered.

7. How many blocks are needed to surround two blocks? All sides and all corners must be covered.

8. Each side of the cube is a different color. What color is covered by the hand?

Problem Solving Review

Solve.

1. How thick is the tuna sandwich? A slice of bread is 15 mm thick. The filling is spread 10 mm thick.

2. Erica is 86 cm tall. She has to reach 18 cm above her head to touch the doorknob. How far is the doorknob from the floor?

3. Dennis and Harley were in the 100 m race. When Harley crossed the finish line, Dennis was 7 m behind. How far had Dennis run so far?

4. Sari lives on the road between Hillcrest and Lake Wilcox. It is 10 km from her house to Hillcrest. It is 15 km in the other direction from her house to Lake Wilcox. How far is it from Hillcrest to Lake Wilcox?

5. Polly's cage is 75 cm high and 39 cm wide. Scooter's cage is 88 cm high and 52 cm wide. How much wider is Scooter's cage?

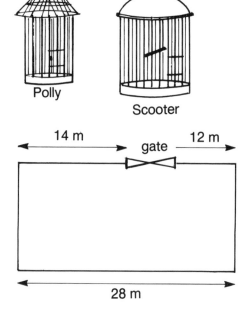

6. The fence needs a gate. How wide should the gate be?

Tell how you would solve the problem.

7. How much farther is it from Halifax to St. John's than from Halifax to Fredericton?

8. Each side of a building is 10 m long. How far must Craig walk to walk around the building?

Chapter Checkup

A survey was taken to find students' favorite lunch hour activity.

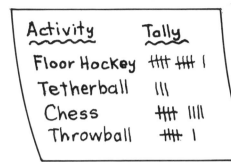

Activity	Tally
Floor Hockey	༦༦༦ ༦༦༦	
Tetherball	|||
Chess	༦༦༦ ||||
Throwball	༦༦༦	

1. Choose a symbol and its meaning.

2. Draw a pictograph.

3. What is the favorite lunch activity?

4. How many more students prefer floor hockey than prefer chess?

5. How many students were surveyed?

6. Draw a horizontal bar graph to show the favorite lunch hour activity.

7. Take a survey of your classmates to find their favorite sandwich. Make a tally sheet, choose a scale, and draw a vertical bar graph.

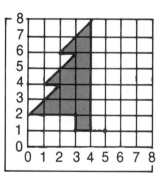

8. Copy the diagram on an 8 by 8 grid. Plot the points needed to complete the symmetrical tree. Join them.

9. Write the ordered pairs that you used.

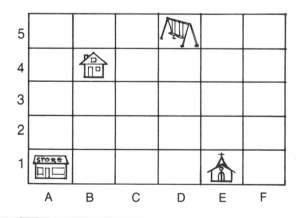

Write the region.

10.

11.

12.

13.

291

Cumulative Checkup

Find.

1. perimeter

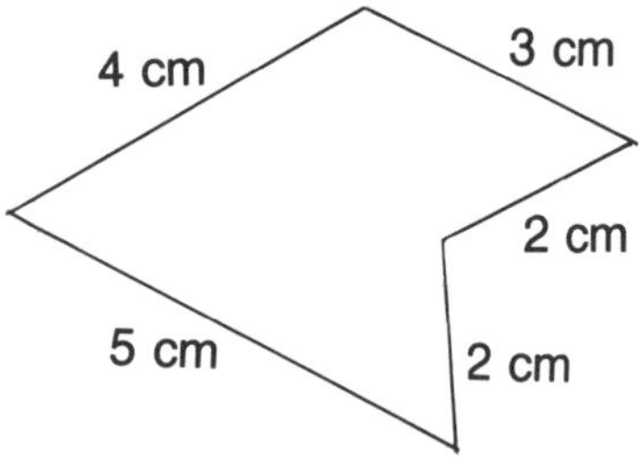

4 cm
3 cm
2 cm
5 cm
2 cm

2. area

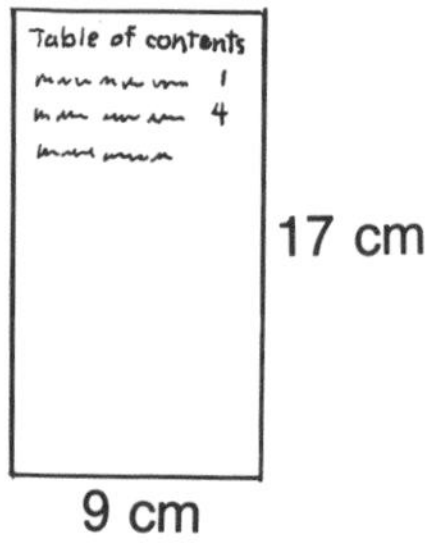

Table of contents

17 cm

9 cm

3. volume

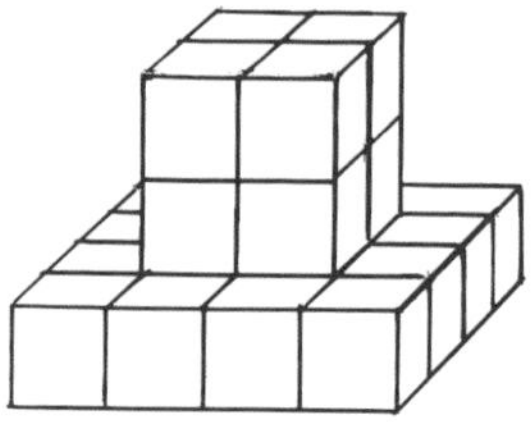

Write the time.

4.  morning

5.  evening

6.  afternoon

7.  morning

8.  evening

9.  afternoon

10.  morning

11.  afternoon

How much is colored? Write the decimal.

12.

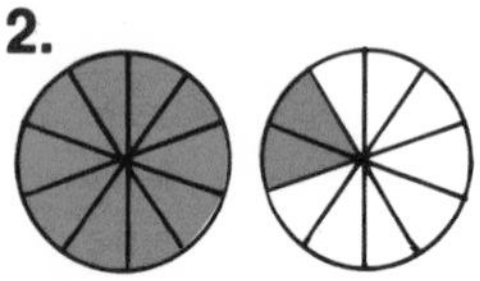

13.

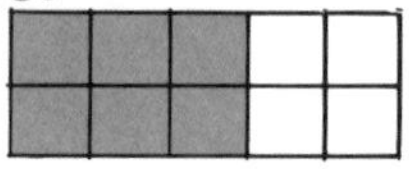

14.

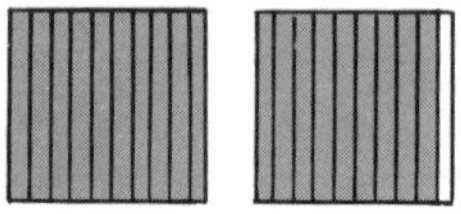

15.

Write the decimal.

16. five-tenths

17. one-tenth

18. ten-tenths

Is the angle equal to, greater than, or less than a right angle?

19.

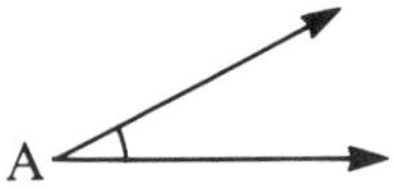

A

20.

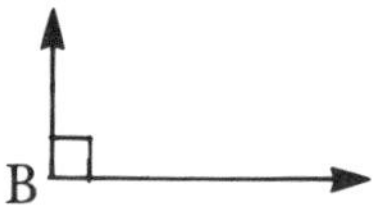

B

21.

C

12/Decimals and Fractions

Many sports scores are given in decimals.
In this chapter you will learn about
decimals in hundredths and how
to add and subtract them. You will learn
how to add and subtract fractions too.

Hundredths

How much is painted?

3 tenths

$\frac{3}{10}$

ones	tenths
0	3

0.3

5 hundredths

$\frac{5}{100}$

ones	tenths	hundredths
0	0	5

0.05

$\frac{35}{100}$ **or**

$\frac{3}{10}, \frac{5}{100}$

ones	tenths	hundredths
0	3	5

0.35

35 hundredths

or 3 tenths 5 hundredths

WORKING TOGETHER

How much is colored?

1.

☐ hundredths

2.

☐ hundredths
or ☐ tenths ☐ hundredths

3.

☐ hundredths
or ☐ tenths ☐ hundredths

Use a square marked in hundredths. Color this much.

4. 8 hundredths

5. 41 hundredths

6. 6 tenths

7.
ones	tenths	hundredths
0	0	7

8.
ones	tenths	hundredths
0	4	5

9.
ones	tenths	hundredths
0	1	8

10. 0.09

11. 0.14

12. 0.72

How much is colored?

1.

☐ hundredths

2.

☐ hundredths
or ☐ tenths ☐ hundredths

3.

☐ hundredths
or ☐ tenths ☐ hundredths

Use a square marked in hundredths. Color this much.

4. 1 hundredth

5. 99 hundredths

6. 4 tenths 4 hundredths

7.

ones	tenths	hundredths
0	0	9

8.

ones	tenths	hundredths
0	2	4

9.

ones	tenths	hundredths
0	8	3

10. 0.10

11. 0.01

12. 0.15

Count by hundredths.

13. 0.01, 0.02, ☐

14. 0.08, ☐, ☐

15. 0.49, ☐, ☐

Write the decimal.

16. 4 hundredths

17. 18 hundredths

18. 2 tenths 1 hundredth

19. 32¢

20. 5¢

21. 98¢

22. 1 cm = ☐ m

23. $\frac{8}{100}$

24. 12 cm = ☐ m

Try This

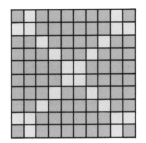
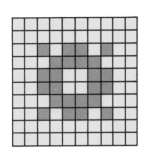

Use a square marked in hundredths.
Create a design by coloring 0.24
in one color and 0.76 in another.

Comparing and Ordering Decimals

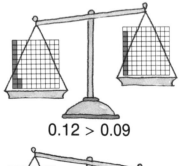

0.12 > 0.09

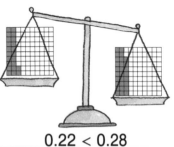

0.22 < 0.28

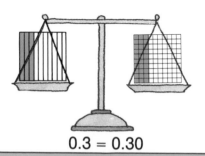

0.3 = 0.30

Compare the ones.

If the ones are the same, compare the tenths.

If the tenths are the same, compare the hundredths.

WORKING TOGETHER

Copy and complete.

1. 1 tenth = ☐ hundredths

2. 2 tenths = ☐ hundredths

3. 40 hundredths = ☐ tenths

4. 23 hundredths = ☐ tenths ☐ hundredths

How much is colored? Use >, <, or = to make a true statement.

5. 0.51 ◯ 0.15

6. 0.46 ◯ 0.7

Find the decimals on the number lines. Complete the statements.

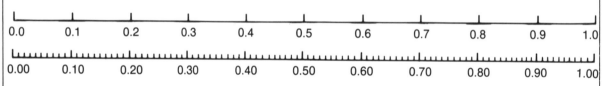

7. 0.26 ◯ 0.52   8. 0.7 ◯ 0.70   9. 0.34 ◯ 0.3

Copy and complete.

1. 10 hundredths = ☐ tenth

2. 5 tenths = ☐ hundredths

3. 0.06 = ☐ tenths ☐ hundredths

4. 0.70 = ☐ tenths ☐ hundredths

Use >, <, or = to make a true statement.

5.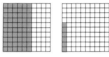

0.60 ◯ 0.06

6.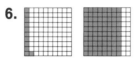

0.11 ◯ 0.8

7.
```
 0.0    0.1    0.2    0.3
 0.00  0.10   0.20   0.30
```

0.2 ◯ 0.17

Use squares marked in hundredths to show the decimals.
Then use >, <, or = to make a true statement.

8. 0.13 ◯ 0.18

9. 0.64 ◯ 0.46

10. 0.07 ◯ 0.7

11. 0.02 ◯ 0.01

12. 0.9 ◯ 0.90

13. 0.82 ◯ 0.28

14. 0.4 ◯ 0.38

15. 0.20 ◯ 0.2

16. 0.63 ◯ 0.29

Order from least to greatest.

17.
0.42
0.5
0.4
0.51

18.
0.98
0.19
0.8
0.09

19.
0.01
0.11
0.1
1.00

Try This

What travels around the earth without rockets? Put the numbers in order from least to greatest to find the answer.

N 0.7 M 0.11 O 0.69 E 0.1 H 0.06 T 0.01 O 0.21

Decimals Greater Than 1.00

3 dollars and 6 cents **$3.06**

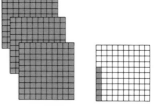

ones	tenths	hundredths
3	0	6

3 **and** 6 hundredths

3.06

WORKING TOGETHER

How much is colored?

1.

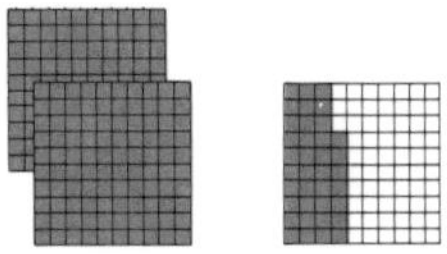

2.

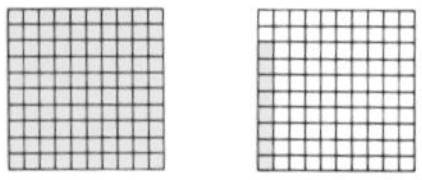

3.

Use squares marked in hundredths. Color this much.

4. 1.25   **5.** 3.03   **6.** 2.71

Complete.

7. 8.09 = ☐ ones and ☐ hundredths   **8.** 5.32 = ☐ ones and ☐ hundredths

9. 7.94 = ☐ ones ☐ tenths ☐ hundredths

10. 100 hundredths = 1 _?_   **11.** 10 hundredths = 1 _?_

Show on a number line. Then order from least to greatest.

12. 2.26, 1.84, 2.9, 1.35   **13.** 1.04, 0.40, 1.01, 1.4

How much is colored? Write the decimal.

1.

2.

3.

Use squares marked in hundredths. Color this much.

4. 2.9

5. 4.11

6. 1.40

Write the decimal.

7. 3 ones 14 hundredths

8. 8 dollars 5 cents

9. 6 ones 4 hundredths

10. 78 cents

11. 243 cents

12. $25\frac{15}{100}$

13. A tree is 275 years old. How many centuries is that? A century is 100 years.

14. Ella needs a rope 3 m and 45 cm long. How many metres is that?

15. In the Olympics, Ben Johnson ran the 100 m race in 10 and 22 hundredths seconds.

16. Sula has 4 dollar bills, 8 dimes, and 2 pennies. How much money does she have?

Count by hundredths.

17. 5.97, 5.98, ☐, ☐, ☐

18. 0.96, 0.97, ☐, ☐, ☐

Order from least to greatest.

19. 2.79, 5.12, 2.17, 1.35

20. 4.03, 0.37, 2.71, 4.3

KEEPING SHARP

How fast can you give the answers?
Have a partner time you.

8	7	5	7	6	6	8	8	9	9	9	8
×6	×7	×9	×3	×6	×9	×4	×7	×8	×9	×7	×8

299

Adding Decimals

Andrea's scores at a gymnastics competition were: vault 8.15, uneven bars 8.80, beam 7.90, and floor 8.85. What was her total score?

Add.   8.15 + 8.80 + 7.90 + 8.85

Line up the places.	Add hundredths. Regroup.	Add tenths. Regroup.	Add ones.
8.15 8.80 7.90 + 8.85	1 8 . 1 5 8 . 8 0 7 . 9 0 + 8 . 8 5 . 0	2 1 8 . 1 5 8 . 8 0 7 . 9 0 + 8 . 8 5 . 7 0	2 1 8 . 1 5 8 . 8 0 7 . 9 0 + 8 . 8 5 3 3 . 7 0

Her total score was 33.70.

WORKING TOGETHER

Regroup.

1. 12 hundredths = ☐ tenths ☐ hundredths   2. 15 tenths = ☐ one ☐ tenths

3. 20 hundredths = ☐ tenths ☐ hundredths   4. 34 tenths = ☐ ones ☐ tenths

Add.

5. 6.35
  + 2.41

6. 4.13
  + 2.65

7. 13.46
  + 23.61

8. $4.27
  + 4.36

9. 9.35
  + 3.47

10. 2.87
  + 5.89

11. $3.68
  + 5.76

12. 14.09
  + 8.55

EXERCISES

Regroup.

1. 53 hundredths
= ☐ tenths ☐ hundredths

2. 17 tenths
= ☐ one ☐ tenths

3. 10 hundredths = ☐ tenth ☐ hundredths

4. 18 tenths = ☐ one ☐ tenths

5. 23 hundredths = ☐ tenths ☐ hundredths

6. 32 tenths = ☐ ones ☐ tenths

Find the sum.

7.
```
  0.63
+ 0.14
```

8.
```
  3.49
+ 2.30
```

9.
```
  6.14
+ 2.08
```

10.
```
  $3.45
+ 8.46
```

11.
```
  5.63
+ 2.87
```

12.
```
  4.59
+ 3.92
```

13.
```
  6.14
+ 4.97
```

14.
```
  $42.08
+  7.87
```

15. 6.42 + 8.09 + 2.80

16. 13.34 + 8.71 + 24.20

Solve.

17. Last year Cindy could jump 0.79 m. Now she can jump 0.05 m higher. How high can she jump?

18. When Michel was born he had a mass of 3.85 kg. He has gained 25.75 kg. What is his mass now?

Try This

Use the numbers from 0.1 to 0.9. Give a set of four addends that have the sum 1.0.

Make as many different sets as you can.

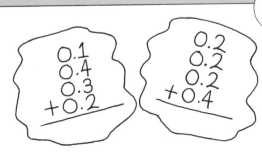

```
0.1
0.4
0.3
+ 0.2
```

```
0.2
0.2
0.2
+ 0.4
```

Subtracting Decimals

Pearson School had a Terry Fox Day run.
The course was 8.50 km long.
Li ran 5.75 km. How far did he
still have to go?

Subtract.   8.50 − 5.75

Need more hundredths. Regroup 1 tenth.	Subtract hundredths.	Need more tenths. Regroup 1 one.	Subtract tenths. Subtract ones.
4 10 8 . 5̸ 0̸ − 5 . 7 5 .	4 10 8 . 5̸ 0̸ − 5 . 7 5 . 5	14 7 4̸ 10 8̸ . 5̸ 0̸ − 5 . 7 5 . 5	14 7 4̸ 10 8̸ . 5̸ 0̸ − 5 . 7 5 2 . 7 5

Li still had 2.75 km to go.

WORKING TOGETHER

Regroup.

1. ☐ 15
   4 . 8̸ 5̸

2. 5 ☐
   1 3 . 6̸ 0̸

3. ☐ ☐
   7̸ . 0̸ 2

4. ☐
   ☐ 2̸ ☐
   5 9̸ . 3̸ 6̸

5. 6 tenths 4 hundredths = 5 tenths ☐ hundredths

Subtract.

6. 8.47
   − 2.15

7. 9.63
   − 4.28

8. $23.46
   − 11.09

9. 7.80
   − 3.52

10. 45.49
    − 12.84

11. $6.03
    − 3.71

12. 8.25
    − 4.86

13. 31.40
    − 12.94

Regroup.

1. 4 tenths 2 hundredths = 3 tenths ☐ hundredths

2. 7 tenths 1 hundredth = ☐ tenths 11 hundredths

3. 5 ones 0 tenths 6 hundredths = 4 ones ☐ tenths 6 hundredths

4. 8 ones 3 tenths 5 hundredths = 7 ones ☐ tenths 15 hundredths

Subtract.

5. $\begin{array}{r} 9.37 \\ -2.42 \\ \hline \end{array}$ 6. $\begin{array}{r} 6.45 \\ -1.14 \\ \hline \end{array}$ 7. $\begin{array}{r} 8.71 \\ -4.36 \\ \hline \end{array}$ 8. $\begin{array}{r} \$27.48 \\ -15.29 \\ \hline \end{array}$

9. $\begin{array}{r} 5.26 \\ -1.88 \\ \hline \end{array}$ 10. $\begin{array}{r} 63.07 \\ -48.25 \\ \hline \end{array}$ 11. $\begin{array}{r} 18.41 \\ -9.18 \\ \hline \end{array}$ 12. $\begin{array}{r} \$97.22 \\ -1.39 \\ \hline \end{array}$

13. 87.04 − 42.61   14. $54.38 − $6.93   15. 12.8 − 6.91

Solve.

16. Kim finished 4.85 km of the course. Lee finished 3.74 km. Joan finished 4.69 km. How much farther did Kim run than Joan?

17. Alex entered the 8.50 km run too. He ran 3.35 km, rested, and then ran 2.60 km. How much farther did he have to go to finish the course?

Copy and complete the Magic Square. The sum of every row, column, and diagonal is the same.

	0.91	
1.17	0.65	0.13
		1.04

PRACTICE

Write the decimal.

1.

2.

3.

4. 3 hundredths

5. 42 hundredths

6. 7 tenths 1 hundredth

7. 6 ones 2 tenths 5 hundredths

8. 8 ones 5 hundredths

9.

ones	tenths	hundredths
0 •	4	9

10.

ones	tenths	hundredths
9 •	0	8

Use >, <, or = to make a true statement.

11. 0.26 ◯ 0.35

12. 0.09 ◯ 0.1

13. 0.8 ◯ 0.80

14. 5.07 ◯ 0.79

15. 2.03 ◯ 2.30

16. 6.31 ◯ 6.50

Order from least to greatest.

17. 0.41, 0.29, 0.47, 0.27

18. 9.41, 9.04, 0.94, 0.41

Add or subtract.

19.   0.69
       + 0.27

20.   0.46
       − 0.18

21. $7.18
        − 2.74

22. $8.37
        + 1.35

23.   39.31
       − 12.83

24. 42.86
       + 3.65

25. 58.04
       − 2.68

26.   6.53
       + 9.99

Solve.

27. Owen can jump 1.41 m. Adele can jump 0.09 m farther. How far can Adele jump?

28. Vicki's score on beam was 8.75. Marie's score was 9.10. How much higher was Marie's score?

Decimal Puzzles

Add or subtract
to get the number
in the display.

Use only the keys shown.

You may use the keys
more than once.

Write the number
sentence.

1.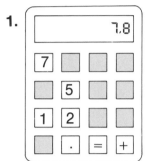

2.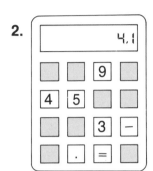

3.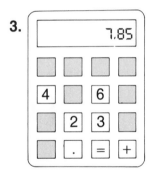

4.

5.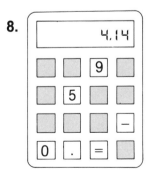

6.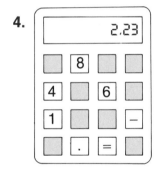

7.

8.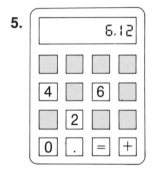

Decimal Names for Fractions

  Other names for $\frac{1}{2}$ ➡ $\frac{5}{10}$ or 0.5 $\frac{50}{100}$ or 0.50

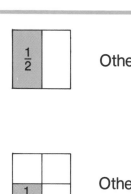 Other names for $\frac{1}{4}$ ➡ $\frac{25}{100}$ or 0.25

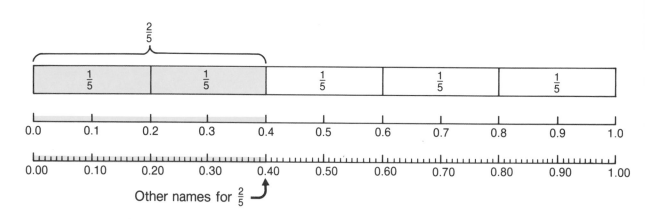

Other names for $\frac{2}{5}$ ↰

WORKING TOGETHER

Give a fraction for the colored part. Then give a decimal.

1.   **2.**   **3.**

4.   **5.**   **6.**

Give the fraction.

7. 0.5   **8.** 0.06   **9.** 0.3   **10.** 0.87   **11.** 0.01

EXERCISES

Copy and complete.

1.

$\frac{1}{2} = \frac{\square}{10} = 0 . \square$

2.

$\frac{7}{10} = \square . \square$

3.

$\frac{1}{4} = \frac{\square}{100} = \square . \square$

4.

$\frac{81}{100} = \square . \square$

5.

$\frac{3}{4} = \frac{\square}{100} = \square . \square$

6.

$\frac{50}{100} = \square . \square$

7.

$\frac{3}{5} = \frac{\square}{10} = \square . \square$

8.

$\frac{10}{100} = \square . \square$

9.

$\frac{4}{5} = \frac{\square}{10} = \square . \square$

Write the decimal.

10. $\frac{9}{10}$

11. $\frac{1}{5}$

12. $\frac{5}{100}$

13. $\frac{18}{100}$

14. $\frac{1}{2}$

Try This

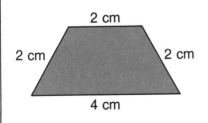

Trace the shape. Cut out 3 copies of it.
1. Put the pieces together to form a triangle.
2. The area of each piece is what fraction of the area of the triangle?
3. The perimeter of each piece is what fraction of the perimeter of the triangle?

307

Comparing and Ordering Fractions

Use the number strip.

Compare $\frac{5}{10}$ and $\frac{7}{10}$. Which is greater?

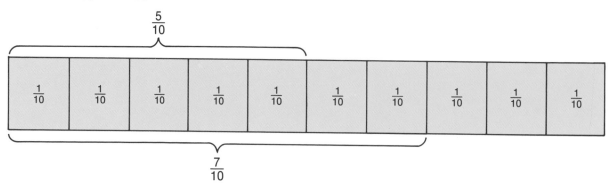

$$\frac{5}{10}$$

$$\frac{7}{10}$$

$\frac{7}{10}$ is greater than $\frac{5}{10}$. $\frac{7}{10} > \frac{5}{10}$

WORKING TOGETHER

Show with number strips. Order from least to greatest.

1. $\frac{3}{4}$, $\frac{4}{4}$, $\frac{2}{4}$, $\frac{1}{4}$

2. $\frac{2}{5}$, $\frac{5}{5}$, $\frac{1}{5}$, $\frac{4}{5}$, $\frac{3}{5}$

Fold a strip of paper into eighths. Find these fractions.
Use >, <, or = to make a true statement.

3. $\frac{1}{8} \bigcirc \frac{7}{8}$

4. $\frac{4}{8} \bigcirc \frac{3}{8}$

5. $\frac{5}{8} \bigcirc \frac{7}{8}$

6. $\frac{8}{8} \bigcirc 1$

Use >, <, or = to make a true statement.

7. $\frac{3}{4} \bigcirc \frac{2}{4}$

8. $\frac{1}{3} \bigcirc \frac{3}{3}$

9. $\frac{5}{6} \bigcirc \frac{6}{6}$

10. $\frac{9}{10} \bigcirc \frac{8}{10}$

11.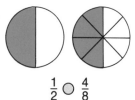

$\frac{1}{2} \bigcirc \frac{4}{8}$

12.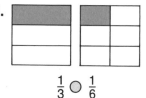

$\frac{1}{3} \bigcirc \frac{1}{6}$

13.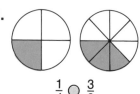

$\frac{1}{4} \bigcirc \frac{3}{8}$

Use a strip of paper marked in tenths. Complete the statement.

1. $\frac{1}{10}$ ○ $\frac{4}{10}$ 2. $\frac{2}{10}$ ○ $\frac{1}{10}$ 3. $\frac{10}{10}$ ○ $\frac{5}{10}$ 4. $\frac{8}{10}$ ○ $\frac{7}{10}$

Use >, <, or = to make a true statement.

5. $\frac{3}{3}$ ○ $\frac{2}{3}$ 6. $\frac{1}{4}$ ○ $\frac{4}{4}$ 7. $\frac{2}{6}$ ○ $\frac{5}{6}$ 8. $\frac{3}{8}$ ○ $\frac{5}{8}$

9. $\frac{4}{5}$ ○ $\frac{3}{5}$ 10. $\frac{4}{5}$ ○ $\frac{5}{5}$ 11. $\frac{1}{6}$ ○ $\frac{6}{6}$ 12. $\frac{7}{8}$ ○ $\frac{6}{8}$

13.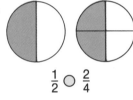

$\frac{1}{2}$ ○ $\frac{2}{4}$

14.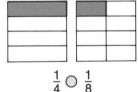

$\frac{1}{4}$ ○ $\frac{1}{8}$

15.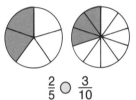

$\frac{2}{5}$ ○ $\frac{3}{10}$

Which is less?

16. $\frac{1}{2}$ of an hour or $\frac{1}{4}$ of an hour?

17. $\frac{1}{10}$ of a pie or $\frac{3}{10}$ of a pie?

Which is more?

18. $\frac{1}{2}$ of the class or $\frac{3}{4}$ of the class?

19. $\frac{1}{2}$ of a dollar or $\frac{1}{10}$ of a dollar?

A **programmer** writes instructions for a computer. The program tells the computer how to make the words, pictures, and sounds. The programs are stored on disks, tapes, or cartridges.

1. Load a program into the computer and use it.

Adding Fractions

Ron's scarf is blue, green, and red.

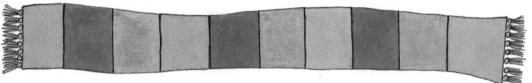

Four-tenths of the scarf is blue, three-tenths is green, and three-tenths is red. How much of the scarf is blue or green?

Add.

4 tenths + 3 tenths = 7 tenths

$$\frac{4}{10} + \frac{3}{10} = \frac{7}{10}$$

$\frac{7}{10}$ of the scarf is blue or green.

WORKING TOGETHER

Complete the addition statement.

1.

$$\frac{1}{3} + \frac{1}{3} = \frac{\square}{3}$$

2.

$$\frac{1}{2} + \frac{1}{2} = \frac{\square}{2}$$

3.

$$\frac{2}{5} + \frac{2}{5} = \frac{\square}{5}$$

4.

$$\frac{1}{8} + \frac{4}{8} = \frac{\square}{\square}$$

5.

$$\frac{3}{10} + \frac{6}{10} = \frac{\square}{\square}$$

6.

$$\frac{2}{6} + \frac{1}{6} = \frac{\square}{\square}$$

7. $\frac{1}{5} + \frac{3}{5} = \frac{\square}{\square}$

8. $\frac{2}{4} + \frac{1}{4} = \frac{\square}{\square}$

9. $\frac{1}{10} + \frac{1}{10} = \frac{\square}{\square}$

310

EXERCISES

Copy and complete the addition statement.

1.

$\frac{1}{5} + \frac{1}{5} = \frac{\square}{\square}$

2.

$\frac{1}{8} + \frac{2}{8} = \frac{\square}{\square}$

3.

$\frac{1}{3} + \frac{2}{3} = \frac{\square}{\square}$

4.

$\frac{1}{10} + \frac{2}{10} = \frac{\square}{\square}$

5.

$\frac{1}{6} + \frac{4}{6} = \frac{\square}{\square}$

6.

$\frac{20}{100} + \frac{25}{100} = \frac{\square}{\square}$

Add.

7. $\frac{1}{8} + \frac{1}{8}$

8. $\frac{2}{10} + \frac{5}{10}$

9. $\frac{1}{6} + \frac{1}{6}$

10. $\frac{5}{8} + \frac{2}{8}$

11. $\frac{9}{10} + \frac{1}{10}$

12. $\frac{4}{10} + \frac{5}{10}$

13. $\frac{1}{4} + \frac{1}{4}$

14. $\frac{3}{8} + \frac{2}{8}$

15. $\frac{6}{10} + \frac{1}{10}$

16. $\frac{3}{5} + \frac{2}{5}$

17. $\frac{3}{6} + \frac{1}{6}$

18. $\frac{5}{100} + \frac{6}{100}$

Solve.

19. George ran $\frac{5}{10}$ of the marathon, rested, and then ran $\frac{2}{10}$ more. How much of the distance did he run?

20. Five of the 11 players on the Grade 4 soccer team are girls. What fraction are girls?

 KEEPING SHARP

Multiply or divide.

1. 284
  $\times 6$

2. 418
  $\times 5$

3. 593
  $\times 8$

4. 627
  $\times 9$

5. $4\,\overline{)\,232}$

6. $7\,\overline{)\,378}$

7. $3\,\overline{)\,167}$

8. $8\,\overline{)\,280}$

311

Subtracting Fractions

Katie knitted $\frac{5}{8}$ of an afghan.

Her kitten unravelled $\frac{2}{8}$ of it.

How much of the afghan was left?

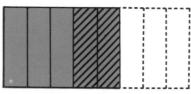

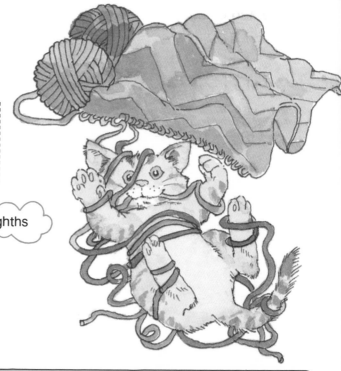

Subtract.

5 eighths − 2 eighths = 3 eighths

$$\frac{5}{8} - \frac{2}{8} = \frac{3}{8}$$

$\frac{3}{8}$ of the afghan was left.

WORKING TOGETHER

Complete the subtraction statement.

1.

$\frac{4}{6} - \frac{3}{6} = \frac{\square}{6}$

2.

$\frac{6}{8} - \frac{1}{8} = \frac{\square}{8}$

3.

$\frac{3}{3} - \frac{1}{3} = \frac{\square}{3}$

4.

$\frac{4}{8} - \frac{3}{8} = \frac{\square}{\square}$

5.

$\frac{9}{10} - \frac{2}{10} = \frac{\square}{\square}$

6.

$\frac{4}{5} - \frac{2}{5} = \frac{\square}{\square}$

7. $\frac{2}{2} - \frac{1}{2} = \frac{\square}{\square}$

8. $\frac{3}{5} - \frac{2}{5} = \frac{\square}{\square}$

9. $\frac{8}{10} - \frac{5}{10} = \frac{\square}{\square}$

312

Copy and complete the subtraction statement.

1.

$\frac{4}{5} - \frac{3}{5} = \frac{\square}{\square}$

2.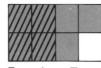

$\frac{7}{8} - \frac{4}{8} = \frac{\square}{\square}$

3.

$\frac{5}{6} - \frac{4}{6} = \frac{\square}{\square}$

4.

$\frac{8}{10} - \frac{1}{10} = \frac{\square}{\square}$

5.

$\frac{2}{3} - \frac{1}{3} = \frac{\square}{\square}$

6.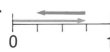

$\frac{3}{4} - \frac{2}{4} = \frac{\square}{\square}$

Subtract.

7. $\frac{9}{10} - \frac{6}{10}$

8. $\frac{6}{8} - \frac{5}{8}$

9. $\frac{5}{5} - \frac{1}{5}$

10. $\frac{4}{8} - \frac{1}{8}$

11. $\frac{5}{10} - \frac{2}{10}$

12. $\frac{3}{6} - \frac{2}{6}$

13. $\frac{4}{4} - \frac{1}{4}$

14. $\frac{7}{10} - \frac{6}{10}$

15. $\frac{3}{8} - \frac{2}{8}$

Solve.

16. Kurt had a can of paint. One day it was $\frac{7}{10}$ full. The next day it was $\frac{4}{10}$ full. How much did he use?

17. Sarah jogged $\frac{5}{8}$ of the distance to school. She walked the rest of the way. What fraction of the distance did she walk?

Try This

Give the mixed number.

1. If $\square$ is 1, then ⬜▷ is $\square$.

2. If ⬡ is 1, then  is $\square$.

3. If ⊞ is 1, then is $\square$.

4. If ⬧ is 1, then is $\square$.

313

Copy and complete.

1.

$\frac{1}{4} = \frac{\square}{100} = \square . \square$

2.

$\frac{3}{5} = \frac{\square}{10} = \square . \square$

3.

$\frac{1}{2} = \frac{\square}{10} = \square . \square$

Write the decimal.

4. $\frac{8}{10}$

5. $\frac{3}{4}$

6. $\frac{6}{100}$

7. $\frac{49}{100}$

Use >, <, or = to make a true statement.

8. $\frac{2}{3} \bigcirc \frac{1}{3}$

9. $\frac{1}{4} \bigcirc \frac{3}{4}$

10. $\frac{7}{8} \bigcirc \frac{5}{8}$

11. $\frac{4}{5} \bigcirc \frac{2}{5}$

12.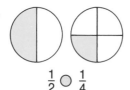

$\frac{1}{2} \bigcirc \frac{1}{4}$

13.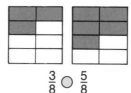

$\frac{3}{8} \bigcirc \frac{5}{8}$

14.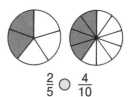

$\frac{2}{5} \bigcirc \frac{4}{10}$

Add or subtract.

15. $\frac{1}{10} + \frac{2}{10}$

16. $\frac{6}{10} - \frac{3}{10}$

17. $\frac{2}{8} + \frac{5}{8}$

18. $\frac{1}{4} + \frac{2}{4}$

19. $\frac{7}{8} - \frac{6}{8}$

20. $\frac{3}{5} + \frac{1}{5}$

21. $\frac{4}{6} + \frac{1}{6}$

22. $\frac{2}{3} - \frac{1}{3}$

23. $\frac{1}{3} + \frac{1}{3}$

24. $\frac{3}{5} - \frac{1}{5}$

25. $\frac{3}{6} - \frac{2}{6}$

26. $\frac{4}{4} - \frac{3}{4}$

Solve.

27. Tim read $\frac{3}{10}$ of his book on Monday and $\frac{4}{10}$ on Tuesday. How much did he read?

28. A box of cat food was $\frac{3}{4}$ full. A week later it was $\frac{1}{4}$ full. How much of the box was used that week?

Computers in the Future

A computer cannot think. But it can do almost anything if people can teach it how.

Today, computers are used in space exploration.

- to train astronauts in giant space simulators

- to operate robots such as the Canadarm

- to navigate spacecraft and permit docking between two objects

- to control gas and power levels in a space suit and jet packs

Think about movies and books that have machines with computers in them.

1. Do you think these computerized machines will ever really exist? Explain.

2. Write a paragraph about a computer that you would like to see in the future.

More Than One Combination

Carla has a pair of brown pants and a pair of navy pants. She has a white sweater, a yellow one, and a red one. How many different outfits can she wear?

Think. One sweater and one pair of pants make an outfit.

Plan and do. Carla makes a chart to show all the combinations.

Sweater	Pants
white	brown
white	navy
yellow	brown
yellow	navy
red	brown
red	navy

Look back. Carla has a choice of 6 outfits.
What if Carla also had a pair of black pants?
How many combinations could she make?

WORKING TOGETHER

Use the coins shown here. ➡
What amounts up to 32¢ could you spend without receiving any change?

1. Cross out all the amounts you could not spend.

2. Record how you could spend the possible amounts.

1¢ = 1¢	7¢ = 5¢ + 1¢ + 1¢	13¢
2¢ = 1¢ + 1¢	8¢	14¢
3̶¢̶	9¢	15¢
4̶¢̶	10¢	16¢
5¢ = 5¢	11¢	17¢
6¢ = 5¢ + 1¢	12¢	18¢

PROBLEMS

Use a chart to show some combinations.

1. Brent had 4 pairs of sweat pants and 3 T-shirts in his suitcase. How many different outfits could he wear?

2. Admission to a puppet show is 20¢. In how many ways can you pay the admission?

Pennies	Nickels	Dimes	Amount
20			

3. How many 3-digit numbers can you make using the digits 1, 3, and 4? Digits cannot be used more than once in any one number. How many can you make if digits can be used more than once?

4. What amounts can you spend without getting any change back?

Find as many solutions as possible. Draw pictures to help you.

5. André, Barb, and Clint are running a race. How many ways can they finish first, second, and third?

6. A glass of lemonade costs 6¢ and cookies cost 4¢ each. What did Franz buy if he spent 22¢?

7. A carpenter is making benches and 3-legged stools. She has 31 legs that can be screwed into seats. How many stools and benches can she make?

8. How can the worm crawl to the opposite corner of the cube (from A to G)? It travels along 3 edges only.

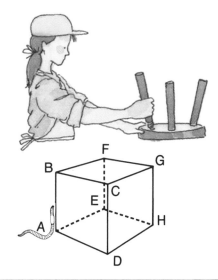

Problem Solving Review

Solve.

1. The counter is 120 cm from the floor. The cupboard is 35 cm above the counter. The cupboard is 75 cm high. What is the distance from the floor to the top of the cupboard?

2. How tall is Susette? She is shorter than her father. Her father is 151 cm tall. The difference in height between Susette and her father is 30 cm.

3. How far does the winning player run? Players in the race must run 8 m to the goal. Then they balance an egg on a spoon and bring it back to a bowl at the starting line. The first player to bring back 3 eggs wins.

4. Bonnie's uncle loaded 15 bags of dog food in his station wagon. Each bag was 10 kg. His own mass is 100 kg. Did he exceed the 600 kg load limit for the station wagon?

5. Nigel has 7 more hockey cards than Rita. Rita has 4 more hockey cards than Vince. Vince has 10 hockey cards. How many cards does Nigel have?

6. Some children were at a party. I counted 20 shoes and 5 hats. How many children did not have hats? Holly's answer was 15 children. Is this reasonable? Explain.

7. Jean bought 8 L of gasoline to fill the tank in her truck. The tank holds 40 L of gasoline. How many litres were in the tank before she filled up?

8. Some months have 31 days and some months have 30 days. How many months have 28 days?

9. I have 28¢ in my pocket. How many different combinations of coins could I have?

Chapter Checkup

Write the decimal.

1.
2.
3.

4. 5 hundredths   5. 71 hundredths   6. 6 ones 7 hundredths

7. 3 ones 1 tenth 4 hundredths   8. 2 tenths 8 hundredths

9. $\frac{7}{10}$ 10. $\frac{11}{100}$ 11. $\frac{1}{4}$ 12. $\frac{2}{5}$

Use >, <, or = to complete the statement.

13. $\frac{5}{6}$ ◯ $\frac{1}{6}$ 14. $\frac{2}{5}$ ◯ $\frac{3}{5}$ 15. $\frac{6}{8}$ ◯ $\frac{7}{8}$ 16. $\frac{9}{10}$ ◯ $\frac{1}{10}$

17. 0.34 ◯ 0.32   18. 0.54 ◯ 0.45   19. 0.07 ◯ 0.2

20. 0.18 ◯ 0.21   21. 0.9 ◯ 0.09   22. 0.8 ◯ 0.80

23. 3.14 ◯ 2.31   24. 8.02 ◯ 0.94   25. 6.3 ◯ 8.03

Add or subtract.

26.   5.47
    − 3.16

27.   2.41
    + 6.27

28.   6.18
    + 1.33

29.   7.82
    − 2.57

30.   12.96
    + 50.34

31.   58.15
    − 12.78

32.   47.65
    + 21.68

33.   9.04
    − 6.80

34. $\frac{2}{5} + \frac{2}{5}$ 35. $\frac{3}{10} + \frac{4}{10}$ 36. $\frac{1}{4} + \frac{2}{4}$ 37. $\frac{6}{8} + \frac{1}{8}$

38. $\frac{5}{6} - \frac{4}{6}$ 39. $\frac{9}{10} - \frac{6}{10}$ 40. $\frac{4}{5} - \frac{3}{5}$ 41. $\frac{2}{3} - \frac{1}{3}$

Cumulative Checkup

Multiply or divide.

1. 453×7 **2.** 800×6 **3.** $88 \div 4$ **4.** $48 \div 2$

5. 5×700 **6.** $75 \div 3$ **7.** 19×68 **8.** $368 \div 4$

9. $95 \div 7$ **10.** 92×74 **11.** $369 \div 9$ **12.** 7×102

Match the shape with the word.

13. 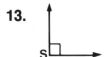 **14.**   **15.**

| line of symmetry |
| angle |
| line |
| hexagon |
| line segment |
| quadrilateral |
| octagon |
| right angle |
| pentagon |

16.   **17.**   **18.**

19.   **20.**   **21.**

Is the blue shape the flip image of the red shape?

22.  **23.**

Is the blue shape the slide image of the red shape?

24.  **25.**

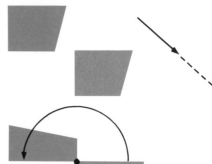

Is the blue shape the turn image of the red shape?

26.  **27.**

Extra Practice

Set 1 (Use after page 7.)

Add.

1. 6
   + 3

2. 2
   + 8

3. 0
   + 7

4. 7
   + 2

5. 4
   + 4

6. 5
   + 4

7. 4
   + 6

8. 3
   + 4

9. 5
   + 5

10. 7
    + 3

11. 9
    + 1

12. 2
    + 6

13. 7 + 1
14. 2 + 5
15. 3 + 2
16. 9 + 0
17. 5 + 3

Set 2 (Use after page 7.)

Add.

1. 9
   + 7

2. 8
   + 6

3. 9
   + 7

4. 8
   + 5

5. 4
   + 9

6. 4
   + 7

7. 6
   + 7

8. 7
   + 8

9. 8
   + 9

10. 7
    + 7

11. 9
    + 6

12. 2
    + 9

13. 8 + 8
14. 9 + 3
15. 9 + 5
16. 8 + 5
17. 6 + 6

18. 7 + 5
19. 4 + 8
20. 5 + 7
21. 5 + 6
22. 7 + 6

Set 3 (Use after page 8.)

Add.

1. 9
   + 7

2. 19
   + 7

3. 27
   + 7

4. 37
   + 7

5. 47
   + 7

6. 57
   + 7

7. 6
   + 5

8. 16
   + 5

9. 26
   + 5

10. 36
    + 5

11. 46
    + 5

12. 56
    + 5

13. 7
    + 4

14. 17
    + 4

15. 27
    + 4

16. 37
    + 4

17. 47
    + 4

18. 57
    + 4

Set 4   (Use after page 11.)

Subtract.

1. 10 −3	**2.** 7 −5	**3.** 8 −4	**4.** 9 −2	**5.** 7 −3	**6.** 6 −5

7. 9 −5	**8.** 10 −8	**9.** 8 −3	**10.** 7 −0	**11.** 5 −4	**12.** 4 −4

13. 10 − 6   **14.** 9 − 6   **15.** 8 − 2   **16.** 6 − 2   **17.** 10 − 1

18. 6 − 4   **19.** 5 − 0   **20.** 7 − 6   **21.** 8 − 1   **22.** 10 − 5

Set 5   (Use after page 11.)

Subtract.

1. 16 −9	**2.** 14 −6	**3.** 12 −4	**4.** 17 −8	**5.** 14 −5	**6.** 18 −9

7. 11 −8	**8.** 17 −9	**9.** 13 −5	**10.** 12 −9	**11.** 15 −8	**12.** 16 −7

13. 14 − 9   **14.** 12 − 7   **15.** 13 − 6   **16.** 11 − 2   **17.** 12 − 8

18. 11 − 3   **19.** 13 − 4   **20.** 12 − 5   **21.** 15 − 9   **22.** 12 − 6

Set 6   (Use after page 11.)

Subtract.

1. 17 −8	**2.** 27 −8	**3.** 37 −8	**4.** 47 −8	**5.** 57 −8	**6.** 67 −8

7. 12 −4	**8.** 22 −4	**9.** 32 −4	**10.** 42 −4	**11.** 52 −4	**12.** 62 −4

13. 13 −8	**14.** 23 −8	**15.** 33 −8	**16.** 43 −8	**17.** 53 −8	**18.** 63 −8

Set 7 (Use after page 11.)

Add or subtract.

1. 8
  +7

2. 16
  −8

3. 13
  −8

4. 9
  +9

5. 9
  +4

6. 7
  +9

7. 15
  −6

8. 10
  −8

9. 7
  +5

10. 4
  −0

11. 15
  −8

12. 9
  −2

13. 8 + 5

14. 16 − 8

15. 11 − 3

16. 15 − 7

17. 3 + 5

18. 7 + 1

19. 14 − 6

20. 13 − 4

21. 8 + 0

22. 9 − 8

Set 8 (Use after page 13.)

Find the missing number.

1. $6 + \square = 15$

2. $12 - \square = 6$

3. $14 - \square = 7$

4. $\square + 7 = 14$

5. $\square + 4 = 13$

6. $12 - \square = 8$

7. $6 + \square = 13$

8. $14 - \square = 9$

9. $3 + \square = 12$

10. $15 - \square = 7$

11. $9 + \square = 18$

12. $\square + 9 = 12$

13. $18 - \square = 9$

14. $\square + 2 = 11$

15. $16 - \square = 7$

Set 9 (Use after page 19.)

Write the standard form.

1. 5 hundreds 6 tens 8 ones

2. 4 thousands 7 hundreds 9 ones

3. 8 thousands 3 hundreds

4. 8000 + 900 + 2

5. 9000 + 60 + 4

6. 4000 + 700 + 60 + 5

7. four thousand seven hundred twenty-nine

8. one thousand six hundred forty

9. six thousand twelve

10. two thousand seven

Set 10 (Use after page 21.)

Use >, <, or = to make a true statement.

1. 6349 ○ 6234

2. 536 ○ 563

3. 7280 ○ 7802

4. 2600 ○ 2000 + 60

5. 762 ○ 722

6. 9010 ○ 9000 + 1

7. 3792 ○ 3927

8. 6003 ○ 6000 + 30

9. 747 ○ 856

10. 4900 ○ 5000

11. 5076 ○ 5067

12. 1736 ○ 1667

13. 8297 ○ 8299

14. 325 ○ 265

15. 479 ○ 740

Set 11 (Use after page 25.)

Copy and complete.

		Round to the nearest		
		ten	hundred	thousand
1.	4628			
2.	5050			
3.	2285			
4.	7351			
5.	6149			

Set 12 (Use after page 27.)

Write the standard form.

1. 9 ten thousands 8 thousands 4 hundreds 5 tens 6 ones

2. 8 hundred thousands 2 ten thousands 9 thousands 5 hundreds 8 tens

3. 5 ten thousands 5 thousands 2 tens 2 ones

4. 4 hundred thousands 6 thousands 8 hundreds 7 ones

5. 20 000 + 9000 + 200 + 80

6. 6000 + 700 + 40 + 7

7. 800 000 + 70 000 + 8000 + 900

8. 90 000 + 2000 + 80 + 6

9. three hundred forty thousand one hundred fifteen

10. eighteen thousand two hundred ten

11. fifty thousand two hundred eighty

Set 13 (Use after page 41.)

Add.

1. 43 + 48	2. 216 + 66	3. 46 + 37	4. $3.25 + 3.65	5. 28 + 34
6. 613 + 427	7. 18 + 77	8. 109 + 23	9. 37 + 14	10. 18 + 342

11. 75 + 39   12. 526 + 48   13. $2.09 + $0.56   14. 86 + 719

Set 14 (Use after page 43.)

Add.

1. 486 + 142	2. 299 + 610	3. 495 + 1262	4. 627 + 3472	5. $85.40 + 2.96

6. 782 + 316   7. $7.91 + $1.94   8. 5376 + 1822

9. 4067 + 2091   10. $39.50 + $7.08   11. 576 + 6621

Set 15 (Use after page 45.)

Add.

1. $4.93 + 4.29	2. 468 + 267	3. 109 + 392	4. 67 + 647	5. 355 + 355
6. 909 + 98	7. 138 + 684	8. $0.99 + 3.85	9. 629 + 286	10. 284 + 326

11. $7.32 + $1.99   12. 1075 + 647   13. $1.36 + $59.57

Set 16   (Use after page 51.)

Find the sum.

1. 284
   137
   + 28

2. 436
   292
   + 187

3. 97
   409
   + 238

4. 89
   74
   18
   + 63

5. 80
   75
   468
   + 287

6. 57 + 395 + 216

7. 457 + 31 + 179

8. 89 + 242 + 63 + 15

Set 17   (Use after page 53.)

Add.

1. 1874
   + 7329

2. 369
   + 2978

3. 4075
   + 3955

4. 7692
   + 528

5. $47.97
   + 3.23

6. $75.99
   + 15.62

7. 478
   + 936

8. 2649
   + 1782

9. 576
   + 759

10. 2079
    + 5942

11. 843 + 268

12. $43.67 + $9.64

13. 3678 + 5555

Set 18   (Use after page 65.)

Subtract.

1. 58
   − 29

2. 147
   − 28

3. 936
   − 818

4. $4.23
   − 2.05

5. 362
   − 244

6. $9.47
   − 7.19

7. 64
   − 28

8. 235
   − 18

9. 470
   − 213

10. 248
    − 119

11. 54 − 17

12. 284 − 36

13. 457 − 139

14. 762 − 57

Set 19   (Use after page 67.)

Subtract.

1. 8397   2. 4628   3. $27.46   4.   675   5. $76.95
   − 4486   − 384   − 9.23   − 380   − 68.43

6. 2044 − 720   7. 2495 − 974   8. 8435 − 6831   9. $72.43 − $67.11

10. 785 − 92   11. 1467 − 932   12. 637 − 428   13. 2038 − 516

Set 20   (Use after page 69.)

Subtract.

1. 226   2.   546   3. $75.64   4. 7532   5. 7082
   − 38   − 288   − 47.92   − 4389   − 690

6. $46.37   7. 2384   8. 7257   9. 2975   10.   3100
   − 3.98   − 1196   − 384   − 980   − 2340

11. 8462 − 7289   12. 3728 − 847   13. 1865 − 873   14. $43.72 − $27.90

Set 21   (Use after page 73.)

Subtract.

1. 2592   2. $42.23   3. 3414   4. 9431   5. 6867
   − 1694   − 3.47   − 2735   − 5563   − 888

6. 7123   7. 4675   8. 5335   9. $26.47   10. $62.94
   − 4235   − 2797   − 3468   − 7.99   − 14.96

11. 5160 − 3981   12. $17.24 − $9.99   13. 7543 − 3795   14. 4784 − 3996

Set 22 (Use after page 75.)

Subtract.

1. 4302
    − 1149

2. 6004
    − 2862

3. 2065
    − 1784

4. $80.00
    − 45.26

5. 3001
    − 1622

6. 5064
    − 4195

7. 9000
    − 7625

8. $32.03
    − 21.67

9. 3070
    − 1798

10. 2000
    − 962

11. $50.00 − $43.27

12. 9060 − 182

13. 2404 − 218

Set 23 (Use after page 89.)

Match the angle with its description.

1.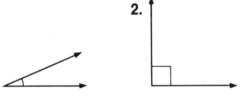

2.

3.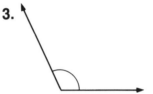

4.

| smaller than a right angle | a right angle | larger than a right angle |

Set 24 (Use after page 93.)

Name the polygon or solid.

1.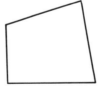

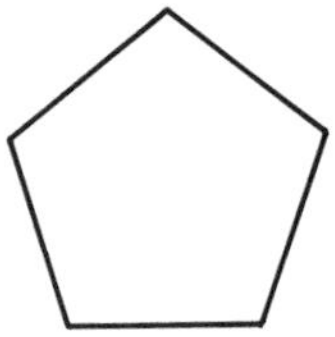

2.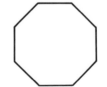

3.

4.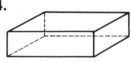

5.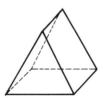

6.

7.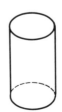

8.

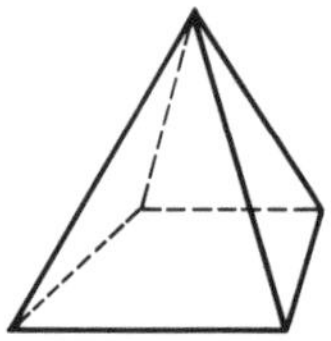

328

Set 25   (Use after page 105.)

Does the picture suggest a slide, a flip, or a turn?

1.

2.

3.

4.

5.

6.

Set 26   (Use after page 123.)

Multiply.

1. 6×0 2. 9×5 3. 7×4 4. 8×0 5. 8×3

6. 7×6 7. 8×6 8. 6×3 9. 7×8 10. 9×9

11. $\begin{array}{r} 9 \\ \times 0 \\ \hline \end{array}$ 12. $\begin{array}{r} 6 \\ \times 5 \\ \hline \end{array}$ 13. $\begin{array}{r} 7 \\ \times 1 \\ \hline \end{array}$ 14. $\begin{array}{r} 7 \\ \times 9 \\ \hline \end{array}$ 15. $\begin{array}{r} 8 \\ \times 8 \\ \hline \end{array}$

16. $\begin{array}{r} 7 \\ \times 7 \\ \hline \end{array}$ 17. $\begin{array}{r} 8 \\ \times 9 \\ \hline \end{array}$ 18. $\begin{array}{r} 7 \\ \times 5 \\ \hline \end{array}$ 19. $\begin{array}{r} 6 \\ \times 6 \\ \hline \end{array}$ 20. $\begin{array}{r} 6 \\ \times 9 \\ \hline \end{array}$

Set 27   (Use after page 127.)

Find the product.

1. $\begin{array}{r} 10 \\ \times 5 \\ \hline \end{array}$ 2. $\begin{array}{r} 100 \\ \times 7 \\ \hline \end{array}$ 3. $\begin{array}{r} 10 \\ \times 9 \\ \hline \end{array}$ 4. $\begin{array}{r} 10 \\ \times 7 \\ \hline \end{array}$ 5. $\begin{array}{r} 100 \\ \times 4 \\ \hline \end{array}$

6. $\begin{array}{r} 100 \\ \times 3 \\ \hline \end{array}$ 7. $\begin{array}{r} 10 \\ \times 4 \\ \hline \end{array}$ 8. $\begin{array}{r} 10 \\ \times 6 \\ \hline \end{array}$ 9. $\begin{array}{r} 100 \\ \times 6 \\ \hline \end{array}$ 10. $\begin{array}{r} 10 \\ \times 8 \\ \hline \end{array}$

11. 10×4 12. 100×8 13. 9×100 14. 2×10

Set 28   (Use after page 131.)

Multiply.

1. 30
   ×5

2. 67
   ×2

3. 85
   ×7

4. 39
   ×4

5. 50
   ×8

6. 28
   ×6

7. 40
   ×4

8. 20
   ×9

9. 41
   ×5

10. 63
    ×6

11. 7 × 18

12. 23 × 6

13. 5 × 95

14. 80 × 3

15. 38 × 8

16. 74 × 3

17. 7 × 24

18. 9 × 59

Set 29   (Use after page 133.)

Multiply.

1. 431
   ×6

2. 208
   ×2

3. 163
   ×7

4. 560
   ×8

5. 242
   ×3

6. 243
   ×8

7. 119
   ×4

8. 618
   ×7

9. 802
   ×4

10. 319
    ×3

11. 4 × 907

12. 425 × 5

13. 6 × 516

14. 527 × 2

15. 618 × 9

16. 3 × 805

17. 364 × 4

18. 9 × 935

Set 30   (Use after page 135.)

Find the product.

1. 9 × 2 × 6

2. 4 × 3 × 8

3. 8 × 2 × 6 × 3

4. 6 × 2 × 7

5. 5 × 4 × 3

6. 3 × 0 × 7

7. 4 × 6 × 2 × 9

8. 3 × 8 × 9

9. 7 × 6 × 9

10. 7 × 5 × 8

11. 2 × 5 × 2 × 5

12. 8 × 4 × 6

Set 31 (Use after page 145.)

Divide.

1. $4\overline{)36}$ 2. $5\overline{)45}$ 3. $2\overline{)18}$ 4. $3\overline{)21}$ 5. $4\overline{)20}$

6. $2\overline{)16}$ 7. $3\overline{)24}$ 8. $4\overline{)28}$ 9. $3\overline{)27}$ 10. $5\overline{)15}$

11. $32 \div 4$ 12. $16 \div 4$ 13. $12 \div 2$ 14. $30 \div 5$ 15. $18 \div 3$

Set 32 (Use after page 147.)

Find the missing factor.

1. $\square \times 6 = 54$ 2. $9 \times \square = 36$ 3. $6 \times \square = 30$ 4. $\square \times 80 = 320$

5. $4 \times \square = 36$ 6. $\square \times 70 = 490$ 7. $\square \times 8 = 64$ 8. $9 \times \square = 27$

9. $\begin{array}{r} \square \\ \times 9 \\ \hline 63 \end{array}$ 10. $\begin{array}{r} 5 \\ \times \square \\ \hline 45 \end{array}$ 11. $\begin{array}{r} 6 \\ \times \square \\ \hline 42 \end{array}$ 12. $\begin{array}{r} \square \\ \times 9 \\ \hline 90 \end{array}$ 13. $\begin{array}{r} \square \\ \times 3 \\ \hline 120 \end{array}$

Set 33 (Use after page 151.)

Write the family of facts for the array.

1. O O O O O 2. ▲ ▲ ▲ ▲ ▲ 3. □ □ □ 4. ★ ★
   O O O O O   ▲ ▲ ▲ ▲ ▲   □ □ □   ★ ★
   O O O O O   ▲ ▲ ▲ ▲ ▲   □ □ □   ★ ★
   O O O O O   ▲ ▲ ▲ ▲ ▲   □ □ □   ★ ★
                 ▲ ▲ ▲ ▲ ▲   □ □ □   ★ ★
                 ▲ ▲ ▲ ▲ ▲   □ □ □   ★ ★
                                          ★ ★
                                          ★ ★

Set 34 (Use after page 155.)

Divide.

1. $8\overline{)72}$ 2. $6\overline{)54}$ 3. $7\overline{)28}$ 4. $4\overline{)32}$ 5. $6\overline{)42}$

6. $9\overline{)63}$ 7. $3\overline{)18}$ 8. $6\overline{)12}$ 9. $7\overline{)49}$ 10. $8\overline{)56}$

11. $24 \div 6$ 12. $40 \div 8$ 13. $42 \div 7$ 14. $12 \div 3$

15. $36 \div 6$ 16. $18 \div 9$ 17. $45 \div 9$ 18. $24 \div 8$

Set 35 (Use after page 157.)

Divide.

1. $9\overline{)0}$ 2. $1\overline{)5}$ 3. $1\overline{)9}$ 4. $3\overline{)0}$ 5. $4\overline{)0}$

6. $1\overline{)8}$ 7. $2\overline{)0}$ 8. $1\overline{)0}$ 9. $1\overline{)7}$ 10. $1\overline{)2}$

11. $4 \div 1$ 12. $0 \div 6$ 13. $6 \div 1$ 14. $0 \div 8$ 15. $0 \div 5$

Set 36 (Use after page 159.)

Divide.

1. $8\overline{)27}$ 2. $3\overline{)17}$ 3. $2\overline{)15}$ 4. $6\overline{)38}$ 5. $4\overline{)22}$

6. $4\overline{)17}$ 7. $5\overline{)37}$ 8. $7\overline{)44}$ 9. $3\overline{)23}$ 10. $9\overline{)59}$

11. $8\overline{)66}$ 12. $4\overline{)31}$ 13. $6\overline{)20}$ 14. $5\overline{)19}$ 15. $3\overline{)26}$

16. $41 \div 6$ 17. $47 \div 5$ 18. $17 \div 2$ 19. $35 \div 4$ 20. $86 \div 9$

Set 37 (Use after page 171.)

Which unit, centimetre, metre, or kilometre, is best for measuring this?

1. height of a door

2. distance from Regina to Winnipeg

3. length of a pencil

4. thickness of a hamburger

5. length of a Terry Fox Day run

6. length of a hall

Set 38 (Use after page 173.)

Find the perimeter.

1.
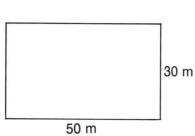

2.
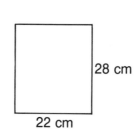

3.
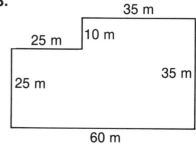

332

Set 39 (Use after page 177.)

Find the area.

1.
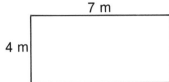
60 cm
30 cm

2.

7 m
4 m
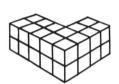

3.
36 cm
30 cm
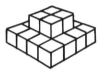

Set 40 (Use after page 181.)

Build the shape with centimetre cubes. Find the volume.

1.

2.

3.

Set 41 (Use after page 189.)

Copy and complete.

1. 6 h = ☐ min

2. 5 d = ☐ h

3. 7 min = ☐ s

4. 4 years = ☐ months

5. 10 weeks = ☐ d

6. 2 years = ☐ weeks

7. 5 min 6 s = ☐ s

8. 7 weeks 3 d = ☐ d

9. 2 h 13 min = ☐ min

Set 42 (Use after page 199.)

What fraction of the whole is colored?

1.

2.

3.

4.
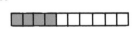

5.

6.

7.

8.

333

Set 43 (Use after page 201.)

What fraction of the set is colored?

1.

2.

3.

4.

Set 44 (Use after page 203.)

How much is colored?

1.

2.

3.

Set 45 (Use after page 205.)

Copy and complete the fractions.

1.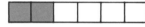

$\frac{1}{3} = \frac{\square}{6}$

2.

$\frac{2}{4} = \frac{4}{\square}$

3.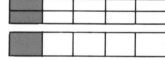

$\frac{1}{5} = \frac{\square}{10}$

4.

$\frac{1}{2} = \frac{5}{\square}$

5.

$\frac{2}{\square} = \frac{4}{\square}$

6.

$\frac{4}{\square} = \frac{8}{\square}$

Set 46 (Use after page 211.)

How much is colored? Write the decimal.

1.

2.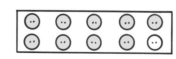

3.

4.

5.

6.

Set 47 (Use after page 213.)

Use >, <, or = to make a true statement.

1.
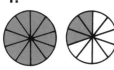

2.

3.

1.3 ○ 0.7   0.5 ○ 0.2   0.9 ○ 1.1

4. 3.0 ○ 3   **5.** 6.7 ○ 6.9   **6.** 7.2 ○ 6.8   **7.** 4.5 ○ 4.2

8. 0.9 ○ 9   **9.** 5.6 ○ 6.5   **10.** 1.0 ○ 1   **11.** 2.9 ○ 3.1

Set 48 (Use after page 215.)

Add.

1. 6.3
      + 4.2

2. 27.1
      + 18.0

3. 16.5
      + 29.3

4. 0.4
      + 0.9

5. 304.6
      + 25.7

6. 193.2
      + 80.6

7. 431.9
      + 4.7

8. 85.6
      + 30.2

9. 1.1
      + 0.9

10. 937.8
      + 25.5

11. 1.7 + 3.4   **12.** 18.6 + 9.0   **13.** 304.7 + 82.3   **14.** 16.2 + 18.9

Set 49 (Use after page 217.)

Subtract.

1. 6.7
      − 4.3

2. 15.2
      − 2.7

3. 43.2
      − 11.6

4. 74.7
      − 25.2

5. 87.8
      − 29.6

6. 9.1
      − 8.9

7. 15.3
      − 8.6

8. 89.0
      − 76.9

9. 27.9
      − 25.8

10. 493.6
      − 85.9

11. 54.7 − 6.8   **12.** 19.5 − 18.8   **13.** 15.0 − 12.7   **14.** 705.3 − 130.4

15. 34.2 − 34.1   **16.** 43.6 − 2.5   **17.** 91.4 − 8.9   **18.** 732.4 − 18.0

Set 50 (Use after page 227.)

Multiply.

1. 81 ×3	**2.** 39 ×7	**3.** 46 ×5	**4.** 38 ×9	**5.** 89 ×6	**6.** 57 ×3
7. 34 ×6	**8.** 25 ×7	**9.** 75 ×4	**10.** 71 ×6	**11.** 69 ×8	**12.** 80 ×8

Set 51 (Use after page 229.)

Multiply.

1. 378 ×4	**2.** 257 ×3	**3.** 908 ×6	**4.** 340 ×5	**5.** 697 ×5
6. 263 ×8	**7.** 374 ×9	**8.** 250 ×4	**9.** 636 ×5	**10.** 761 ×8

11. 563 × 5 **12.** 281 × 8 **13.** 7 × 689 **14.** 4 × 426

Set 52 (Use after page 231.)

Multiply.

1. $4.28 ×6	**2.** $7.81 ×9	**3.** $0.53 ×4	**4.** $3.80 ×7	**5.** 37¢ ×5
6. $1.73 ×3	**7.** $7.92 ×5	**8.** $6.23 ×7	**9.** 56¢ ×2	**10.** $8.44 ×8

Set 53 (Use after page 237.)

Find the product.

1. 67 ×40	**2.** 83 ×60	**3.** 32 ×70	**4.** 50 ×50	**5.** 78 ×80	**6.** 36 ×10

7. 30 × 60 **8.** 50 × 37 **9.** 80 × 82 **10.** 20 × 51 **11.** 90 × 30

12. 10 × 58 **13.** 60 × 24 **14.** 40 × 19 **15.** 70 × 64 **16.** 40 × 27

Set 54 (Use after page 239.)

Multiply.

1. 48 ×62	**2.** 37 ×23	**3.** 18 ×44	**4.** 58 ×17	**5.** 86 ×33	**6.** 29 ×63
7. 30 ×29	**8.** 62 ×19	**9.** 76 ×67	**10.** 87 ×54	**11.** 39 ×45	**12.** 50 ×72

13. 67 × 32   **14.** 19 × 28   **15.** 31 × 79   **16.** 54 × 32   **17.** 23 × 95

Set 55 (Use after page 249.)

Divide.

1. 3)69   **2.** 6)60   **3.** 4)84   **4.** 3)93   **5.** 1)63

6. 9)99   **7.** 2)86   **8.** 4)48   **9.** 5)55   **10.** 2)64

11. 62 ÷ 2   **12.** 40 ÷ 4   **13.** 97 ÷ 1   **14.** 39 ÷ 3   **15.** 93 ÷ 3

Set 56 (Use after page 251.)

Divide.

1. 5)75   **2.** 2)38   **3.** 4)64   **4.** 3)51   **5.** 7)91

6. 8)96   **7.** 4)72   **8.** 5)60   **9.** 6)96   **10.** 7)84

11. 42 ÷ 3   **12.** 96 ÷ 4   **13.** 78 ÷ 6   **14.** 76 ÷ 2   **15.** 98 ÷ 7

Set 57 (Use after page 253.)

Divide.

1. 3)59   **2.** 7)80   **3.** 5)62   **4.** 4)51   **5.** 3)70

6. 4)63   **7.** 6)73   **8.** 8)98   **9.** 6)97   **10.** 5)79

11. 95 ÷ 7   **12.** 43 ÷ 3   **13.** 83 ÷ 5   **14.** 81 ÷ 6   **15.** 90 ÷ 8

16. 91 ÷ 6   **17.** 58 ÷ 4   **18.** 95 ÷ 4   **19.** 49 ÷ 3   **20.** 79 ÷ 2

Set 58 (Use after page 259.)

Divide.

1. $3 \overline{)159}$ 2. $7 \overline{)217}$ 3. $5 \overline{)155}$ 4. $2 \overline{)128}$ 5. $6 \overline{)186}$

6. $8 \overline{)328}$ 7. $6 \overline{)240}$ 8. $4 \overline{)208}$ 9. $3 \overline{)183}$ 10. $7 \overline{)140}$

11. $250 \div 5$ 12. $160 \div 4$ 13. $400 \div 8$ 14. $328 \div 4$

15. $279 \div 9$ 16. $144 \div 2$ 17. $164 \div 2$ 18. $219 \div 3$

Set 59 (Use after page 277.)

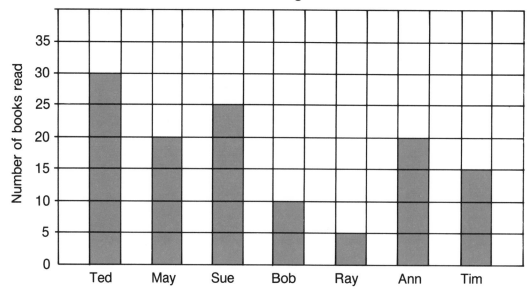

Books Read during the Readathon

1. Who read the most books during the Readathon?

2. How many books did Sue read?

3. Which 2 children read the same number of books?

4. Who read the least number of books? How many was that?

5. How many more books did Ann read than Tim?

6. How many books did Ted and Sue read together?

Set 60 (Use after page 281.)

Draw a horizontal bar graph to show the information in the tally sheet.

1.

Sport	Tally
Soccer	JHT JHT JHT III
Basketball	JHT II
Football	JHT IIII
Baseball	JHT JHT II

2.

Fruit Juice	Tally
Orange	JHT JHT
Apple	JHT JHT JHT
Grape	JHT JHT JHT JHT
Pineapple	JHT

Set 61 (Use after page 285.)

Write the letter at this position.

1. (3,1)   **2.** (1,5)   **3.** (2,1)

4. (5,3)   **5.** (3,6)   **6.** (2,3)

7. (5,5)   **8.** (6,2)   **9.** (1,2)

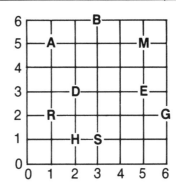

Set 62 (Use after page 297.)

Use >, <, or = to make a true statement.

1.

0.12 ◯ 0.02

2.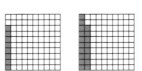

0.08 ◯ 0.18

3.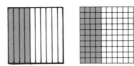

0.4 ◯ 0.40

4. 0.50 ◯ 0.5   **5.** 0.75 ◯ 0.56   **6.** 0.37 ◯ 0.39

Set 63 (Use after page 301.)

Add.

1. 6.29
    + 4.06

2. 3.15
    + 2.59

3. 2.48
    + 0.36

4. 0.94
    + 0.88

5. $36.23
    + 4.98

6. 5.62 + 4.08 + 3.70   **7.** 12.17 + 13.42 + 9.20   **8.** 6.04 + 9.50 + 8.30

Set 64 (Use after page 303.)

Subtract.

1. 8.34
   − 2.68

2. 7.59
   − 5.46

3. 13.02
   − 4.19

4. $86.18
   − 75.67

5. 43.66
   − 28.78

6. 86.03 − 54.16   **7.** 8.21 − 6.19   **8.** 58.34 − 18.71   **9.** 42.56 − 29.79

Set 65 (Use after page 309.)

Use >, <, or = to make a true statement.

1. $\frac{3}{4}$ ◯ $\frac{2}{4}$ 2. $\frac{6}{8}$ ◯ $\frac{7}{8}$ 3. $\frac{10}{10}$ ◯ $\frac{4}{10}$ 4. $\frac{3}{5}$ ◯ $\frac{5}{5}$

5.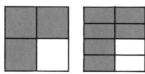

$\frac{3}{4}$ ◯ $\frac{6}{8}$

6.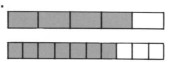

$\frac{4}{5}$ ◯ $\frac{7}{10}$

7.

$\frac{2}{3}$ ◯ $\frac{3}{6}$

Set 66 (Use after page 311.)

Add.

1. $\frac{7}{10} + \frac{2}{10}$ 2. $\frac{3}{6} + \frac{2}{6}$ 3. $\frac{2}{10} + \frac{5}{10}$ 4. $\frac{3}{100} + \frac{6}{100}$ 5. $\frac{3}{8} + \frac{5}{8}$

6. $\frac{2}{4} + \frac{1}{4}$ 7. $\frac{1}{5} + \frac{3}{5}$ 8. $\frac{2}{8} + \frac{3}{8}$ 9. $\frac{5}{10} + \frac{4}{10}$ 10. $\frac{1}{3} + \frac{1}{3}$

Set 67 (Use after page 313.)

Subtract.

1. $\frac{8}{8} - \frac{3}{8}$ 2. $\frac{3}{4} - \frac{2}{4}$ 3. $\frac{5}{6} - \frac{4}{6}$ 4. $\frac{3}{3} - \frac{2}{3}$ 5. $\frac{7}{10} - \frac{4}{10}$

6. $\frac{2}{4} - \frac{1}{4}$ 7. $\frac{9}{10} - \frac{6}{10}$ 8. $\frac{6}{8} - \frac{1}{8}$ 9. $\frac{3}{5} - \frac{1}{5}$ 10. $\frac{4}{6} - \frac{2}{6}$

INDEX